The Flammarion Guide to

WORLD WINES

English translation © Copyright Studio, Paris, France
Originally created by Copyright Studio, as *Les Vins du monde*
© Copyright Studio, Paris, France 1999
Translation: Elizabeth Ayre
Copyediting: Lisa Davidson
Graphic design: Jacques Hennaux
Jacket design: Nicolas Trautmann, Studio Flammarion
Typesetting: Isabelle Chojnacki
Editorial assistant: Sophie Greloux

For this English-language edition
© Flammarion 2000

ISBN: 2-08013-685-2
N° d'édition: FA3685-X-00
Dépôt légal: October 2000

Printed in Spain

The Flammarion Guide to
WORLD WINES

FRANÇOIS COLLOMBET
JEAN-PAUL PAIREAULT

Flammarion

Contents

From early vintages to the first production of fine wines

Wine, like wheat, is one of the most ancient commodities produced by mankind, and certainly the most prestigious. In Rome and Athens, wine was associated with the gods Bacchus and Dionysus. Nectar and ambrosia were the preferred drinks of the gods of Olympus, and although water and milk were consumed more widely during Antiquity, wine was drunk for the pleasure and intense sense of well-being it offered.

Wine was seen as a heavenly creation well before it became the "blood of Christ" used in sacraments and rituals. Yet Christianity played a crucial role in the expansion and development of wine and wine production.

Bacchus With Grapes,
Greco-Roman art,
Paris, Musée du Louvre.

Opposite page:
Saint-Émilion,
Château la Gaffelière,
detail of a Roman mosaic.

The Last Supper, *by Joos van Cleve, 16th c., Paris, Musée du Louvre.*

The earliest roads lead to Rome

Evidence of grape vines, or *Vitus vinifera,* as well as an early form of wine production, were found in Transcaucasia as early as 3000 B.C. Early vines, originally found in forests as liana and creepers, were domesticated and then gradually spread as early civilizations shifted westward. The vine probably was first transplanted to Italy by the Etruscans, one thousand years before Christ.

It would take centuries to advance from early techniques such as selecting Vitus vinifera and mastering propagation by cuttings to more sophisticated viticultural methods. The evolution of wine production was linked closely to the development of commercial trade. Wine production and transportation flourished in Antiquity to meet the growing demand of wealthy customers. Pottery became highly sought after, and amphoras soon grew more popular than goatskin bottles. The pottery left valuable archaeological traces indicating the routes which the Greeks and Phoenicians used to travel to the West, spreading the wine trade.

Rome became a vast center for importing and consuming wine.

During the late Roman Republic and Roman Empire, thousands of gallons of wine were consumed each week, and Campania, a rich agricultural region, became a wine hub that played as pivotal a role in its time as Bordeaux did in the Middle Ages.

Defining quality

Was a wine's quality maintained when great quantities were produced? Most likely not. Unless they used it for medicinal purposes, the Greeks drank their wines watered down, and the widespread use of pitched vessels hindered the development of its aromatic qualities. Poets may have waxed lyrical over the virtues of Roman wines, but they were undoubtedly far from what we consider fine wines today. In the first place, wine storage depended largely on chance. Wine was either drunk locally and stored in open jars; "forced" by adding honey to withstand transport; or "heated," where, after approximately one-third of the liquid had evaporated, condensed form remained, most likely simi-

lar to "cooked" wine. In addition, the Romans tended to store wine above their kitchens, not in cellars away from the heat, resulting in further evaporation. Adding water to wine was certainly required before it could be drunk.

Later it became common to flavor wines. Myrrh, incense, anise, pepper and cinammon were added to enhance the taste. This practice persisted over the years and probably originated due to the poor qualities of the wine, as no great wine was produced during Antiquity.

European vineyards in Italy, Spain, Gaul and the Rhineland date back to this period, but it took centuries for the taste and quality of wine to improve.

From wine produced by monks to the first fine wines

The cultivation of vines declined in the late Middle Ages as Mediterranean countries themselves declined. Beginning in the seventh century, Arab invasions resulted in the spread of Islam, which forbade the drinking of wine. The situation was

Greek amphora.

scarcely better outside the Mediterranean Basin, where few could afford the luxury of drinking wine, which often involved paying the *disette*. In the late Middle Ages, the Church was the principal wine producer and ensured its survival. Monks not only produced wines, but also contributed to their expansion by adapting them to the tastes of northern countries like Flanders, Germania and England. As Christianity spread, new trade routes opened up toward the north. The process of adapting grape varieties to harsher climates led to a more rigorous selection process to guarantee quality. The first noble grape varieties appeared. Beginning in the eleventh century, wine production flourished in the northern countries under the auspices of abbeys.

Winegrowing regions evolved considerably during the seventeenth century with the emergence of the Lowlands and England as the great maritime powers. Although the wine trade was active in the early seventeenth century, it had not yet reached an international scale, since wines could not withstand the shipping process. The Dutch, the great lords of the seas, therefore began shipping vast quantities of eau-de-vie, which was hardier and could withstand long journeys without going off. They obtained the liqueurs in France, mostly from the Charente region.

Demand was great, fostering the development of vineyards throughout all of southwestern France, which also supplied robust wines shipped from the port of Bordeaux.

The port was bolstered by the decline in German wine production and gained a strong enough position to weather the Franco-Dutch War toward the end of the century. During the war, the Dutch turned to Spain and Portugal for wine. Meanwhile, the English waged a bitter battle with them over control of Sherry and Port production, which had supplanted the Bordeaux clarets when the English government imposed a ban on French wines during the wars against Louis XIV of France. When France and England restored trade relations in the early eighteenth century, Bordelais producers actively promoted their highly refined wines to stave off an invasion of Spanish and Portuguese wines.

This advertising strategy sat well with the aristocracy at the time, as it was striving for greater sophistication in taste. With the cooperation of English merchants, Girondin dignitaries launched the first true selections of fine wines, which were produced on specific sites, aged in barrels and stored in bottles. New processes were introduced; these included sterilization using sulfur and clarification with egg whites. A tradition of quality wine was born, which would flourish with the active participation of English traders.

Grape-harvesting scene in Saumur, illuminated manuscript by Pol de Limburg, 15th c.

Transporting the grapes, illuminated manuscript from The Book of Hours, *15th c., Musée de Chantilly.*

The Marriage at Cana
by Bernard David, 15th c.,
Musée du Louvre.

Soil and climate: a question of moderation

Soil and climate play a vital role in determining the quality of a wine. Humidity is also required for vines to flourish. In addition to moisture found in the topsoil and subsoil, fog and morning dew help maintain an optimal humidity rate of approximatey 70 percent. Rainfall, even heavy rainfall, can be withstood if it occurs periodically throughout the growing cycle; in this case, it is less harmful than excessive sunshine.

Napa Valley, Sterling Vineyards, palm trees in the vineyards.

Graves, Bordeaux: characteristic soil from some of the world's finest vineyards.

Poor soil

Which soil types are best for vine-growing? Nearly all types, providing that they are poor, as vines produce their finest fruit in very poor soils. The elements that constitute arable soil may vary, but the soil's poverty is a major factor (the restricted yield of poor soils helps concentrate flavor and richness in the grapes).

Gravel is as good as sand or stone. Great vintages throughout France are produced on a variety of soil types, which influence the different colors, flavors and aromas of wines. Granite schists produce light, pleasantly fresh wines; calcareous or limestone soil enhances the degree of alcohol and the subtlety of the nose; soil rich in clay produces wines that are ruddy in color, tannic and full-bodied.

All soil types in which vines grow absorb heat and retain moisture to varying degrees. Rocky soil is one of the best types of soil for storing heat during the day and emitting it at night. Darker soil has a greater capacity to absorb sunlight. Hillsides and slopes are often prime sites for vineyards as they are most likely to provide optimal sunlight. In

addition, raked terrain absorbs heat better and retains less cold air than flat land surfaces do.

A leading role for the subsoil

The preference for poor soil types stems from the nature of the vine, whose roots can reach deep into the ground if no groundwater level or compact sublayer blocks them. Subsoil plays a crucial role for grapes growing in poor soil types. If the roots don't grow down into the ground, they grow laterally over the surface, and the vines are exposed to excess sun or humidity. If there is too much sunlight, the stomata of the leaves tend to get clogged, hindering photosynthesis and stunting the ripening of the grapes. If there is too much humidity, for example in heavy downpours, the plants swell with water and the grapes burst.

If the roots dig deep into the subsoil, there will be sufficient water without risk of excess moisture. Vines that produce good grapes have a limited yield, and a good grape ripens slowly, without rotting or drying up. Water must be available in moderate amounts. The three basic soil charac-

Napa Valley: fans are used to protect against frost.

Saint-Émilion:
Roman ridges.

teristics essential to winegrowing are large-grained soil composition, good drainage and depth, all of which keep water from coming into direct contact with the roots.

Sunshine, but in moderation

Climatic conditions play a more vital role with grapes than they do with any other type of fruit. The ripening period spans approximately forty-five days, and once the grapes are ripe, frost, hail, winds and other severe climatic conditions can wipe out entire crops. Sunshine is required for the grapes to ripen, but never in excess. Excess sunshine deprives the wine of acidity, which gives it its subtlety. Three conditions are required for healthy vines: light, heat and humidity. Light is necessary for the absorption of chloryphyll, with required minimum levels at 20,000 lux—which even a cloudy summer or spring sky can provide. The sun does not have to be shining continuously, which would expose the vines to drought.

Ideally, temperatures should not rise above 82° F to 86° F, nor fall below 50° F. Yet vines can survive harsh winters, enduring temperatures as low as –13° F, even –22° F. Spring frosts can be devastating, particularly in flat regions where cold air amasses. Winegrowers now fight frost by watering the plants just before frost sets in. The ice acts as a protective shield, creating a kind of igloo effect.

Napa Valley:
the vineyard after the vines
have been cut back.

Good wine requires water

Although vines need water, irrigation is legally banned in many Appellation Contrôlée regions. It is, however, required in very hot regions like Chile and California. Watering is beneficial to growth provided that it occurs in springtime, well before the grape-harvesting period. Over-watering or watering too late into the growing cycle tends to dilute the grape juice. Moderation is the best practice.

Climatic conditions and vintage year wines

The vintage year indicates when a wine was produced, and is a reference to the climatic factors of a given year. In a single region, however, weather conditions may vary considerably from one year to the next, producing differences in the vintages.

It is impossible to predict the quality of a vintage year, as forecasts are not sophisticated enough to predict weather conditions or to determine a given phase in the growth cycle. The relative quality of a vintage year depends on variations in climate.

What is *terroir?*

Terroir literally means "soil," but the concept is more complex than equating it with the given properties of soil. Along with topsoil and subsoil, it also includes such factors as micro-climate, drainage and the angle of the slope with respect to the sun. Hence, a variety of factors give a *terroir* its own distinctive character and status.

The island of Santorini: vines struggle to grow in the volcanic soil.

Sauternes: rootstocks.

Grape varieties: the mark and identity of wine

Over one thousand grape varieties are produced by winegrowers throughout the world. A handful of them, the famous "international" grape varieties—ten in all—may soon overshadow the others, and even force some varieties out of existence. A wine's character is essentially determined by its grape variety (or varieties), which influences up to 90 percent of its flavor, body, bouquet and longevity. This may sound like an overstatement, but in addition to climate and soil, the grape variety plays a major role in forging a wine's identity, and there is an increasing number of varietals, or wines named after their grape type.

Médoc, Bordeaux: Cabernet Franc grape variety.

Choosing the grape can be difficult for the wine-grower, given the importance of the decision. Although classic soil/grape variety combinations traditionally exist—the relationship between limestone and Chardonnay, for example—there is no fixed constant between a given soil/grape combination and quality, which is the ultimate goal. Moreover, the plants generally live forty to fifty years, with quality increasing proportionally with age (vines under four years of age are not eligible for the appellation label). There are over four thousand grape varieties in existence, all descendants of the Indo-European species *Vitis vinifera*. Wine lovers are familiar with only forty of these varieties, and the more classic internationally recognized grapes represent only a handful.

Red and white grape varieties can be distinguished by their flavor and pleasantness. In addition to "fine" or "noble" grape varieties noted for their strength and original aromas, there are "semi-fine" varieties, whose outstanding qualities are often linked to a certain winegrowing region, and "common" varieties, which have greater yields, if less quality.

THE TEN GREAT CLASSIC GRAPE VARIETIES

Five red grape varieties:
Cabernet Sauvignon
Pinot Noir
Merlot
Cabernet Franc
Syrah

Five white grape varieties:
Riesling
Chardonnay
Gewürztraminer
Sauvignon Blanc
Muscat

Grape varieties are also distinguished by their robustness, resistance to disease, yield and growth rates. According to a system devised in the late nineteenth century based on the maturation rate of the Chasselas Doré, grape varieties can range from Fourth epoch (late ripening), to Second epoch (early mid-season ripening) to Precocious (very early ripening).

The choices are many, and the practice of assemblage, or blending wines by "marrying" and mixing them, varies the taste of wine even more, giving them an infinite number of subtle flavors. The global tendency to promote only a few exclusive champion varieties is discouraging. The top grape varieties may have unbeatable qualities, but the many varieties considered "inferior" have rich, agreeable characters worth preserving. It is impossible to mention all grape varieties here, or even to look at each of the greatest classic varieties; the four grape types explored here are merely examples illustrating the variety of characteristics and qualities.

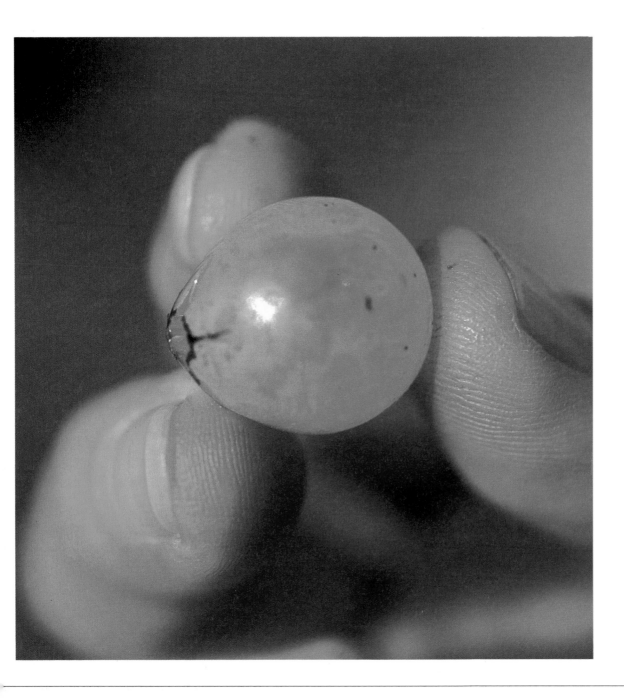

SIGNATURE GRAPE VARIETIES

It is becoming more and more common for labels to indicate a wine's original grape variety. This is particularly true in more recently established winegrowing regions, such as California, where virtually all wines are named after their grape variety. In countries in which wine production is a longstanding tradition, however, the association between grape varieties and geographical origin is so well-entrenched that the latter suffices. If "Barolo" is indicated on a label, for example, it is implicit that the wine is produced from the Nebbiolo grape.

A look at the four great grape varieties

Cabernet Sauvignon

This is the red grape variety par excellence, with a reputation for being the world's finest. The most prestigious Médoc wines are produced from Cabernet Sauvignon, which confirms its position as a noble grape. It is highly resistant, even to spring frosts, and is easy to grow.

The dusty blue-black grapes are covered with a thick skin and are gathered in tight clusters that protect them from heavy rains and insects. The Cabernet's only drawback is its late maturation. Its relatively low yield adds to the grape's nobility and enhances its rich aromatic palette. Black-currant is predominant, along with resinous, spicy, smoky notes, and sometimes a hint of licorice or kelp.

The highly tannic wines need to age slowly, preferably in oak barrels, and are easily compatible with more supple varieties like Cabernet Franc and Merlot.

Cabernet Sauvignon, seen as a prestigious grape variety worldwide, has traveled widely. Although it is rare in New Zealand, South Africa and Spain, the grape is commonly grown in California, Italy and Bulgaria. Cabernet Sauvignon is also grown in Romania and the Balkans, and even holds its own in China and Japan these days.

Pinot Noir

The only trait shared by Pinot Noir and Cabernet Sauvignon is their nobility. Pinot Noir is no globetrotter and is difficult to domesticate, and is one of the greatest challenges in winemaking. It thrives in cooler climates and is less resistant to vineyard hazards. One of the advantages of Pinot Noir, however, is its early maturation, producing fruity wines with notes of raspberry and black currant. It is lower in tannin than the other great red-grape varieties, so the wines do not need to age for long periods of time.

Pinot Noir is well-represented in France, as it is the grape variety of red Burgundy and is very common in Champagne. But the grape is also found in Germany and northeastern Italy and in the Neuchâtel region of Switzerland.

Chardonnay

Chardonnay has become the most fashionable white-grape variety, due in part to the fact that it produces all of the great white wines of Burgundy. It is also the most adaptable, given its hardiness, resistance to cold, very early maturation and high yield. In the cellar, Chardonnay is easy to vinify and responds well to a variety of treatments and techniques, from the Champagne process to aging in oak barrels. It produces a great number of quality wines with highly distinct personalities.

In addition to producing Burgundy's finest white wines, Chardonnay is used in Champagne and has had tremendous success in California. Its success there has somewhat overshadowed the excellent results obtained in Australia and Italy, where the grape has managed to adapt to the heat.

Riesling

A white grape variety of German origin, Riesling is Chardonnay's top challenger. The grape is well represented in Germany, yet even more common in Russia and the former Soviet republics—with over 36,000 acres planted in the Ukraine. Its yield varies from country to country: very high in Germany, medium in California and low in South Africa. Wherever it grows, Riesling is a hardy grape that is highly resistant to cold. Its most outstanding feature is its exceptional depth and aroma of flavor, enhanced by the soil's characteristics, as is the grape's mellowness or acidity.

Cabernet Sauvignon.

France

The winemaking tradition in France dates to ancient times: the Phoenicians and the Greeks began to grow grapes in the sixth century B.C. The great vineyards were first established under the Romans during the first century A.D. The key factors determining the layout of the vineyards were the orientation of the land and proximity to water—the best wines today are still produced by vineyards near the Gironde, Rhône, Marne, Loire and Rhine rivers.

No other country has such a wide range of climates and such diversified soil types. Furthermore, all of the greatest classic grape varieties are grown, producing an extraordinarily rich range of wines from the twelve principal winegrowing regions: Bordeaux, Burgundy, Champagne, the Loire Valley, Alsace, Côtes du Rhône, Jura and Savoy, Provence, the Southwest, Languedoc and Roussillon. In the wake of the devastating outbreak of phylloxera, a classification system was set up in the early twentieth century to guarantee quality standards as well as place of origin.

The village of Saint-Émilion in Bordeaux.

The label: a question of rank and standard

How can wine lovers find their way around among the tens of thousands of wines produced annually in France? Besides the color of the wine and the shape of the bottle, the label is the only source of information. It guarantees a wine's quality.

Labels indicate:

1. The name and address of the bottler, stipulating if it is a grower or a shipper;

2. The category of wine: Vin de Table, Vin de Pays, VDQS or AOC
- Vin de Table: the degree of alcohol must be indicated. The wine may be a blend of wines from different European Union countries.

- Vin de Pays: a higher-ranking Vin de Table with the geographical region of production indicated. The grape varieties and production area are regulated.
- VQPRD: Vin de Qualité Produit dans une Région Délimitée. This is the official European Union term to designate wines above table wine status, and includes top-quality wines. Although VQPRD does not appear on French labels, the European designation has been in effect since 1962. It encompasses VDQS (Vin Délimité de Qualité Supérieure), an official guarantee that the wines are produced in a specified area, are made from approved grape varieties and meet standards on yield, production methods, etc.; and AOC (Appellation d'Origine Contrôlée).

The wine label identifies the wine and the person responsible for it. The name of the bottler, who is the last person to intervene in the production process, must by law appear on the label. The label also gives a wine's classification: Vin de Table, Vin de Pays, VDQS (Vin Délimité de Qualité Supérieure) or AOC (Appellation d'Origine Contrôlée).

AOC wines: the peak of perfection

The AOC classification offers five guaranteed standards based on a series of texts, amendments, regulations and special clauses that led to the creation of the INAO* in 1947.

1. - Production area: the geographical delimitation of the vineyard within a wine-growing region based on traditional criteria, and geological and production factors of the *terroir*.

2. - Grape varieties: those yielding the best wines on a given *terroir*, depending on weather conditions.

3. - Yield per acre: this is highly regulated, as is growing and tending the vines and maximum yield, which can never exceed the stipulated limit, given in gallons per acre.

4. - Minimum alcohol content, prior to the addition of any sugar.

5. - Vinification methods, which aim to preserve traditional vinification techniques.

INAO: Institut National des Appellations d'Origine, the French government agency overseeing production conditions of AOC wines.

How to read a label

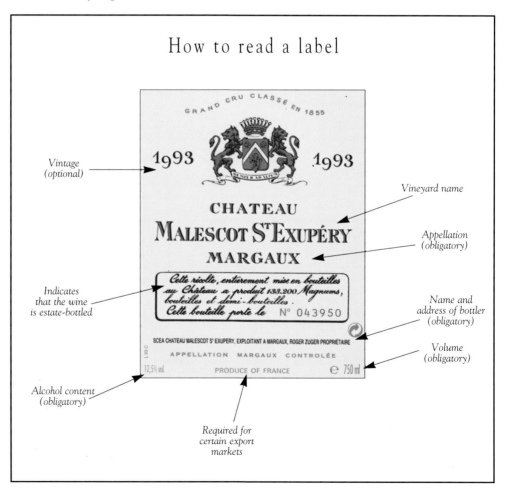

Vintage (optional)

Vineyard name

Appellation (obligatory)

Indicates that the wine is estate-bottled

Name and address of bottler (obligatory)

Volume (obligatory)

Alcohol content (obligatory)

Required for certain export markets

Burgundy

Burgundy is one of the most fascinating wine-producing regions, its glorious past embodied in its many castles and monasteries. The Burgundy vineyard area extends over 68,000 acres of AOC, which have been partitioned to such an extent that they resemble a kind of mosaic. This is particularly pronounced in the Yonne and Côte d'Or *départements,* less so toward the south in the Saône-et-Loire and Rhône. But in the first two regions, even the tiniest plot of land on the slopes seems to have been meticulously selected.

This mosaic yields a great variety of wines, adding to the region's mystique, for only two grape varieties are dominant in producing Burgundy wines, Pinot Noir for Burgundy reds and Chardonnay for whites, which seem to thrive in the semi-continental climate. Their interaction with the great variety of different soil types (although the soil is principally chalky) is quasi-miraculous in producing the great diversity of wines.

The winegrowing regions of Burgundy begin 110 miles southeast of Paris, with the exceptional wines of Chablis, then descend to the remarkable Côte de Nuits and Côte de Beaune. Farther south lie the Chalonnais, the Mâconnais and near Lyon, the Beaujolais.

Chablis

The Yonne *département* runs across the northern part of Burgundy, featuring the great appellation of Chablis, reserved exclusively for dry white wines.

Located between Auxerre and Tonnerre, Chablis once covered a vast winegrowing region of 100,000 acres. The region's wines were once relished by the aristocracy and easily transported to Paris via the Yonne and Seine rivers. The wine became so popular that greater amounts needed to be produced, and the vineyards were expanded to the detriment of its quality.

With the advent of the railroad, massive amounts of wine could travel from the Midi to reach Parisians, who suddenly couldn't get enough of it. In addition to this new competitor, the phylloxera blight hit in the late nineteenth century, as did a series of late frosts in the twentieth century which winegrowers were unable to combat. In response, many landowners in the area surrounding Chablis abandoned viticulture.

Vignerons in Chablis proper persevered, however, and to work more efficiently, agreed to cultivate only the best soil. The appellation was thus reduced to some 1,000 acres, and as a result of this rigorous selection, the quality exceeded that of what it once used to be.

The Chablis region, which today covers 10,000 acres, managed to overcome the various setbacks, and outside France

BURGUNDIAN APPELLATIONS
From the general to the particular

Appellations indicate the soil and place of origin that determine the quality of a wine. These include, in ascending order of quality:

1- a general regional or generic appellation, which applies to all wines produced in Burgundy.

2 - a district appellation, which indicates a more specific region, such as a subregion—Côte de Nuits, Beaujolais, Mâcon, etc.

3 - a commune name, which concerns all wines produced on that commune or parish—Chablis, Meursault, Gevrey-Chambertin and Pommard, for example.

4- a vineyard (cru-name), indicating a given parcel of land, which in Burgundy is often called a "climat" or "clos."

The thirty-one Grands Crus Classés are identified by their vineyard (cru) name: Chambertin, Montrachet, Corton, Clos de Vougeot, etc. Premiers Crus mention the commune name as well, for example, Chambolle-Musigny-les-Amoureuses.

The more specific the appellation, or name, the better the wine. To take one of the best wines as an example, a Romanée-Conti (vineyard name) is greater than a Vosne-Romanée (commune name), which is better than a Côte de Nuits (district name), which in turn is superior to a Burgundy (generic name).

today, the name Chablis is virtually synonymous with fine dry white wines. Its worldwide reputation is so great that imitation Chablis wines have cropped up in the United States, Australia and Argentina. An important step occurred in 1997 when imitation Californian Chablis was banned in Japan. Although Chardonnay is today the only variety authorized for AOC Chablis, it produces a variety of very distinctive wines.

Chablis are ranked according to four levels of quality: Grands Crus (Great Growths), followed by Premiers Crus (First Growths), then Chablis and Petit Chablis. The greatest Chablis wines are grown on soil that contains at least 50 percent limestone. The topsoil is thin and in many places the white, marly, calcium-rich subsoil (known as Kimmeridge Clay) shows through.

Good Chablis are green-tinged, yellow-gold in color. Aged in vats, they have a delicate, light perfume. More and more, Chablis is being fermented and aged in oak barrels, resulting in richer, more full-bodied wines. The bouquet is often floral, with notes of apple and sometimes almond, hazelnut or hay. They are distinguished by their assertiveness and finely judged acidity.

Grands Crus (Great Growths)

Seven vineyards totaling 250 acres northeast of Chablis make up the Grands Crus of Chablis. The vineyards include Blanchots, Bougros, Les Clos, Grenouilles, Les Preuses, Valmure and Vaudésir.

These seven crus are clearly superior to the other Chablis wines. Another one which might have been included is La Moutonne between Les Preuses and Vaudésir. The yield is 370 gallons per acre. Labels may indicate the name of the vineyard after the Chablis Grand Cru appellation.

Premiers Crus (First Growths)

The vineyards are spread out over a 2.5-mile radius around Chablis. There are twenty-nine in all, with eleven main ones. The vineyards and the towns from which they come are as follows:
• Mont-de-Milieu (communes of Fyé and Fleys);
• Montée de Tonnerre, divided into Chapelot and Pied-d'Aloup (commune of Fyé);
• Fourchaume, which is divided into Vaupulent, Côte de Fontenay, Vaulorent and l'Homme-Mort (communes of La Chapelle-Vaupelteigne, Poinchy, Fontenay and Maligny);
• Vaillons, divided into Châtains, Séché, Beugnons and Les Lys (commune of Chablis);

• Montmains, divided into Forêts and Butteaux (commune of Chablis);
• Mélinots, divided into Roncières and Les Epinottes (commune of Chablis);
• Côte de Léchet (commune of Mily);
• Beauroy, divided into Troesmes (communes of Poinchy and Beine);
• Vaucoupin (commune of Chichée);
• Vosgros, divided into Baugiraut (commune of Chichée);
• Les Fourneaux, divided into Moreing and Côte des Prés-Girots (commune of Fleys).

The yield is restricted to 422 gallons per acre, and on the label, the Chablis Premier Cru appellation may be followed by the name of the vineyard.

Chablis

The vineyards producing simple Chablis (on a wine label, Chablis without any further qualification) also surround the city, but are more far-flung. These are the areas that were developed after catastrophic frosts nearly decimated the region, reducing it to a few hundred acres. Although the yield is limited to 422 gallons per acre throughout the region, quality ultimately depends on the landowner. The quality is often quite high for these light, very dry and assertive wines.

Petit Chablis

These are produced mostly from grapes grown in the Chablisian hinterlands with the least favorable exposure. The wines are drunk young and are traditionally sold in bulk.

Bourgogne Irancy

Irancy, the hometown of Soufflot, the architect who built the Pantheon in Paris, gives a good idea of what the Yonne wine-producing region was like over one century ago. The slopes of this large village, which lies in a basin, are well exposed to

SIX APPELLATION CATEGORIES
Burgundy's record number

Burgundy has the greatest density of rootstocks per acre (approximately 5,265 per acre), and although the region produces ten times less the amount of wine as Bordeaux does, it has twice the number of appellations (approximately one hundred distinct appellations).

Bourgogne
This is the general appellation which, under certain conditions, covers all wines produced in the delimited region of Burgundy. Red wines are produced from Pinot Noir, although César and Tressot are used in the Yonne *département*. White wines are made from Chardonnay and Pinot Blanc (red wines: 10 percent, white wines: 10.5 percent minimum).

Bourgogne Aligoté
White wines made from Aligoté with a maximum 12 percent of Chardonnay (9.5 percent minimum).

Bourgogne Passetoutgrains
Red or rosé wines made by vatting together Pinot Noir (at least one-third) and Gamay Noir à Jus Blanc (7.5 percent minimum).

Bourgogne Ordinaire or Bourgogne Grand Ordinaire
Red, rosé and white wines. Red wines are made from Pinot and Gamay and also from Tressot and César in the Yonne. Chardonnay is used for quality whites, followed by Pinot Blanc, Aligoté, Melon de Bourgogne and in the Yonne, Sacy (red wines: 9 percent, white wines: 9.5 percent minimum). Maximum yield per acre is 520 gallons.

Bourgogne Mousseux
All "sparkling" versions of the above-mentioned white, red and rosé wines.

Crémant de Bourgogne
On October 17, 1975, Crémants de Bourgogne were given the same rank as other crémants from Alsace, the Loire, Bordeaux and Limoux when a new appellation—Crémant de Bourgogne—was created. "Crémant" refers to wines that are only partly sparkling with respect to Champagne, with less pressure behind the cork. Crémant de Bourgogne Sec—approximately four million bottles are produced each year—is one of the crémants that comes closest to Champagne, due to the Chardonnay grapes. (Blancs de Blanc wines are made solely from Chardonnay grapes.) Pinot Noir, Aligoté, Melon and Sacy also can be used in making Crémant de Bourgogne. Some exceptionally fine rosés are made from Pinot Noir and Gamay. Crémants have a minimum alcohol content of 8.5 %. They are produced by a secondary fermentation in the bottle.

---

the sun. The vineyard's reputation was assured in 1977 when the name Irancy was officially added to the Burgundy appellation.

The red Irancy wines have a superb purple color (there are rosés as well), and in good years are full-bodied and have great finesse. Their bouquet becomes highly characteristic as the wines age. Most are made from the Pinot Noir grape, although the César, the historic local grape variety dating back to the Gauls, produces a few surprisingly good wines. The addition of César is what gives Irancy wines their distinctive taste, which is unlike that of any other wine. It adds tannin lacking in the Pinot Noir, and allows the wine to keep well. The vineyards, alternating with cherry orchards, occupy 375 acres of the communes of Vincelottes and Cravant (the famous Côte de Palotte).

Sauvignon de Saint-Bris

Officially classified as VDQS since 1974, Saint-Bris (152 acres) is soon to become an AOC. The wine is produced exclusively from the Sauvignon grape variety from the communes of Saint-Bris-le-Vineux, Chitry and Irancy. The aromatic headiness is due to the soil's chalky bed.

Vézelay

This small vineyard was revived in 1986 by Marc Meneau, the owner of the Auberge de l'Espérance. Year after year, it expands over the famous Vézelay slope under the protection of the great Romanesque Sainte-Marie-Madeleine basilica. History has come full circle: the Dukes of Burgundy owned a walled vineyard here at one time.

Côte de Nuits

Côte de Nuits covers some 12 miles, from the northern border of the commune of Fixin to the southern border of Corgoloin. The slopes lie toward the east, opposite the Saône River, and contain a great variety of soil types, with a subsoil of limestone and marl.

COMMUNAL APPELLATIONS and GRANDS CRUS OF CÔTE DE NUITS

AOC communal Grands Crus Reds
- Fixin
- Gevrey-Chambertin, Chambertin
- Chambertin-Clos de Bèze
- Charmes-Chambertin
- Chapelle-Chambertin
- Griotte-Chambertin
- Latricière-Chambertin
- Mazis-Chambertin
- Ruchottes-Chambertin
- Morey-Saint-Denis Bonnes Mares (part of it)
- Clos Saint-Denis
- Clos de la Roche
- Clos de Tart
- Clos des Lambrays
- Chambolle-Musigny, Musigny
- Bonnes Mares
- Vougeot, Clos de Vougeot
- Flagey-Échézeaux
- Vosne-Romanée Romanée-Conti
- Romanée
- Romanée-Saint-Vivant
- La Tache
- Richebourg
- Nuits-Saint-Georges

The region produces very few white wines, and the predominant grape variety is Pinot Noir.

There are as many Grands Crus and Premiers Crus as there are communes. Some are so prestigious that they are famous throughout the world. Traveling north to south, you'll find:

Marsannay

The wines produced on the communes of Marsannay-la-Côte and Couchey, on the northern bordern of the Côte de Nuits, are included in the Côte de Nuits appellation. The vineyard experienced a revival following the acquisition of the AOC classification in 1987 and was replanted primarily with Pinot. One exception was Marsannay rosé, which has a remarkable strawberry aroma and is Burgundy's best rosé. Chardonnay and Pinot Blanc produce fine white wines with exceptional finesse in the Côte de Dijon.

BURGUNDY GRAPE VARIETIES

For red wine, the predominant grape variety is Pinot Noir, sometimes called Noiren or Noirien. White wines are made from Chardonnay, also called Aubaine, Beaunois, and Pinot Blanc, which is sometimes added to Chardonnay. The Aligoté grape and Melon de Bourgogne (Muscadet) are used for generic wines.

Fixin

This commune may not be world famous, but the wine it produces provides a superb introduction to the Côte de Nuits (it is the northernmost of the Côte de Nuits wine communes). There are nine Premiers Crus, considered by wine lovers to be nearly as great as the prestigious wines in neighboring Gevrey-Chambertin.

Gevrey-Chambertin

Gevrey-Chambertin occupies 1,075 acres of vineyards, the largest communal appellation. Some twenty Premiers Crus and eight Grands Crus are produced, including the regal Chambertin and Chambertin-Clos de Bèze. The color, bouquet, finesse and smoothness make them truly heavenly wines. Wines produced in the surrounding vineyards are almost as good in quality and deserve to add their name to that of Chambertin.

Chapelle-Chambertin, Charmes-Chambertin, Griotte-Chambertin, Latricière-Chambertin, Mazis-Chambertin and Ruchottes-Chambertin are all magnificent Grands Crus, while the Premiers Crus include notable wines like Clos Saint-Jacques, Lavaut, les Combottes and Varoilles.

Morey-Saint-Denis

There are four Grands Crus and part of a Cinquième Cru (Fifth Growth) on this excellent 250-acre vineyard which, oddly enough, remains little known. This is quite surprising, and the vineyard deserves a better reputation. Clos Saint-Denis, Clos de la Roche, Clos de Tart, Clos des Lambrays and part of Bonnes Mares yield superb full-bodied, rich reds with great breed, and there are eighteen fine Premiers Crus.

Chambolle-Musigny

"Silky" and "lacey" are two words often used in describing Chambolle-Musigny, in particular its two Grands Crus, Musigny and Bonnes Mares. The delicate, elegant, subtle wines have a good measure of finesse and are a wine lover's dream. But the Grands Crus should not overshadow the Premiers Crus—such as Les Amoureuses (meaning 'women in love') and Les Charmes, superb in elegance and bouquet—produced on this 500-acre region.

Vougeot

Of the 225 acres under vine in this commune, the Grand Cru Clos de Vougeot alone occupies 125 acres, enclosed by a stone wall. Some magnificent wines are produced here, but the area is so fragmented, with several dozen property-owners sharing the surface, that quality depends on the skill of the winemaker. Not all of the Clos de Vougeot wines currently produced are still fit to be served at royal tables, as they once were.

Flagey-Échezeaux

The commune exists, but there is no appellation. It produces two Grands Crus: Échézeaux, with 75 acres of vineyards, and Grands Échézeaux, which is limited to 22.5 acres and produces wines superior to the former. Few bottles are sold as Échézeaux. Most are marketed as Vosne-Romanée, and by law the label can bear the Vosne-Romanée Premier Cru qualification.

Vosne-Romanée

The five Grands Crus coexist on a 500-acre surface area. Among them is the world-famous Romanée-Conti, the legendary wine produced on a tiny 4.5-acre vineyard. Romanée-Conti is truly unforgettable, unbeatable in quality, very expensive and quite rare. The estate produces only 5,000 to 10,000 bottles annually, and only a select few will ever have the privilege of tasting one. They are described as being as smooth as velvet, beautifully balanced and lingering on the palate.

The Romanée-Conti estate owns nearby Richebourg (20 acres) and La Tâche (15 acres), so it may be possible to get a little closer to this magnificent wine. There is also Romanée (2.5 acres) and Romanée-Saint-Vivant (24 acres). These Grands Crus are excellent and less expensive.

The twelve Premiers Crus include such treasures as La Grande-Rue (3.8 acres bordering on Romanée-Conti) and Les Malconsorts (6.3 acres). These too need to be laid down, although for shorter periods of time (eight to ten years), and are rare. The vineyards of Vosne-Romanée are great in quality, not surface area.

Nuits-Saint-Georges

The 950-acre appellation extends into the neighboring commune of Prémeaux, with the southern lots producing the most assertive, full-bodied wines. There are no Grands Crus here, but nearly forty Premiers Crus, with such favorites as Les Saint-Georges (19 acres), round and powerful, and Les Vaucrains (15 acres), both of which should be laid down.

Côte-de-Nuits-Villages

Five communes located at the two extremes of the Côte de Nuits are entitled to this subregional appellation: Fixin and Brochon to the north; and Prissey, Comblanchien and Corgoloin to the south. The entire area represents 812 acres with a limited yield of 370 gallons per acre, producing primarily light, fruity red wines.

Côte de Beaune

Côte de Beaune is a long strip of land running down from the Côte de Nuits along the Saône. The slope covers 7,500 acres, nearly double that of the Côte de Nuits. The gently sloping hills create a less austere landscape, with soil that is gravely, argilo-calcareous and iron-rich in parts, ideal for red wines; or of marl whitened with limestone debris, perfect for whites. Pinot Noir and Chardonnay are planted according to soil type.

Burgundy's noble grapes produce only two Grands Crus here—Le Corton in red and Le Montrachet in white—but this by no means relegates the Côte de Beaune to second-class status. There is a fine panoply of Premiers Crus, including outstanding reds and dry whites which rank among the best in the world.

One difficulty is that Côte de Beaune wines are relatively inaccessible. A great number of parcels are difficult to find and it is hard to know where one cru ends and another begins, as there are no signs. Yet, like in the Côte de Nuits, each commune features a patchwork of specific parcels; these include, from north to south:

Ladoix-Serrigny

The slope begins at Ladoix, as does the Grand Cru of Corton—whose name is so prestigious that it overshadows its place name. Ladoix's claim to fame is its small share in the Grand Cru AOCs of Corton and Corton-Charlemagne, but its top vineyards and Premiers Crus (La Maréchaude, La Toppe-au-Vert, La Courtière, Les Petites-Lolières and Les Grandes-Lolières) often use the appellation Aloxe-Corton.

Aloxe-Corton and Pernand-Vergelesses

The Cortons are produced primarily on these two communes. This renowned family comprises red wines and some rare extraordinary white wines. The whites include Le Corton-Charlemagne, Le Charlemagne and the very rare Corton. Most people associate Corton with reds, all of which use the Corton appellation and may include the name of the vineyard, as in Corton-Clos du Roi, Corton-Bressandes and Corton-Renardes.

All wine lovers hope to have the rare privilege of tasting a Corton. The whites, grown on slopes facing south (an exception), are powerful and full-bodied, golden in color and have a splendid bouquet with hints of almond. Corton red ranks among

CÔTE DE BEAUNE GRANDS CRUS AND APPELLATIONS

- Ladoix-Serrigny, appellation: Ladoix
- Aloxe-Corton, appellations: Corton and Corton-Charlemagne
- Chorey-lès-Beaune, appellation: Chorey
- Savigny-lès-Beaune, appellations: Savigny-Lès-Beaune and Savigny-Côte-de-Beaune
- Beaune, appellation: Beaune
- Pernand-Vergelesses, appellation: Pernand-Vergelesses
- Pommard, appellation: Pommard
- Volnay, appellation: Volnay
- Monthélie, appellation: Monthélie
- Auxey-Duresses, appellation: Auxey-Duresses
- Saint-Romain, appellation: Saint-Romain
- Saint-Aubin, appellation: Saint-Aubin
- Meursault, appellations: Meursault and Blagny
- Puligny-Montrachet, appellations: Chevalier-Montrachet, Bâtard-Montrachet, Bienvenues-Bâtard-Montrachet, Montrachet, Puligny-Montrachet, Côte-de-Beaune
- Chassagne-Montrachet, appellations: Montrachet, Bâtard-Montrachet, Criots-Bâtard-Montrachet, Chassagne-Montrachet, Côte-de-Beaune
- Santenay, appellations: Santenay and Santenay Côte-de-Beaune
- Cheilly-lès-Maranges, appellation: Cheilly-Lès-Maranges
- Sampigny-lès-Maranges, appellation: Sampigny-Lès-Maranges
- Dezize-lès-Maranges, appellation: Dezize-Lès-Maranges

Burgundy's greatest. It has a deep garnet color and is rich, powerful and full-bodied with notes of overripe or cooked berries. Corton has stolen the limelight from many Premiers Crus which are of good quality and definitely more affordable.

Savigny-lès-Beaune

A great majority of red wines and a few whites are produced on the 950 acres divided into two separate zones, north and south of the small Rhoin River. Wines produced in the south, toward Beaune, are light and inferior in quality to those in the north, growing closer to Aloxe-Corton. The latter have a bright ruby color, and rich, full-bodied flavor, particularly if produced on more reputable parcels such as Vergelesses, Dominode, Lavières and Marconnets.

Chorey-lès-Beaune

This village, located east of Savigny-lès-Beaune, has a magnificent chateau, but no Premier or Grand Cru wines. The vineyards bordering Savigny are planted in soil that is too rich for great wines, although the communal appellation wines are pleasant enough.

Beaune

As the historic "Capital of Burgundian Wines" and wine trade center, Beaune is a great place to visit, and not only to see the Hospices de Beaune charity hospital. There are also nearly 1,250 acres of vineyards. The northern vineyards produce red wines of excellent breed near Savigny. These include Beaune-les-Grèves, as well as Les Marconnets, Le Clos du Roi, Le Clos des Fèves, Les Cent Vignes and Les Bressandes. The southern regions, near Pommard, produce wines with a brilliant clear color, suppleness and a delicate fruitiness.

Pommard

At one time, Pommard was so exceedingly popular in England that the neighboring communes began to market their wine under this appellation, which has become nearly synonymous with Burgundy red. The 850 acres under vine are well worth the interest, notably the parcels Les Epenots and Les Rugiens located west of the national highway; this region produces exceptionally powerful wines.

Despite their sturdiness and high alcohol content, the other Premiers Crus (twenty-one in all) are generally somewhat softer and subtler in character.

Volnay

Just as a good Corton wine is distinguished by its powerful, robust character, Volnay wines play up their femininity, elegance and delicateness. A Volnay is to Côte de Beaune what a Chambolle-Musigny is to Côte de Nuits—the crown jewel. Although the appellation's 550 acres don't produce any Grands Crus, Les Caillerets deserves to rank as one, as do other Premiers Crus like Champans and Bousse-D'Or. One advantage of Volnay wines is that they can be drunk relatively young and slightly chilled.

Monthélie

This 325-acre wine commune deserves to be much better known. A gem of a wine is produced by Les Champs-Fulliot, an extension of Les Caillerets, one of the best vineyards of Volnay.

Auxey-Duresses

The vineyards, two-thirds of which are planted with Pinot Noir and one-third with Chardonnay, cover approximately 425 acres with full southern exposure. The reds are somewhat reminiscent of Volnays, while the whites recall the great Meursaults. The best vineyards include Les Duresses, Reugne and La Chapelle.

Saint-Romain

This picturesque village, with the ruins of the local chateau, is well worth a visit, but unfortunately no Premiers Crus are produced. Its white wines are of good quality, however. Some wines are blended with other wines grown nearby and are sold as Côte de Beaune-Villages.

Meursault

This 1,050-acre wine region produces fabulous white wines. It matters little that the best parcels (Les Genevrières, Les Perrières, Les Charmes, La Goutte-d'Or and Les Poruzots) are not ranked as Grands Crus. They are still famous for the magnificent whites which have a brilliant golden-green color. The wines are dry yet have a subtle luxuriousness, and intense complex aromas of toasted almonds or hazelnuts. Meursault reds are rarer, and most are legally marketed as Volnays.

Puligny-Montrachet and Chassagne-Montrachet

Although the two communes are linked by the noble Montrachet family, they are not identical. The former produces nearly only white wines, while the latter produces primarily reds. The two share some of the Grands Crus, although they each have exclusivity over certain Grands Crus.

Puligny owns all of Chevalier-Montrachet (17.5 acres), a beautifully balanced white with a subtle bouquet; and Bienvenues-Bâtard-Montrachet (7.5 acres), with a great measure of finesse, but perhaps a slightly less intense flavor.

Puligny and Chassagne share Montrachet (18.7 acres), whose wines are often described as being the world's greatest dry white wines. The vineyard lies halfway up the slope on soil rich in silica, limestone and clay and reddish in color from the ferrous oxide. Pale-colored, highly perfumed wines that are mellow yet vigorous are produced. It is truly a regal wine.

Around it lies Bâtard-Montrachet (30 acres). The wines are less well-rounded and subtle, yet are rich and powerful and have a bouquet with notes of toasted bread.

Chassagne owns all of Criots-Bâtard-Montrachet (3.7 acres), exclusively producing a very powerful, fruity white wine, a result of the full southern exposition. These magnificent wines shouldn't over-shadow the Premiers Crus of Chassagne or Puligny, which include Les Folatières, Le Clos de la Garenne, Les Colombettes and Les Pucelles.

Saint-Aubin

Saint-Aubin is located back in the Côte d'Or hills behind Puligny-Montrachet and Chassagne-Montrachet—tough acts to follow. If Saint-Aubin disappoints, it is for one simple reason: the vineyards are located slightly too high above the favored strip of the slope's mid-section for really top-quality wines. The commune has 590 acres under vine, 390 of which produce six Premiers Crus. One of the hamlets of Saint-Aubin is Gamay, which gives its name to the famous Beaujolais grape variety.

The production of wines other than Premiers Crus consists of a few whites and a majority of simple, light reds marketed under the appellation Côte-de-Beaune-Villages.

Santenay

The 1,000 acres of vineyards produce mainly pleasant red wines which, although they may lack a certain fullness, are agreeably rustic. There are several attractive Premiers Crus—Les Graviers, La Comme and Les Maladières, for example.

Maranges, Cheilly, Dezize and Sampigny-lès-Maranges

The last three villages of the Côte de Beaune share a Premier Cru, the Les Maranges vineyards. Nearly all of the well-structured, deeply colored reds are marketed as Côte-de-Beaune-Villages. Their quality is often as appealing as the price.

Côte Chalonnaise

Côte Chalonnaise, which is not an appellation, is frequently referred to as the "Mercurey region," as Chalon-sur-Saône is no longer the great wine-trading port it was during the Empire. Yet the region, which spans some 15 miles as the Côte de Beaune tails off, does have several interesting vineyards. They are more dispersed than those in the Côte de Beaune and, although the favored slopes generally face east (as in the Côte de Beaune), some face southeast or south. The soil types are similar enough in character, however, to produce a similarity among the reds and whites in both districts. Four communes have their own appellation. Like elsewhere in Burgundy, Pinot Noir is the predominant grape variety, occupying 67 percent; Chardonnay, for white wines, occupies 10 percent. Aligoté represents 13.5 percent, yielding the famous Aligoté de Bouzeron, among others. Lastly, Gamay represents 9.5 percent of the grape variety, which makes up two-thirds of Burgundy's Passetoutgrains—which is a mixing or vatting together of Pinot Noir and Gamay—at least one-third Pinot Noir and two-thirds Gamay.

Rully

The northernmost of the Chalonnais wine communes, Rully produces high-quality red wines, but owes its reputation to its white wines, made from Aligoté and Chardonnay. The white wines have a high degree of acidity and are naturally inclined to sparkle. They produce an excellent Crémant de Bourgogne.

Mercurey

The 1,500 acres of this appellation, which spills over into the two neighboring communes, produce mainly red wines. Pinot Noir is grown on iron-rich soil high in clay and limestone, which imparts qualities similar to those of Côte-de-Beaune-Villages and produces high-quality wines.

Givry

Like Mercurey, Givry produces mainly red wines. Although the appellation's wine-growing area is three times smaller than that of Mercurey and much less famous, the wines are by no means minor. They are sometimes more tannic and more vigorous than Mercurey wines, and age better as a result.

Montagny

This commune applies exclusively to white wines. The predominant grape is Chardonnay, and the wines are frequently light, some having a good measure of finesse. Although several vineyards can market their wines as Premiers Crus, few bottles bear the classification.

Bourgogne Côte Chalonnaise

This AOC (since 1990) spans forty-four communes between Chagny and Saint-Gengoux-le-National in the cantons of Chavigny, Givry, Buxy and Mont-de-Saint-Vincent. Red wines are produced from Pinot Noir and whites from Chardonnay. Aligotés are also becoming more popular.

Mâcon

The production area is relatively large, spanning nearly 30 miles from Tournus to Mâcon in southern Burgundy. It is known for its characteristic white wines—with some excellent ones made from Chardonnay. In contrast, its reds (sometimes produced exclusively from Pinot Noir, sometimes Gamay, sometimes a blend of both) are less well known.

The region's wide variety of wine styles stems from its five specific appellations. The first three apply to reds and whites, in ascending quality: Mâcon, with no indication of source; Mâcon Supérieur; and Mâcon, followed by the name of the commune in which the wine was grown (there are forty-three authorized communes).

Pouilly-Fuissé

Pouilly-Fuissé is the great white wine of the Mâconnais. It is produced in five communes: Solutré, Pouilly, Fuissé, Chaintré and Vergisson.

Pouillys, pale gold in color with green overtones, are made exclusively from Chardonnay grown on soil rich in limestone. They are very dry, yet silky and vigorous enough to be bottle-aged for two to three years, and sometimes longer for the better Pouilly-Fuissé.

Pouilly-Loché and Pouilly-Vinzelles

These have somewhat less breed than Pouilly-Fuissé wines, with less vigor and body. Yet as a rule they have as much fruitiness and color.

Saint-Véran

This appellation covers eight communes and applies to dry, light wines produced in conditions similar to those in Pouilly. They are lighter, however, and have a less distinctive bouquet.

Beaujolais

"Three rivers flow into Lyon—the Rhône, the Saône and the Beaujolais" goes a popular saying. And indeed the Beaujolais does flow, generally into carafes.

Beaujolais is Burgundy's largest wine-producing region, with 55,000 acres under vine, just over one-half of the total land surface producing AOC Burgundy wines. Vineyards carpet the slopes from southern Mâcon to Lyon.

Two types of soil are distinguished:
- In the north, the Haut-Beaujolais soil is granitic with slate rubble, and the sub-soil is rich in manganese.

- In the south, the Bas-Beaujolais soil is calcareous with some clay. The lesser Beaujolais are produced here.

Whites and rosés play a minor role in the region. The production is predominantly red, produced from Gamay Noir à Jus Blanc.

Gamay wines are violet-tinged in color, pleasantly fruity and so light that for years Beaujolais has been the "café" wine, served in pots, bottles and carafes.

Beaujolais is world-renowned due to the sharp business acumen of wine producers and marketing experts. To get the best out of Gamay grapes, wine producers developed a specific vinification method based largely on carbonic maceration. This is known as "Beaujolais vinification." The method preserves the fruitiness of Gamay and allows for rapid production of wines, which preferably should be drunk young—the famous Beaujolais Primeurs, which can be marketed as early as November 15 each year. With the help of a few great marketing strategies, the date has become synonymous with ritualistic drinking and festivities. Signs are posted everywhere, billing "Le Beaujolais nouveau est arrivé" (New Beaujolais is here!). The wine is flown to such cities as London, Brussels and New York, and the partying begins.

One thing should be clarified however: People drink Beaujolais Primeur, not Beau-

BEAUJOLAIS GRAPE VARIETY

Gamay Noir à Jus Blanc is the sole grape variety used in making Beaujolais reds.

jolais Nouveau, on November 15; it can be sold by producers under the denomination until January 31. Beaujolais Nouveau generally can be sold during the year following its harvest, although sales must stop by August 31.

Beaujolais' success naturally has caused the quality to vary.

The best part of these wines is the pleasure of drinking them with others; the worst is the terrible hangover after drinking too much—and this holds for both simple Beaujolais and Beaujolais Supérieur. It applies much more rarely to the Beaujolais Crus and to the some thirty-five Beaujolais-Villages.

Beaujolais Crus

The permitted yield is 420 gallons per acre (versus 530 gallons per acre and more for ordinary Beaujolais), producing wines capable of aging two to five years. Each cru has its own distinctive character. Beaujolais Crus from north to south include:

Saint-Amour

The wine is as agreeable as its name suggests (*amour* meaning "love"). It should be drunk within two years, when its suppleness and fruitiness are at a peak.

Juliénas

This fruity wine is among the sturdiest, and its high tannin makes it longer-lasting than Saint-Amour.

Chénas

Like Juliénas, it is very full-bodied and can be remarkably vigorous.

Moulin à Vent

Moulin à Vent is not a place name; the appellation is named after a windmill that stands on a hill above Les Thorins. The vineyard is divided between the communes of Chénas and Romanèches-

Thorins. The wine is classy enough to resemble a good breed Burgundy as it ages. It is the most corpulent and tasty of all Beaujolais Crus.

Fleurie

The wine is as fresh and elegant as its name, with a highly floral bouquet. It is light and soft even in its first year, and takes on a soft velvety quality as it ages. Most wine lovers have difficulty waiting for the wine to age, however, as it is so wonderful to drink.

Chiroubles

A supple, fruity, well-balanced wine that is generally of good value.

Morgon

Morgon is a big, powerful Beaujolais, whose sturdiness makes it well-suited for aging.

Régnié

Once a Beaujolais-Villages, Régnié was admitted as a cru in 1988, an apt move given its suppleness and fruitiness.

Brouilly

Brouilly is the largest cru, with vines in six communes. It produces vigorous, flavorful wines characteristic of Gamay. Best drunk after two years in the bottle.

Côte de Brouilly

These full-bodied wines grown on the sunny slopes of Mont Brouilly have great character. They're best drunk after three to four years in the bottle.

Jura and Savoy

This region east of Burgundy is better known to most people for its cross-country ski trails than its wines. The vineyards, introduced during the Roman conquest, cover 3,000 acres amid forests and pastures and are divided up into many small estates.

Jura

Grown on the limestone-rich silt of the mountain tops (1,000 feet average altitude), the various vines receive enough sunlight to weather the harsh winters. The production is highly diversified. There are relatively light reds, made from Poulsard, sometimes flavored with Pinot Noir, as well as rosés. But the range of white wines is unforgettable. Dry whites and sparkling whites made from Chardonnay (called Melon d'Arbois here) coexist with two highly original regional specialties, Vin Jaune (yellow wine) and Vin de Paille (straw wine).

Rare and therefore expensive, Vin Jaune is produced in very limited quantities and is an exclusive specialty of the Jura. Originating for the most part from the area near Château Châlon, it is produced from Savagnin (Naturé) and is processed in a way similar to that of Sherry. The grapes are harvested late and pressed in the same manner as for white wine. The juice is then sealed in barrels containing yellow wine. They are stored for a minimum of six years, during which a film forms on the top, effectively sealing it off from the air. The film contributes the unusual yellow color and nutty fragrance—the "taste of yellow." It is marketed in small 22-ounce bottles and is best drunk at room temperature. It is a wine that can last for excep-

APPELLATIONS
From the general to the particular

Jura
- Vin Jaune
- Vin de Paille
- Côtes-du-Jura
- Arbois
- Arbois-Pupillin
- Château-Châlon
- L'Étoile
- Crémant du Jura

Savoy
- Savoy wines
- Savoie-Apremont
- Savoie-Mondeuse
- Rousette de Savoie
- Seyssel
- Crépy

tionally long periods of time, sometimes for up to one century. Vin de Paille derives its name from the process of allowing the grapes, which are harvested early, to dry out on wattles (originally on straw mats) to concentrate the sugar and reduce acidity. After three to four months, the grapes lose 50 percent of their weight and the sugar becomes concentrated. They are then pressed in well-ventilated rooms. After the pressing, a long fermentation process yields a richly sweet wine that is sold in 12-ounce bottles and has great longevity.

Savoy

Following along the Rhône, the Savoy vineyards stretch from the southern side of Lake Geneva to the Isère Valley. The vineyards, occupying 3,750 acres on lowish Alpine slopes, are scattered over the valley. Mondeuse is the local grape variety; Gamay and Pinot Noir are used to produce simple red wines that are best drunk slightly chilled. The region produces mainly white wines, made from the predominant Roussette (or Altesse) grape variety. There is also Jacquère, Molette and Chasselas grapes (the Fendant of Switzerland). Many white wines produced in Savoy, most of which are dry and spirited, can be either *mousseux* (sparkling) or *perlants* (wine which is naturally slightly sparkling or crackling).

Côtes du Rhône

Some of the finest vineyards grow along the banks of the rivers. The vineyards of the Côtes du Rhône extend approximately 120 miles (105,000 acres) from Vienne to Avignon, stretching over sheer, high cliffs on both sides.

The Côtes du Rhône vineyards are some of the oldest in France. The Phoenicians and Romans grew vineyards in the Rhône Valley, which was used intensively by merchants and invading armies. For years, Côtes du Rhône wines were unjustly underrated. Today this is changing, however, and the wines are gaining in reputation, with many wine lovers appreciating the robustness and richness of the Grands Crus, which are fine enough to rank among France's best wines.

The vineyards are divided into two areas, corresponding to highly different soil types and climate:
– Northern Côtes du Rhone, from Vienne to Valence, where the soil is granite-rich, with hot summers and autumns and high humidity regulated by the river.
– Approximately 24 miles south, around Avignon, Orange and Châteauneuf-du-Pape, the southern Côtes du Rhône has sandy soil rich in gravelly alluvium deposits and drift boulders. Summers are dry and the area is swept by the mistral wind each year.

Northern vineyards

Wine producers in this region share a staunch allegiance to the Syrah grape variety, the only one used for red wines. It produces deep-colored, tannic wines with concentrated aromas. Whites are made from Viognier alone or from Marsanne and Roussanne, most often combined.

Nearly all of the great Côtes du Rhône are described here in eight AOCS, some of which represent wines that rank on a par with the great Bordeaux and Burgundies.

EIGHT APPELLATIONS

- Côte Rôtie (right bank): red wine.
- Condrieu (right bank): white wine.
- Château-Grillet (right bank): white wine.
- Saint-Joseph (right bank): red and white wines.
- Hermitage (left bank): red and white wines.
- Crozes-Hermitage (left bank): red and white wines.
- Cornas (right bank): red wine.
- Saint-Péray (right bank): red and white wines, slightly sparkling wines.

Côte Rotie

On the right bank of the Rhône, 4 miles from Vienne and above the village of Ampuis, the Côte Rôtie is on a hillside terraced steeply with old stone walls. The slope consists of two parts: the Côte Brune and the Côte Blonde. Syrah is the predominant grape variety for both, although the white grape variety Viognier is sometimes added to round out the wine and add a measure of finesse to the bouquet. In this way, after being blended and aged in oak barrels, the wines are garnet-colored, heady and powerful, with an assertive bouquet. They are best aged in the bottle for at least five years, preferably longer.

Condrieu

The commune of Condrieu, located 3 miles from Ampuis, lords over 230 acres of terraced vineyards. Only white wines made entirely from Viognier grapes are allowed to use the appellation. The magnificent white wine produced is sometimes dry, sometimes semi-sweet, golden in color with a subtle flowery, spicy bouquet. A disadvantage is its scarcity, for production is limited and nearly all of what little there is goes to the region's great restaurants.

Château-Grillet

Château-Grillet, even more scarce and more exceptional, stands apart from other French wines. The appellation applies to only one estate—a tiny 6.7-acre vineyard south of Condrieu, straddling the communes of Verin and Saint-Michel-sous-Condrieu. The vineyard is perched on a steep slope above the Rhône, somewhere between 525 and 820 feet high in altitude. Its sole grape variety, Viognier, gives it its

CÔTES DU RHÔNE GRAPE VARIETIES

Syrah is the sole grape used for red wines. Viognier, Roussanne and Marsanne are used for white wines.

high alcohol content and delicate perfume. The wine is aged 18 months in oak barrels. It has qualities similar to those of Condrieu, with perhaps a bit more suppleness and a greater measure of finesse. If you can find a bottle (its production rarely exceeds 12,000 bottles), it should be drunk young. It is one of the truly great white wines of the Rhône Valley and one of the most exceptional white wines in the world. The same family has run the estate since 1820.

Hermitage and Crozes-Hermitage

Once a favorite with the great and powerful, Hermitage remains on the whole excellent in terms of quality. The 312 acres of terraced vineyards grow on the slopes above Tain-l'Hermitage. The red wine grape is the Syrah—yielding full-bodied wines that are rich in alcohol—while the white wine grapes are Marsanne and Roussanne. The whites are soft, sweet and fruity, yet dry and low in acidity. Both reds and whites are long-lasting. The 2,750 acres of Crozes-Hermitage surround the winegrowing regions of Hermitage and produce reds and whites which, although lighter, often resemble Hermitages.

Saint-Joseph

Some 2,030 acres of vineyards on the right bank of the Rhône, opposite Hermi-

tage and producing the same grape varieties, occupy terrain that is less granitic and less precipitous. The reds and whites are more supple and light and are ready after five years in the bottle.

Cornas

This 190-acre wine-producing region lies near the city of Valence in the foothills of the Cévennes Mountains. Syrah is the predominant grape variety.

The very dark wine, if well vinified, can be a bit hard at first taste, but in general is full-bodied. It goes very well with game.

Saint-Péray

Near Cornas, growing on arid slopes, lies the 88-acre vineyard of Saint-Péray. Marsanne and Roussanne grape varieties produce spirited white wines that are some-

times more well-rounded and fruitier than certain Champagnes. This rare but excellent aperitif is relatively unknown.

Clairette de Die and Châtillon-en-Diois

This winegrowing region, located on the right bank of the Drôme River, produces a semi-sparkling white wine made from Clairette and Muscat grapes. It is called "de tradition" (not to be confused with "brut") and makes a very agreeable aperitif with distinctive apple aromas. Châtillon, above Die, is a recent AOC producing simple, light reds and whites.

Southern vineyards

From Montélimar to Avignon, many changes occur, not only in terms of soil and climate, but also grape varieties, which are multiple here. Simple Côtes du Rhônes wines are produced in the region, as well as Côtes-du-Rhône-Villages. The region owes its prestige to a small number of stellar appellations, for the most part Châteauneuf-du-Pape and Gigondas.

Châteauneuf-du-Pape

This is the largest appellation area of the Côtes du Rhône. The popes of Avignon introduced wine production to the area.

THREE TYPES OF REGIONAL APPELLATIONS

- Côtes-du-Rhône
- Côtes-du-Rhône-Villages
- Côtes-du-Rhône Primeur

The alcohol content is a sign of quality. Alcohol adds body and strength and improves wine. The diversity is expressed in the number of authorized grape varieties: Grenache, Cinsault, Syrah, Mourvèdre for reds; Clairette, Picpoul, Bourboulenc and Roussanne for whites (these being the main ones).

Vast terraces of varying height are covered with pebbles, which absorb heat very well. Exceptionally, thirteen grape varieties are authorized here. Although the yield is restricted to 375 gallons per acre for both reds and whites, the vineyard is large enough to ensure an abundant production, which includes the best and the lesser wines as well. A traditional Châteauneuf-du-Pape is a well-rounded, full-bodied, robust wine that grows smoother with age. The current trend among certain wine producers to use carbonic maceration in vinifying wines is unfortunate. The wines may be more appealing in the short term, but they lose a degree of their substance and well-roundedness.

Gigondas

The soil on these 3,000 acres resembles that of Châteauneuf-du-Pape. Thirteen grape varieties are authorized, but only Grenache, Cinsault, Syrah, Mourvèdre and Clairette are actually used.

The reds, by far the majority, somewhat resemble those of Châteauneuf-du-Pape, although they have a less rich and complex bouquet. Other AOC wines of the south include Lirac and Tavel, producing very dry and fragrant rosés when carefully vinified. Among the Côtes-du-Rhône-Villages, special mention goes to Rasteau, particularly for its natural sweet wines, and to Beaumes-de-Venise for its magnificent Muscat.

Tavel

Tavel has the great distinction of being the best rosé produced in France, if not one of the best rosés in the world. The list of Tavel lovers is a long one, from writers to kings.

The appellation produces nothing but rosé wine; the area covers Tavel and a small sector of the adjacent commune of Roquemaure. The 2,375 acres of vineyards, 9 miles from Châteauneuf-du-Pape on the opposite bank, are located on the edge of an area of uncultivated land. The wines grow in sandy soil, with alluvial deposits rich in clay and a gravely substratum—for the better parcels—carried here by the Rhône and its tributaries.

THE THIRTEEN GRAPE VARIETIES OF CHÂTEAUNEUF-DU-PAPE

Grenache and Cinsault are the most common, followed by Syrah, Mourvèdre, Clairette and Picpoul, as well as Muscardin, Vaccarèse, Cournoise, Picardan, Roussanne, Terret Noir and Bourboulenc.

APPELLATIONS

- Châteauneuf-du-Pape (left bank): red and white wines
- Gigondas (left bank): red and rosé wines
- Vacqueyras (left bank): red, rosé and white wines
- Tavel (right bank): rosé wines
- Lirac (right bank): red, rosé and white wines

Neighboring appellations
Coteaux du Tricastin (left bank): red, rosé and white wines
Côtes du Ventoux (left bank): red, rosé and white wines
Côtes du Luberon (right bank): red and rosé wines
Côtes du Vivarais (right bank)
Coteaux de Pierrevert (right bank): two VDQS

Provence, Côte d'Azur and Corsica

The magical combination of sea, stone and sun established Provence and Corsica as the cradle of viticulture in France. From Toulon to Marseille and Aix-en-Provence, the warm Mediterranean climate builds up such a thirst that most wine producers place a priority on making simple rosés to be served well-chilled. Nothing sells better during the tourist rush.

As a result, red wine production in the vast winegrowing region of Côtes de Provence (nearly 50,000 acres, newly anointed with the AOC classification) has declined. Recent efforts by certain property owners to grow Bordelais grape varieties should be hailed, as they have produced some fairly promising reds. Throughout Provence, four appellations deserve recognition, despite their somewhat limited size. First, Bandol, which produces the most harmonious tannic reds of the region on 1,250 acres planted predominantly with Mourvèdre. In contrast, Cassis, near Marseille, stands out for its dry, fruity whites. The small region of Palette (50 acres) near Aix-en-Provence produces fresh, refined white wines as well as a few sturdy reds. Lastly, Bellet (100 acres) yields white, red and rosé wines superior in finesse with respect to others in the region.

Bandol

Northwest of Toulon, the 3,250 acres of the Bandol appellation benefit from the proximity of the sea, sandy limestone soil and abundant sunshine that allows them to easily exceed the minimum 11 % required for qualification.

Bandol wines may therefore have a bitter taste when young. As a result, they cannot be sold before a minimum of eight months' aging in barrels for whites and rosés, and at least eighteen months for reds. The compulsory eighteen-month aging period for Bandol reds—the most reputable and interesting—allows them to obtain their color, level of tannin and black currant aromas of the Mourvèdre grape.

Cassis

Famous for its magnificent coves, the small fishing port of Cassis is also the site of a quality vineyard, albeit it is somewhat

controversial. Some wine lovers find full-bodied, vigorous and heady Cassis whites to be the best. The writer Frédéric Mistral described them as smelling of rosemary, heather and myrtle. Others claim the dry and strong rosés are best. Whatever your pick, the wine is best drunk during a meal, as the wine's qualities are most pronounced in accompanying seafood, fish and bouillabaisse. Cassis also produces robust reds, although they are less distinctive than the rosés and whites.

Corsica

In the 1960s, following the Algerian War, there was a revival in wine production on the aptly named Ile de Beauté as expatriates returned home. The local grape varieties, Sciacarello and Niellucio, flourish alongside Grenache and Cinsault and produce hardy reds and sturdy rosés.

Sciacarello yields elegant, lively wines which have a bright color. Niellucio (a grape variety related to Sangiovese) produces more robust wines with a good measure of tannin. There are also a few dry white wines of considerable quality. The vineyards of Patrimonio, one of the island's seven AOC wines, resemble a

APPELLATIONS: "VILLAGES" AND CRUS

Five Appellations Villages:

- **Vin de Corse** (generic appellation)
- **Vin de Corse-Coteaux du Cap Corse**
- **Vin de Corse-Calvi**
- **Vin de Corse-Sartène**
Red and rosé wines produced from Sciacarello, Cinsault and Grenache.
- **Vin de Corse-Figari**
A red wine that keeps well made from Grenache and Carcagiolo, a local grape variety specific to the region.
- **Vin de Corse-Porto-Vecchio**

Two Grands Crus:
The appellations Ajaccio and Patrimonio, promoted to Grand Cru status, are not preceded by the Vin de Corse appellation.

kind of enormous amphiteater, growing between a mountain ridge and the bay. Patrimonio is the oldest of Corsica's AOC wines and remains the best.

APPELLATIONS

Curiously enough, the appellations of the Provence-Côte d'Azur wine-producing region were granted during two different periods spanning nearly forty years. The smallest *terroirs* (under 2,470 acres) were the first to be granted the classification, from 1936 to 1948. The largest *terroirs* (over 2,470 acres) were not granted an appellation until the mid-1970s. The former (1936-1948) include four AOC wines: Bandol, Bellet, Cassis and Palette, although Bellet nearly lost AOC status in 1947 when urban development around Nice threatened the vineyards on the hillsides.

The newcomers include three AOC wines: Côtes-de-Provence (1977), Coteaux d'Aix-en-Provence (1986) and Coteaux Varois (1993).

PROVENCE GRAPE VARIETIES

There are many Côtes du Rhône grape varieties in Provence. Carignan, Cinsault, Grenache and Mourvèdre are used to make red and rosé wines. Whites are produced from Sauvignon, Clairette and Ugni Blanc.

Languedoc-Roussillon

Languedoc-Roussillon, the most vast wine-producing region in France, arches along the Mediterranean coast from the Rhône Delta to the Spanish border. Until the mid-1960s, most wines produced were ordinary red wines, light in color and alcohol and used mostly for blending with other wines. But for the past fifteen years, the region has been making great efforts to produce greater quality wines, through large-scale uprooting of high-yield grape varieties, the selection of more aromatic grapes, and more frequent use of carbonic maceration in vinification, well-suited for young fruity wines as it enhances their fruitiness. This tendency to produce higher-quality wines is accelerating as a result of stiffer competition from other European countries.

The vast area of Corbières (extending from Narbonne to Carcassonne and to the area surrounding Perpignan) deserves special mention for its agreeable, highly popular red wines. Corbières has at least one direct competitor in Minervois, where wine dealers have spearheaded moves for more careful grape selection to set an example in terms of quality.

Les Costières in Nîmes and such vineyards as La Clape and Saint-Chinian inside the huge Coteaux du Languedoc zone deserve mention as well.

The AOCs of the region, however, are of greatest interest. The most famous concern the sweet fortified wines produced in Banyuls, Maury and Rivesaltes.

Minervois

Côtes de Cabardès
Côtes de la Malepère

North of the ramparts of Carcassonne, the AOC Minervois is produced alongside two VDQS: Côtes de Cabardès et de l'Orbiel and Côtes de la Malepère. Sixty-one communes share the appellation straddling the Aude and the Hérault, which offers the 10,000 acres of vineyards sun-drenched slopes and terraced hills sheltered from cold winds by the Montagne Noire. The region's rough, gravely soil and dry climate produce excellent red wines composed of Grenache, Syrah and at least 30 percent Mourvèdre. They are sturdy wines with notes of red or wild berries, even violet notes depending on the *terroir*. The rosés are dry and fruity, the whites spirited and aromatic, sometimes with hints of honey and linden or of heather.

Corbières

Corbières, which acquired AOC status in 1985, extends over eighty-seven communes southeast of Carcassonne down to the Mediterranean. This country of contrasting landscapes is filled with rocky hills and uncultivated land, drenched in sunshine and swept by winds; it is divided into four production zones: Corbières Maritimes along the coast; Hautes-Corbières in the mountains; Corbières d'Alaric in the northwest, where the climate is milder; and Corbières Centrales, south of the Vallée de l'Aude.

Ninety-three percent of the wine produced in the region is red wine which, depending on the *terroir* and grape variety—the Carignan being predominant—can be well-rounded and full-bodied; soft and primeur (made to be drunk very young); or powerful and hearty, developing a remarkable bouquet after five or six years in the bottle. Much more scarce are the dry, aromatic white wines and the fresh, fruity rosés.

Fitou

The 5,000 acres under vine in Fitou are divided into two parts: Fitou Maritimes bordering the Etang de Leucate and Etang de Lapalme; and an inland region, ensconced in the Hautes-Corbières. The sheer immensity of the arid, sterile slopes are remarkably well-suited for wine production, making Fitou one of the best wines of

MAIN GRAPE VARIETIES OF THE LANGUEDOC-ROUSSILLON

White wines: Clairette, Picpoul, Mauzac, Ugni Blanc, Listan, Bourboulenc, Terret.
Red wines: Grenache, Carignan, Aramon, Cinsault, Syrah, Mourvèdre, Alicante-Bouschet.
Sweet and richly sweet wines: Grenache, Malvoisie, Maccabeo, Muscat.

the Midi. Made essentially of Carignan, Grenache or Lladoner Pelut, Fitou is a powerful, assertive wine that is deep in tone and rich in alcohol. It must have a minimum nine months in wood before being marketed, and is best drunk after five to six years.

Rivesaltes, Banyuls and Maury

These are the Sweet Fortified Wine appellations, producing a variety of remarkable wines with highly distinctive characters. Rivesaltes is produced on eighty-six communes of the Pyrénées-Roussillon and nine communes of the Aude region. There are three types, whites, reds and Muscat de Rivesaltes—by far the best—which is a remarkable amber color. Banyul wines are superb, with an incredibly rich aroma, whether rosés, known as Grenaches after the grape variety used, or reds, which are somewhere between Madeira and Port. Some Banyuls are considered to be the only wine that can be drunk with chocolate. The vineyards lie on steep schistous terraces overlooking the Mediterranean.

A WHOLE ARRAY OF APPELLATIONS

Fitou is the oldest AOC in the Languedoc region. Thirty-four other appellations have since come into existence, most during the last ten years or so. There will soon be others, for after a long period of stagnation, Languedoc-Roussillon wines are improving all the time.

Languedoc appellations:
There are at least twenty-eight appellations in the Gard, Hérault and Aude *départements*.
• AOC Costières de Nîmes
• AOC Clairette de Bellegarde
• AOC Coteaux du Languedoc
• AOC Coteaux du Languedoc Cabrières
• AOC Coteaux du Languedoc Saint-Christol
• AOC Coteaux du Languedoc la Méjanelle
• AOC Coteaux du Languedoc Montpeyroux
• AOC Coteaux du Languedoc Pic Saint-Loup
• AOC Coteaux du Languedoc Saint-Drézery
• AOC Coteaux du Languedoc Vérargues
• AOC Coteaux du Languedoc Saint-Georges-d'Orques
• AOC Coteaux du Languedoc Saint-Saturnin
• AOC Coteaux du Languedoc-Picpoul du Pinet
• AOC Coteaux du Languedoc La Clape
• AOC Coteaux du Languedoc Quatorze
• AOC Clairette du Languedoc
• AOC Faugères
• AOC Saint-Chinian
• AOC Muscat de Lunel
• AOC Muscat de Mireval
• AOC Muscat de Frontignan
• AOC Muscat de Saint-Jean-de-Minervois
• AOC Corbières
• AOC Minervois
• VDQS Côtes du Cabardès et de l'Orbiel
• VDQS Côtes de la Malpère
• AOC Blanquette de Limoux
• AOC Fitou

Roussillon appellations:
The Pyrénées-Orientales *département* has six AOC appellations.
• Rivesaltes
• Banyuls
• Collioure
• Côtes du Roussillon
• Côtes du Roussillon-Villages
• Maury

Wines of Southwest France

The various vineyards in the southwest of France, scattered over a vast area stretching from east of Bordeaux down to the Spanish border, produce wines that are original and assertive in character. All of them benefit from generous sunshine, and the wines are sturdy enough to accompany the rich local cuisine, including the famous confits and foies gras. Some wines are produced near the Bordeaux area, yet they do not resemble Bordeaux wines in the slightest. This is especially true in the most southern vineyards, which have their own grape varieties.

Bergerac and Côtes de Bergerac

These two appellations are the most general ones of the region and designate light and fruity red or white wines (two-thirds of the production), agreeable when drunk fairly young, after two years. They often are an excellent buy. A semi-sweet Côtes de Bergerac produced from overripe grapes is becoming more popular.

Saussignac

On the left bank of the Dordogne, west of the Monbazillac vineyard, this recent appellation (since 1982) concerns a small production of white wines that are generally dry and fairly strong (12.5 % minimum). The semi-sweet wines are just slightly less sweet than those of Monbazillac. They are essentially marketed on site, but deserve greater recognition.

Monbazillac

Monbazillac is the wine of Bergerac par excellence—so much so that during the Middle Ages when the pope asked a delegation of pilgrims from Bergerac visiting him where exactly Bergerac was, his chamberlain is said to have murmured "Near Monbazillac."

It is made by the same methods as Sauternes (late harvest, grape-by-grape harvesting, overripe grapes on which the noble rot of the *Botrytis cinerea* acts) and from the same grape varieties (Sémillon, Sauvignon and Muscadelle). Although known as the "poor man's Sauternes," in good years it will have much of the full, richly sweetness of its "young" neighbor— young because the vinification techniques for Monbazillac date back to the Renaissance, but weren't transposed to Sauternes until the harvest of 1874.

After a few difficult years (collapse of demand after the Second World War and the abandonment of traditional selective harvesting methods), Monbazillac has made a splendid comeback as a result of the efforts of the local cooperative operating out of the magnificent Château de Monbazillac.

Buzet

In the Lot-et-Garonne *département,* around the city of Agen, the Bordelais grape varieties (Cabernet, Malbec and Merlot) are still grown in this beautiful vineyard on the slopes. Nearly all wine producers here are grouped into co-ops and produce mainly reds which can be very excellent buys.

Cahors

The vineyard of Quercy produces one wine only, a red. But what a wine—the prestigious Cahors, which the English nicknamed "black wine" for its very deep tones.

This wine has a very ancient reputation and tradition. The vineyard dates back to the seventh century, and the wines were exported as far and wide as Russia (where the communion wine, although currently produced in Crimea, is still called Cahors). For years, Cahors was the wine of the rich and powerful. Pope John XXII had it delivered to the Avignon Palace in the early fourteenth century, while François I planted Cahors vines in Fontainebleau.

Varietal blends: 70 percent Auxerrois

Quercy produces exclusively red wines, predominantly using Auxerrois (the local name for Cot, Malbec, still called Cahors in other regions). When used alone, this grape variety produces a very hard deep inky color. This is why small proportions of Merlot, Jurançon, Tannat and Syrah are blended with Auxerrois to make Cahors wines, as well as Dame Noire (or Folle Noire).

Two soil types, three *terroirs*

Most of the vineyards grow in soil rich in alluvial deposits forming terraces and small hills above the Lot, downstream from Cahors. Certain vines grow in the dell of the valley near the river, equally rich in alluvial deposits. In contrast, the vines on the Causse plateau flourish in dolinas—sink-holes rich in red clay and chalky pebbles—and appear to be growing in stone.

The climate conditions for the entire region are Atlantic, with a touch of Mediterranean brought by the autan—the "madman's wind"—and warm sunshine, which is magnified as the light reflects off the white limestone.

APPELLATIONS: A REFLECTION OF DIVERSITY

The twenty-seven appellations in existence, including twenty-two AOC wines, are proof that recent efforts by wine producers to improve quality are paying off. In addition, most of the Hors Appellation wines deserve to be classified as Vin de Pays.

Guyenne vineyards
All wines produced in the Bergerac region are classified as AOC wines, with nine appellations: Bergerac, Côtes de Bergerac, Saussignac, Monbazillac, Montravel, Côtes de Montravel, Haut-Montravel, Pécharmant, Rosette. Côtes de Duras and Côtes du Marmandais vineyards in the Lot-et-Garonne region are classified, respectively, as AOC wines and VDQS wines.

Le Quercy vineyards
All wines produced here are classified as AOC Cahors.

Le Rouergue vineyards
This region produces two VDQS and one AOC: wines from Entraygues, Le Fel, Estaing and Marcillac.

Le Tarn vineyards
Three appellations: AOC Gaillac and AOC Côtes du Frontonnais (with the mention Fronton or Villaudric, depending on area of production) and wine from Lavilledieu, classified VDQS.

Gascony and Pyrénées vineyards
They share nine appellations, seven AOC: Buzet (called Côtes de Buzet until 1988), Côtes du Brulhois, Jurançon, Béarn, Irouléguy and—curiously enough—two AOC wines from the same *terroir:* Madiran for red wines and Pacherenc du Vic Bilh for whites. Côtes de Saint-Mont and Tursan wines are classified as VDQS.

Gaillac

Gaillac vineyards are scattered along the Tarn east of the beautiful city of Albi; they yield a great variety of reds, rosés and whites, including some sparkling whites. Predominant local grape varieties include Duras and Braucol for reds, and Ondenc and Mauzac for whites. Gaillac wines in general are best drunk young and slightly chilled, and can be excellent buys.

Côtes du Frontonnais

Négrette is the main grape variety of Côtes du Frontonnais, located north of Toulouse near Gaillac. The supple wines—primarily reds and some rosés—are best drunk young and chilled. They are as familiar to the residents of Toulouse as Beaujolais wines are to the Lyonnais.

Madiran

North of Pau, this vineyard produces wines that are very deep in tone, similar to those of Cahors. But unlike Cahors, the color is produced by the Tannat grape, which occupies 50 percent of the vineyard. The wines are robust and full-bodied, and although they are far from having great finesse, they have a remarkable roundness. Madiran can bottle-age for ten years or more.

Jurançon

Planted primarily with the rare traditional grape varieties Gros Manseng and Petit Manseng, this vineyard located south of Pau produces mainly sweet Jurançon white wines, as well as a few dry whites. The sweet whites are exceptional in their pungency, firmness and complex nose of spices, nutmeg and cinnamon. Jurançon is a great wine which can age for many years, easily longer than ten years. For the record, we mention the AOC appellations Irouléguy and Béarn (less interesting) and the VDQS Tursan.

Bordeaux

Given the number of prestigious crus it produces, Bordeaux—one of the most important wine-producing regions in the world—seems particularly endowed with the gift of the grape.

The vineyards occupy nearly 285,000 acres, forming a triangle encompassing the left bank of the Garonne, the right bank of the Dordogne and the area around the Gironde.

Soil types range from gravel banks to limestone and clay, and differ too widely to give wines common characteristics, which are instead attributed to the temperate climate due to the proximity of the sea and to specific grape varieties.

Bordeaux wines are produced using several different grapes, which are vinified separately, then blended in varying proportions.

The three main red grape varieties are Cabernet Sauvignon, Cabernet Franc and Merlot, to which Malbec and Petit Verdot are added. The three white grape varieties are Sauvignon, Sémillon and Muscadelle.

With the exception of the great sweet wines, all the fine wines of Bordeaux are red. There is a handful of dry whites as well. There are over four thousand chateaux in the Gironde (wine estates are called "chateaux" here), so the various hierarchies and classifications, although quite sophisticated, play a major role in distinguishing some two hundred wines from the others.

Médoc

Médoc is a corruption of the Latin *in medio aqua,* and takes its name from its geographical position, almost in the middle of the water—for the 42-mile peninsula, which occupies a landmass of some 850 square miles, is never wider than 3 to 6 miles as it stretches from east of the Gironde to the Atlantic. The winegrowing region benefits from the mildness and humidity due to the proximity of the ocean and the estuary. Médoc is divided into two local appellations:

Bas-Médoc, which occupies the northern part and has a soil rich in clay. The area is so riddled with streams and canals that some compare it to the Netherlands.

Haut-Médoc, with its gravely, pebbly soil, produces wines of magnificently fine breed, with a great measure of finesse and such distinction that they are considered the queens of Bordeaux.

MÉDOC GRAPE VARIETIES

As Médoc produces only red wines, only the corresponding Bordelais grapes are found here. Cabernet Sauvignon and Cabernet Franc are predominant. There is also Merlot, as well as a small amount of Malbec and Petit Verdot.

Crus Bourgeois

The first thing to know is that Crus Bourgeois, despite their fine qualities, are not Crus Classés, or officially classified wines. They came into existence when the Bordeaux bourgeois acquired seignorial land. Over the centuries, they obtained good winegrowing land in the Médoc, and the vineyards were christened Crus Bourgeois—the merchants' name for good-quality wines that were not included in the great 1855 classification.

Margaux

This appellation, occupying 3,400 acres, includes five communes: Margaux, Arsac, Cantenac, Labarde and Soussans. The chateaux themselves tend to be clustered around the village of Margaux, but the winegrowing area is very much broken up. Nowhere in Médoc is the soil more stony and the subsoil more gravely. This is most likely why the appellation produces more Crus Classés than any other. Another factor includes a limited yield of an average 420 gallons per acre.

The result are wines with subtle complexity and a superb harmony. Although the greatest—with Château Margaux topping the list—are virtual works of art, the Cinquièmes Crus (Fifth Growths) of the appellation are also a great luxury to drink.

Saint-Julien

The vineyards of Saint-Julien occupy 2,250 acres. The area is small, yet most of it is classified, although no Premier Cru is produced.

Saint-Julien lies on gravely hillocks with a clay-rich subsoil with good drainage. The conditions are so favorable to wine

The incredibly wide variety of growths incited brokers and shippers to develop a classification system early on. Categories range from Crus Paysans, Crus Artisans and Crus Bourgeois Ordinaires to Crus Bourgeois Supérieurs and Grands Crus. The 27,170 acres under vine in the Médoc region today are divided into eight appellations:

Two regional appellations:
Médoc and Haut-Médoc
The Médoc appellation applies to all appellations, but is used principally in the northern Bas-Médoc, where it covers approximately 11,725 acres. The Haut-Médoc encompasses twenty-nine communes, from Blanquefort to Saint-Estèphe and includes the Grands Crus, notably:

Six communal appellations famous throughout the world:
Saint-Estèphe
Saint-Julien
Pauillac
Listrac
Moulis
Margaux

Four of these appellations include fifty-four of the sixty-two crus classified in 1855 (this classification applies only to red wines).

Moulis and Listrac

The two communes, located in the center of Haut-Médoc west of Margaux, have been unfairly bypassed with respect to official classifications, and not a single Cru Classé is produced.

Yet Moulis, with a winegrowing region of 1,370 acres that includes a large gravelly ridge in the hamlet of Grand-Poujeaux, can boast of such crus as Château Chasse-Spleen.

Listrac has more than a beautiful Romanesque church, for its 1,250 acres of vines produce robust yet elegant wines similar to those produced in Moulis.

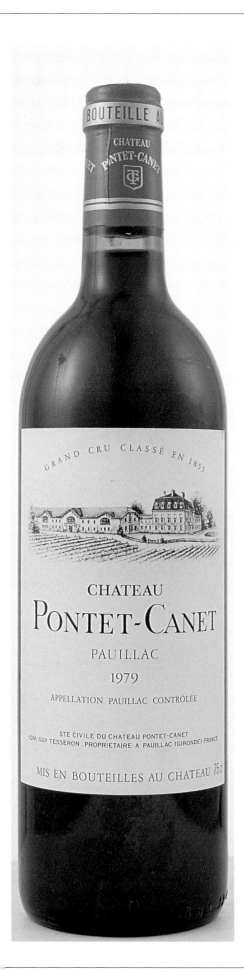

production that the wines easily rival those of Margaux in finesse and delicacy, yet are more robust and full-bodied.

Pauillac

Given the number of inhabitants, Pauillac is the largest commune of the Médoc, a fact owed to the petroleum refinery.

This doesn't prevent the 2,960 acres of glorious vines surrounding it to flourish in the gravely, pebbly soil.

Pauillac produces three Premiers Crus and fifteen Crus Classés which, although they are Cinquièmes Crus (Fifth Growths), are highly exceptional in quality. They are vigorous and are the most virile of Médoc wines, yet their strength is well-balanced by a rare finesse.

Saint-Estèphe

Set against hills with steep slopes, Saint-Estèphe's 3,110 acres of vineyards are the

---

APPELLATIONS: THREE MAJOR CATEGORIES

French regulations stipulate that there should be no hierarchy among AOC wines, yet there are three major appellation categories for Bordeaux wines:

1 - A general appellation: Bordeaux or Bordeaux Supérieur.

The appellation dates from 1911 and applies to all wines produced on vineyards in the Gironde département (excluding forest zones and flat lands near the river rich in alluvial deposits, called *palus*). Some 69 million gallons are produced annually. These include:
Bordeaux whites
Bordeaux dry whites
Bordeaux Supérieur (noble grape varieties, better vinification, higher alcohol content, lower yield per acre, good longevity)
Bordeaux rosés
Bordeaux clarets
Bordeaux Clarets Supérieurs
Bordeaux Sparkling (second fermentation in the bottle using the *méthode champenoise*)
This appellation groups together vineyards that have no local appellation. But there are many producers in the Gironde who vinify several kinds of wines. For most, the appellation applies to only one wine, the others are entitled to a generic appellation.

2 - A "regional" appellation.

3 - A "local" or "communal" appellation

Médoc has two regional appellations:
Médoc, Haut-Médoc
Six "communal" appellations:
Margaux
Moulis
Listrac
Saint-Julien
Pauillac
Saint-Estèphe
Graves has three appellations:
Graves
Graves Supérieurs
Pessac-Léognan

Sauternais has three appellations:
Sauternes
Barsac
Cérons
Entre-Deux-Mers has eight appellations:
Entre-Deux-Mers
Entre-Deux-Mers-Haut-Benauge
Cadillac
Loupiac
Sainte-Croix-du-Mont
Côtes de Bordeaux Saint-Macaire
Sainte-Foy-Bordeaux
Graves de Vayres
Libournais has fourteen appellations, including four for Saint-Émilion:
Saint-Émilion
Saint-Émilion Grand Cru
Saint-Émilion Grand Cru Classé
Saint-Émilion Premier Grand Cru Classé
And five neighboring communes:
Montagne-Saint-Émilion
Saint-Georges-Saint-Émilion
Parsac-Saint-Émilion
Lussac-Saint-Émilion
Puisseguin-Saint-Émilion
Pomerol
Lalande de Pomerol
Néac
Fronsac
Canon Fronsac
The Côtes group (although they are not geographically grouped together, they have formed an association to defend and promote the wines):
Côtes de Blaye
Premières Côtes de Blaye
Côtes de Bourg
Premières Côtes de Bordeaux
Bordeaux Côtes de Castillon
Bordeaux Côtes de Francs

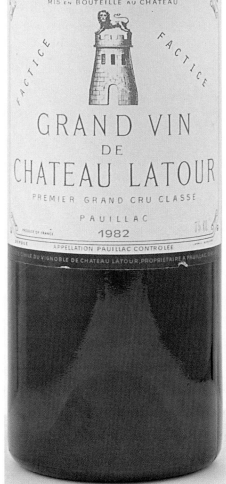

most widely spread out of the Haut-Médoc. The soil is the area's heaviest and least gravely, yielding deep-colored robust wines that lose a certain measure of finesse as a result. There are few Crus Classés in Saint-Estèphe, but on the whole the wines are excellent in quality.

GRAVES GRAPE VARIETIES

For white wines, a small percentage of Muscadelle is sometimes added to the classic Sauvignon and Sémillon. For reds, the traditional Bordelais grape varieties are used: Cabernet Sauvignon, Cabernet Franc and Merlot, and in lesser quantities, Malbec and Petit Verdot.

Haut-Médoc

The global appellation encompasses all of the vineyards surrounding the famous regions of the six communal appellations. Quality thus varies. Wines can be first-class, such as Château La Lagune and Château Cantemerle produced in Ludon, a commune in the southernmost regions 10 miles outside Bordeaux.

Graves

When Aquitaine belonged to the kingdom of England, all well-known wines from Bordeaux came from Graves. The region, stretching from the edge of the Médoc, is a strip of land approximately 6 to 9 miles in width encompassing Bordeaux and running down the Garonne for 36 miles. The vines have virtually disappeared from the city and suburbs as a result of urban development, except for the famous Château Haut-Brion, Château Laville-Haut-Brion and Château La Tour-Haut-Brion.

What has protected these vineyards from urban encroachment? The Graves region has many forests and prairies, as well as vineyards, which are less numerous than in the Médoc and smaller. But more important, the best soil lies in the north, mainly around the communes of

Pessac and Talence (almost immediately adjacent to Bordeaux), Gradignan, Ville-neuve-d'Ornon and Léognan (which boasts six Crus Classés). The greater reputation of Graves du Nord was officially recognized on September 9, 1987, when the Graves region was divided into two, and the north was designated a superior appellation, Pessac-Léognan, occupying nearly 2,500 acres west and southwest of Bordeaux on the communes of Cadanjac, Carrejan, Gradignan, Léognan, Martillac, Mérignac, Pessac, Saint-Médard d'Eyrans, Talence and Villenave-d'Ornon. This new appellation encompasses fifty-five crus, including all of the Graves Crus Classés. Reputed for its red wines produced on soil similar to the sandy, limestone and clay soil of the Haut-Médoc, and a subsoil rich in flintly gravel ("Graves"), the Pessac-Léognan appellation also produces the best white wines in all of Bordeaux.

The rivalry between Graves and Médoc is legendary. Although the Graves reds are quite similar to those of the Médoc, they are slighty less elegant, do not age as well and are more marked by the *terroir*— making them subtly different from Médocs. But choosing between a little less class and a little more body remains a question of taste. Although the white grape varieties are more widespread in the south, there are white wines produced in the north as well. Most are fragrant, fresh dry white wines with a subtle bouquet. They age well, and generally improve in richness and complexity. The sweet white Graves Supérieurs are produced within the Sauternais and can be of very good quality.

Sauternes

Barsac and Cérons

The Sauternais is filled with crests, ridges and hills, occupying 5,750 acres of vineyards ensconced in the southern area of Graves. The appellation is reserved for five communes: on one side, Sauternes, Bommes, Fargues and Preignac; on the other, Barsac, where the countryside is flatter. The latter is entitled to its own appellation (AOC Barsac). The Ciron, a tributary of the Garonne, flows between the two regions, providing just the right humidity required for Sauternes wines. The terrain of flinty gravel, with a subsoil of clay, plays a vital role in producing quality, as does the climate, with its early morning mists followed by bright sunshine. The humidity is required for the development of *Botrytis cinerea*, which covers the grape skin and forms the famous noble rot required for sweet wines.

The best of these wines—the queen of Sauternes being Chateau d'Yquem with its "extravagant perfection"—are unrivaled in class. Ranging from golden yellow to light amber, they develop a sumptuous floral, fruity, honey-rich bouqet , reconciling opulence and sweetness, finesse and strength. A good Sauternes is always expensive, so be wary of those sold for lower prices.

There are several reasons for the higher prices. The yield is restricted to an aver-

SAUTERNES: CRUS CLASSÉS

As with the great Médoc wines, the classification dates from the 1855 Universal Exhibition, with one difference: the attribution of a Premier Cru Supérieur, for Château d'Yquem, followed by eleven Premiers Crus and fourteen Deuxièmes Crus.

Premier Cru Supérieur
Château d'Yquem Sauternes

Premiers Crus
Château Climens Barsac
Château Coutet Barsac
Château Clos Haut-Peyraguey Bommes
Château Lafaurie-Peyraguey Bommes
Château La Tour-Blanche Bommes
Château Rabaud-Promis Bommes
Château Rayne-Vigneau Bommes
Château Sigalas-Rabaud Bommes
Château Rieussac Fargues
Château Suduiraut Preignac
Château Guiraud Sauternes

Deuxièmes Crus
Château d'Arche Sauternes
Château Filhot Sauternes
Château Malle Preignac
Château Romer du Hayot Fargues
Château Lamothe Despujols
Château Lamothe-Guignard
Château Doisy-Daëne Barsac
Château Doisy-Dubroca Barsac
Château Doisy-Védrines Barsac
Château Caillou Barsac
Château Broustet Barsac
Château de Myrat Barsac
Château Nairac Barsac
Château Suau Barsac

age 26 gallons per acre, which is never achieved, even in better years. In addition, noble rot never affects all of the grapes nor affects them at the same time. Because of the variation in the formation of noble rot, the grapes must be picked grape by grape, which makes harvesting time-consuming and costly. As the grapes shrivel, the juice becomes concentrated and richer in sugar, but it also loses nearly half its volume. Lastly, the vinification process requires special methods

and the expertise of the best producers—those who age their wines in wooden casks, then in bottles before marketing them.

Saint-Émilion

Saint-Émilion is a Bordeaux-lover's paradise. Although the winegrowing region, which spans eight communes, is only 13,25 acres, no other produces as many Grands Crus.

Like Graves, the region has a longstanding wine tradition, and the small town of Saint-Émilion is believed to be one of the oldest wine towns in France. Tourists come to see the historic old ramparts and cobbled sidestreets, as well as the Château du Roy and the ruined arches over the Cordeliers Cloister. They also come to sample the famous macaroons sold in bakeries and to see the Jurade wine society, which promotes Saint-Émilion wines. The town of Saint-Émilion, which is classified as a historical monument, is not focusing on urban expansion, but on its wines—and exclusively its reds. Vineyards spill down the Saint-Émilion slopes and spread out over the plain.

The estates are not large, often occupying 5 to 8 acres each; it is rare that they occupy several dozen acres. The vineyards include a whole range of soil types, with two zones clearly distinguished:

• The "slope" zones, found primarily on the limestone plateau and the ridge that is predominantly clay-limestone but in parts clay-siliceous surrounding the town. The ridge is where the best Saint-Émilion crus are produced. The wines are a deep garnet color, full-bodied and powerful. Their bouquet is often very rich, but fades with age.

• The "Graves" zone, occupying a vast plain below the town running down to

SAINT-ÉMILION: CRUS CLASSÉS

Premiers Grands Crus

A Château Ausone, Château Cheval Blanc.

B Château Angélus, Château Beauséjour (Bécot), Château Beauséjour (Duffau Lagarrosse), Château Belair, Château Canon, Clos Fourtet, Château Figeac, Château La Gaffelière, Château Magdelaine, Château Pavie, Château Trottevieille.

Grands Crus

Château Balestard-la-Tonnelle, Château Bellevue, Château Bergat, Château Berliquet, Château Cadet-Bon, Château Cadet-Piola, Château Canon-la-Gaffelière, Château Cap-de-Mourlin, Château Chauvin, Clos des Jacobins, Clos de l'Oratoire, Clos Saint-Martin, Château Corbin, Château Corbin-Michotte, Château Couvent-des-Jacobins, Château Curé-Bon-la Madeleine, Château Dassault, Château Faurie-de-Souchard, Château Fonplégade, Château Fonroque, Château Franc-Mayne, Château Grandes-Murailles, Château Grand-Mayne, Château Grand-Pontet, Château Guadet-Saint-Julien, Château Haut-Corbin, Château Haut-Sarpe, Château la Clotte, Château la Clusière, Château la Coupaude, Château la Dominique, Château la Marzelle, Château Laniote, Château Larcis-Ducasse, Château Larmande, Château Laroque, Château Laroze, Château l'Arrosée, Château la Serre, Château la Tour-du-Pin-Figeac (Giraud Belivier), Château la Tour-du-Pin-Figeac (Moueix), Château la Tour-Figeac, Château le Prieuré, Château Matras, Château Moulin-du-Cadet, Château Pavie-Decesse, Château Pavie-Macquin, Château Petit-Faurie-de-Soutard, Château Ripeau, Château Saint-Georges Côte Pavie, Château Soutard, Château Tertre-Daugay, Château Troplong-Mondot, Château Villemaurine, Château Yon-Figeac.

SAINT-ÉMILION GRAPE VARIETIES

These are the traditional Bordelais red grapes, primarily Cabernet Sauvignon and Cabernet Franc, in addition to Merlot, and a smaller amount of Malbec.

the Dordogne. The zone is a misnomer ("Graves" meaning gravel), for the gravel soils most often are flinty gravel that is somewhat sandy. The zone is thus also called the "plains" zone or the "sandy" zone. In many places there is a hard, compact layer of iron-rich sandstone in the subsoil, called *crasse de fer,* as in the Médoc region. This zone's wines share many common features with those produced in the "slope" zones, but they are more supple, less full-bodied and do not age as well.

Saint-Émilion wines are healthy, straightforward wines. Although they improve tremendously with age, they are round and accessible when drunk young, with a well-pronounced flavor. It is not easy to pinpoint the Saint-Émilion region, given its size and the sheer density of planting. There are some one thousand chateaux, including some three hundred crus (compared with the Médoc's sixty crus for nearly double the land area), and the region has its own classification system.

APPELLATIONS AND CLASSIFICATIONS

The Saint-Émilion appellation, which was not included in the 1855 classification, has its own classification system. Dating only from 1955, the system was revised in 1958 and 1967, then modified in 1984 to conform to European standards. According to the latest revision, made in 1996, there are now two official AOC classifications: Saint-Émilion and Saint-Émilion Grand Cru Classé. The four-tiered appellation which governed Saint-Émilion wines for years has thus been superseded, but the indications will appear on the labels of certain wines for some years to come. The four include:

First group
Saint-Émilion
This appellation zone covers the communes of Saint-Émilion, Saint-Laurent-des-Combes, Saint-Christophe-des-Bardes, Saint-Hippolyte, Saint-Étienne-de-Lisse, Saint-Pey-d'Armens, Saint-Sulpice-de-Faleyrens and Vignonet. It also covers certain communes surrounding Saint-Émilion, namely three communes north of Saint-Émilion and west of Pomerol that are entitled to indicate Saint-Émilion on their labels: Saint-Georges-Saint-Émilion, Montagne Saint-Émilion and Puisseguin-Saint-Émilion. Note that the wines of Parsac and Saint-Georges are often grouped under the Montagne-Saint-Émilion appellation.
  Sables-Saint-Émilion: this is a small sector ensconced between Pomerol and the Dordogne. The vines are planted in sand.

Second group
Saint-Émilion Grands Crus
There are approximately two hundred. These are not specific sites, but a very rigorous selection of wines. Each year in June, wine producers must ask for the entitlement from a committee that carries out tastings. The wines are either approved, set aside or rejected. The wines must be bottled on the estate after being aged for a minimum period of eighteen months. Only red wines of the Saint-Émilion appellation are entitled to be included in this category; no surrounding communes are entitled to it.

Third group
Saint-Émilion Grands Crus Classés
The classification of Premiers Grands Crus Classés (there are thirteen of them) and Grands Crus (fifty-five in all) Classés is unusual for ranking wines. The Grand Cru Classé appellation may be used only by the estates which have been classified themselves. A second tasting is required prior to bottling. The classification is subject to revision every ten years.

Fourth group
Saint-Émilion Premiers Grands Crus Classés
The conditions for entitlement to this group are even more stringent. Thirteen Premiers Grands Crus were selected in 1996, divided into two subcategories: A and B.
A is a classification that applies solely to Château Ausone and Château Cheval-Blanc. The eleven other classified estates fall under the B classification.

Pomerol

The Pomerol appellation occupies just 1,960 acres on the outskirts of Libourne and northwest of Saint-Émilion; the Lalande-de-Pomerol appellation is located in a small neighboring commune. But Pomerol's vineyard is modest only in size.

In contrast to Saint-Émilion, there are few tourist attractions in the village of Pomerol, the only parallel with Saint-Émilion being that it is located in the midst of an area devoted solely to wine production. Although the vineyards are small, there are over 150 wineries, many owning only 5 acres, sometimes less.

They produce solely red wines, each having disinct personalities depending on soil types. There are gravely soils in the southeast, and sandy terrains in the west. Between the two lies a plateau with a clay and iron subsoil.

These characteristics determine the dis-

POMEROL GRAPE VARIETIES

Merlot is predominant, along with Cabernet Franc and, to a lesser degree, Cabernet Sauvignon. No Petit Verdot is used, but a small quantity of Malbec is.

tinctive nature of Pomerol. As the appellation's best soil is rich in clay, Merlot is predominant, while the Cabernet Sauvignon is present to a lesser extent. The combination produces wines that have a deep ruby color and are remarkably round and smooth. They have the finesse of a Médoc and the full-bodiness and generosity of a Saint-Émilion. The *crasse de fer* is said to give Pomerols their truffle-like aroma. Five years' aging is often sufficient for them to reach their peak, although they can still improve if kept longer. Although Pomerols have never been officially classified, an unwritten "customary classification" system exists among experts: the world-famous Château Pétrus takes top rank (Cru Hors Classe), equal to a Premier Grand Cru, followed by the main chateaux or estates worthy of mention.

POMEROL: A "CUSTOMARY CLASSIFICATION"

Although no official hierarchy exists, a "customary classification" is in effect, ranking the wines as follows:

Cru Hors Classe
Château Pétrus
Main estates
Château Beauregard
Château Gazin
Château Certain de May
Château Lafleur
Château La Conseillante
Château Lagrange
Château La Croix
Château Latour-Pomerol
Clos l'Église
Château Nenin
Château l'Église-Clinet
Château Petit-Village
Château l'Évangile
Château La Pointe
Château Feytit-Clinet
Château Rouget
Château La Fleur-Gazin
Château Trotanoy
Château La Fleur Pétrus
Vieux Château Certan

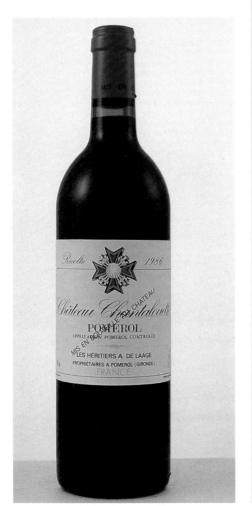

Lalande de Pomerol

AOC Lalande de Pomerol extends the Pomerol region to the north, encompassing the communes of Lalande and Néac. The gravely or sandy-gravely soil produces smooth wines rich in alcohol that can hold their own vis à vis their august neighbor.

Fronsac
and Canon-Fronsac

The fortified village of Fronsac is set in the hills outside Libourne. It gives its name to the wines produced on two-thirds of the hillsides; the other vineyards—which are better exposed to the sun—produce AOC Canon-Fronsac.

The region produces mostly reds, which are flavorful, full-bodied, and robust with notes of spices. They are the best of Bordeaux's secondary appellations.

Between the Garonne and the Dordogne: Entre-Deux-Mers

The Bordelais vineyards are spread out enough (287,500 acres) to incorporate several so-called "minor" regions, some of which offer serious competition to their prestigious neighbors. They are worth a detour. Large quantities of the wines are produced, and you can stumble onto an excellent bottle that can be a very good buy.

This vast zone refers to the area between the Garonne and Dordogne rivers. Entre-Deux-Mers occupies most of the terrain. The area running along the Garonne encompasses the Premières Côtes de Bordeaux and, facing the Graves and Barsac wine districts, Bordeaux-Saint-Macaire, Loupiac and Sainte-Croix-du-Mont. To the northeast lie Graves de Vayres and Sainte-Foy-Bordeaux on the Dordogne.

Entre-Deux-Mers

Entre-Deux-Mers, forming a large triangle bounded by the Garonne and Dordogne rivers, looks like an enormous luxuriant garden of vines. It produces red and dry white wines (with only a few sweet wines). The Entre-Deux-Mers appellation applies strictly to dry white wines produced in the appellation zone. They have varying degrees of fruitiness depending on the amount of Sauvignon. Most are produced by large cooperatives, averaging 20 million bottles annually. Nine communes of the small subdistrict of Haut-Bénauge have three appellations for dry white wines—Entre-Deux-Mers, Bordeaux Haut-Bénauge, and Entre-Deux-Mers Haut-Bénauge—situated in the middle of the triangle, next to Premières Côtes de Bordeaux. The red wines take either the appellation Bordeaux or that of Bordeaux Supérieur. This is one of the few instances in Bordelais wines where a basic AOC establishes two main categories for wines. This is interesting in several respects: First, given the huge land area covered by the vineyards (120,000 acres)—one-half of Bordeaux's vineyards—many "small" Bordeaux are produced. How are they distinguished from the Bordeaux Supérieurs?

Secondly, there are fewer of them, occupying a mere 24,000 acres, or 20 percent of the terrain. What's more, the grape varieties used are nearly identical (on average 55 percent of Merlot for 25 percent Cabernet Sauvignon, 15 percent Cabernet Franc and 5 percent of Malbec and Petit Verdot), but the yield is less, often under 528

gallons per acre. The appellation's wine producers have devised a sort of entrance examination for their wine: At the Maison de la Qualité, located near Bordeaux in Beychac-et-Caillau (the wine cellar is worth a detour), the *agréage* process involves a blind tasting carried out by a committee of impartial experts. The committee either rejects or approves each wine, and the decision is key to a vigneron's success. Wine producers put forth their best effort to be qualified for a Bordeaux appellation and, if possible, to be included among the elite Bordeaux Supérieurs. The latter are proving themselves more and more worthy of the distinction, while still remaining reasonably priced.

Côtes de Bordeaux-Saint-Macaire

Opposite Langon, this appellation extends the Premières Côtes de Bordeaux southeast and occupies over 7,500 acres, including 7,000 acres of red wines. But only 150 acres of gravely clay hillsides near the medieval village of Saint-Macaire are entitled to the appellation. They produce supple, somewhat semi-sweet wines that would be very much like the sweet Sainte-Croix-du-Mont wines if they had just a touch more body and bouquet.

Cadillac

This name is associated with Antoine de la Mothe de Cadillac, the French colonial governor in North America who founded Detroit. The chateau, built by the Ducs d'Épernon, houses one of Bordeaux's great wine fraternities, the Connétablie de Guyenne, devoted to the promotion of sweet white wines. Since 1973, the district of Cadillac and six neighboring communes have their own appellation. Formerly part of the Premières Côtes de Bordeaux, the 6,500-acre vineyard produces rich, fruity sweet white wines which are somewhat similar to the illustrious Barsac and Sauternes wines produced nearby.

Loupiac and Sainte-Croix-du-Mont

These small appellations are ensconced in the Premières Côtes de Bordeaux. The varietal blend is similar to that of wines of the neighboring Sauternais, but the permitted yield is higher. Top-quality richly sweet white wines are produced in Sainte-Croix-du-Mont from late-picked and overripe grapes. The wines, which are less fat than those produced in Loupiac, also have a greater measure of finesse and aromatic richness. These two appellations alone produce one-third of richly sweet wines occupying one-quarter of the land area. This is possible because of the high permitted yield per acre—420 gallons per acre, in comparison to 264 gallons per acre on the left bank of the Garonne. The Sainte-Croix-du-Mont appellation, ensconced in the Premières Côtes de Bordeaux on steep hillsides overlooking the Garonne, produces remarkably good richly sweet wines that have a limpid golden color.

Sainte-Foy-Bordeaux

The 11,500 acres of the Sainte-Foy-Bordeaux appellation, located at the far northeast of the Gironde on the Dordogne's left bank, spans nineteen communes. The region produces reds, which undergo tests to qualify for the appellation (110,880 gallons annually), along with semi-sweet and sweet whites (71,280 gallons), produced in diminishing quantities. Here, as elsewhere, white grape varieties are being uprooted and red varieties planted.

Graves de Vayres

This tiny sector clinging to a bend of the Dordogne between Libourne and Bordeaux received its appellation in 1931 for the communes of Vayres and Arveyres. The appellation's name ("Graves") refers to the gravel-rich soil of the 1,300 acres under vine, producing 242,880 gallons of red wine, which is somewhat reminiscent of Pomerol, and 316,800 gallons of dry white wine.

The Côtes

To geographically lump together Premières Côtes de Bordeaux and such diverse vineyards as Côtes de Blaye, Côtes de Bourg and Côtes de Castillon requires a leap of the imagination. Yet a "Groupe

des Côtes" was created for commercial purposes to support and promote the wines. We have therefore considered them as a group as well.

Premières Côtes de Bordeaux

Occupying the entire southeastern region of the sector, they are part of Entre-Deux-Mers. Yet since 1973 they have had their own appellation for red wines and richly sweet whites. Look at the map: Skirting the Bordelais agglomeration in the north, the Premières Côtes de Bordeaux stretch down the length of the Garonne. Vineyards planted on the limestone hillsides overlooking the river span thirty-six communes down to Saint-Maixant.

The northern area produces warm, deep-colored reds which grow finer with age and have a longstanding reputation (Quinsac, Camblanes, Cénac, Latresne). The 7,500 acres of the vineyard are planted with Cabernet Sauvignon, Cabernet France, Merlot, Malbec, Petit Verdot and Carménère. The southern part, which includes the appellations of Cadillac, Loupiac and Sainte-Croix-du Mont, covers 1,800 acres that produce sweet and semi-dry whites from traditional grape varieties: Sauvignon, Sémillon and Muscadelle. Continuing along the right bank of the Garonne, stop off at Verdelais, to look out over the vineyards which the author François Mauriac so loved.

Côtes de Blaye, Blaye, Premières Côtes de Blaye

Separated from the Médoc by the width of the Gironde, Blaye is a region of rolling hills, its main landmark being the huge fortress that now stands in ruins. The wines of the Blayais region are sold under three appellations: Blaye and Côtes de Blaye are the most common; while the regulations are stricter for the appellation Premières Côtes de Blaye. The grape varieties must be 90 percent noble. A minimum of 10.5% alcohol is required. Reds (85 percent of the varietal blend) are fruity, supple wines that are lighter than the Bourgs. Whites can be dry or sweet (actually semi-sweet).

Côtes de Bourg, Bourg and Bourgeais

There is little difference between the white and red wines produced on the hillsides of Bourg and neighboring Blaye. The old fortified town of Bourg stands at the fork of the Dordogne and the Garonne. The vineyard snaking through the hills produces dry, semi-dry and semi-sweet white wines. The red Bourgs are well-balanced, full-bodied and robust and age well.

Côtes de Castillon

The Côtes de Castillon, where the English defeat in 1453 resulted in the restoration of Guyenne to France, is a huge, peaceful appellation with 7,500 acres under vine. Located opposite Entre-Deux-Mers and next to Saint-Émilion, the Côtes de Castillon appellation spans the communes of Castillon-la-Bataille, Saint-Magne-de-Castillon and Bièves-Castillon, producing 3.96 million gallons annually. The red wines are best drunk as primeurs, although they become full-bodied and rich in alcohol with age. This is one of the regions of Bordeaux where you can still find some excellent buys by selecting the right crus.

Bordeaux-Côtes de Francs

Farther north, the Bordeaux-Côtes de Francs appellation was decreed in 1967 for a small 980-acre vineyard whose red wine production never exceeds 212,000 gallons. Fifty-five acres produce some surprisingly good sweet wines that are worth a detour. A minimum 11.5% alcohol and a residual sugar content of at least 1 ounce per quart is required by law.

Loire

Vines and rivers coexist harmoniously in the Loire region. Over 500 miles of vineyards are scattered along the Loire River, from the Massif Central to the Atlantic and from Saint-Pourçain to Saint-Nazare. Two hundred thousand acres of vines lie within varying reaches of the Loire and its many tributaries. Paradoxically, however, the vines are set back from the river, as it is inclined to flood. Take the back roads that don't follow the course of the river and you'll stumble onto hillsides and small valleys planted with a few acres of vineyards, which produce the great variety of wines from Nevers to Nantes. The Loire, one of Europe's major rivers although it is not suited for commercial navigation, has shaped its banks into a massive garden, and its valley—home to kings and queens over the centuries—into a part of France synonymous with fine food, good conversation and easy living.

The Pays Nantais

Muscadet

This wine-producing region on the left bank of the Loire, south of Nantes, has a mild, humid maritime climate. Its main mark of distinction lies in its grape variety: the Muscadet, which produces dry white wines and remains the only authorized variety for AOC wines (Muscadet de Sèvre et Maine, Muscadet des Coteaux de la Loire and generic Muscadet).

The best Muscadets are those which have been vinified sur lie, a technique whereby wine is bottled directly from the cask or tank without being racked or filtered. The technique preserves the finesse and fruitiness. All Muscadets are pale in color, very refreshing and musky, and go extremely well with shellfish and fish dishes.

Gros-Plant du Pay Nantais, which is somewhat lesser in quality, is a very dry

VDQS white wine that is slightly acidic, to be drunk well chilled.

Anjou and Saumur

These vineyards, growing on gentle slopes east of the Nantais region, are divided into two regional appellations, Anjou and Saumur. They both have a maritime climate but the soil is markedly different. Schist and clay are predominant in Anjou, whereas Saumur has chalky terrain. Stocks of maturing bottles of sparkling Saumur lie in huge caves carved out of the local soft tufa rock, undergoing the same style of secondary fermentation as is found in Champagne. These factors produce highly different wines, despite a common grape variety.

The Anjou wines suffered from overexploitation for years, given the high

ANJOU-SAUMUR GRAPE VARIETIES

Whites: Chenin Blanc predominates, and Sauvignon and Chardonnay are used as well. Reds: Cabernet Franc is the predominant grape, followed by Cabernet Sauvignon, Pineau d'Aunis and Gamay.

demand for exports. But a number of outstanding wines are still to be found.

Anjou, the land of great richly sweet wines

Anjou, along with Sauternes and Barsac, produces the best sweet wines in France. The wines, whether semi-dry, sweet, semi-sweet or richly sweet, require late harvests between October and November.

Savennières

Savennières, a small appellation of scarcely 225 acres, caters to more exclusive palates. It has been limited to a select few for years, a tradition that still holds given its limited production levels and exceptional quality of its crus. The appellation encompasses the commune of Savennières and the village of Epiré, as well as part of Bouchemaine and Possonnière (famous for its windmill), and stretches over four rocky hillsides perpendicular to the Loire. There are two exceptional Savennières crus. Like the Côte d'Or, Savennières is walled, although the expansion of the vineyard has destroyed the walls in part. The most famous is Clos de la Coulée-de-Serrant, as well as Clos du Papillon, Clos des Perrières, Close de la Bergerie and Clos de la Goutte d'Or—named after a remark which Louis XI uttered in tasting the wine:

"It's a drop of gold!" (*goutte d'or* meaning drop of gold).

Coteaux du Layon

The vineyards cover the Layon Valley, scattered along the banks of the Layon from Cléré-sur-Layon to Chalonnes, an old river port where warehouses built by the Dutch once stood.

This amazing valley seems to have been custom-made for the characteristics of the only grape type used for this appellation, Chenin, which basks in the warm, sunny autumns and early morning fog covering the slopes. The humidity and heat are ideal conditions for noble rot to develop. Grape harvesters have only to go from row to row, picking the overripe grapes that have been "roasted" by the early autumn sunshine.

Quarts de Chaume

The 100 acres of this appellation are ideally located on the tip of a hill that runs down to the Layon, and are facing south. Neighboring hillsides shield the vines from northern and easterly winds, and a kind of "sun pocket" results. These are ideal conditions for noble rot to set in, producing sweet wines that are rich in flavor and fruit, considered by some to be the best of the Layon slopes.

Bonnezeaux

No survey of the Layon Grands Crus would be complete with mentioning Bonnezeaux. The name, believed to be Celtic in origin, refers to the former iron deposits in the area. Some 185 acres of the commune of Thouarcé on the right bank of the Layon are under vine. The vineyards face south-southwest on three steep schist slopes—La Montagne, Beauregard and Fesles—above the village of Thouarcé. Vigorous, opulent and very sturdy wines with a highly distinctive fruitiness are produced, whose aroma grows more powerful with age.

Coteaux de l'Aubance

Compared to the Coteaux du Layon, the Coteaux de l'Aubance are dryer and the *terroir's* influence more markedly pronounced. The wines are fruity and very sturdy, although less powerful and have a lesser measure of finesse than the Layon.

The appellation zone (some 250 acres) stretches from south of Angers to span ten communes along the small Aubance river running between the Loire and the Layon. The appellation's white wines, which are extremely popular and sell well, are struggling to exist in one of the best areas of the Anjou-Villages appellation. Cabernet is gradually replacing the Chenin vines, resulting in some good red wines that are promoted by an annual wine contest in Brissac-Quincé.

Anjou

Nearly two hundred communes (20,000 acres) are included in this regional appellation. These days, the trend is to produce fewer rosés and more and more reds from Cabernet Franc, Cabernet Sauvignon and, to a minor extent, Pineau d'Aunis. The quantity of reds and rosés produced now exceeds the volume of white wines: 1.87 million gallons versus 2.4 million gallons for reds and rosés.

A decline in traditional vinification methods, combined with shorter maceration, results in fresher, more aromatic wines.

Anjou whites, produced on soil rich in clay and schist from the Layon and Aubance, are generally dry and made solely of Chenin, although producers have begun to use Chardonnay or Sauvignon grapes to a maximum of 20 percent, which soften the hard edges of Chenin.

Saumur-Champigny

Here, at last, is a red wine that can compete with its great neighbors in Touraine. The Saumur-Champigny, produced from Breton (Cabernet Franc) with at times the addition of Cabernet Sauvignon or Pineau

NIVERNAIS GRAPES

Sauvignon is the predominant grape used in making whites, along with Chasselas. Reds are made primarily from Pinot Noir.

d'Aunis, is a very pleasant wine. It is light, easy to drink, tannic (but not excessively so) and rich in alcohol, with a gentle aroma of violets. It is violet in color when very young and slightly spirited when poured from the cask, then deepens to a blueberry color, taking on red overtones and tawny highlights with age.

Touraine

"Touraine is the garden of France," Rabelais loved to say. He was born not far from Chinon. One of France's most interesting vineyards is found in this spot, which has some of the loveliest chateaux in France. Two *départements* of the Touraine are major wine producers: the Indre-et-Loire to the west, where many Grands Crus are produced; and the Loir-et-Cher to the east, home to many regional appellations.

Bourgueil and Saint-Nicolas-de-Bourgueil

AOC Bourgueil spans 3,000 acres and produces 1.58 million gallons of reds and rosés. It encompasses the twin AOC of Saint-Nicolas-de-Bourgueil, whose 2,250 acres supply 1.2 million gallons. The wines may be sold under the Bourgueil appellation, although the reverse does not apply.

The Cabernet Franc (known locally as the Breton) is the main variety of the appellation area; a maximum of 10 percent of Cabernet Sauvignon is allowed.

Both Bourgueil and Saint-Nicolas-de-Bourgueil wines are fruity, with aromas of raspberry and gooseberry. Saint-Nicolas-de-Bourgueil are grown in gravely soil and are thus more precocious, lighter, and easier to drink. They are often compared to baskets of small red berries.

Chinon

The 4,750 acres of AOC Chinon vineyards on the left bank of the river are scattered around the confluence of the Vienne and

TOURAINE GRAPES

Chenin is the dominant white grape, locally referred to as Pineau de la Loire, followed by Arbois and Sauvignon. Cabernet Franc is predominantly used in red wines, followed by Le Grolleau (called groslot), Pineau d'Aunis, Gamay, Pinot Noir and Le Cot (Malbec).

the Loire rivers. They occupy the valley's south-facing slopes of tufa, as well as the alluvial terrain a dozen or so yards above water level, and produce wines grown in gravel-rich soil and wines from chalky hillsides. An amateur will have difficulty distinguishing a Chinon from a Bourgueil, although the former is lightly perfumed with violets, and the latter with raspberries. Chinon is also softer and lighter, pure red in color, dainty and simple, and the violet perfume is mixed with fruity raspberry notes and a hint of rich loam and truffles from the *terroir*.

Vouvray

If any one wine symbolizes the Touraine, it's Vouvray: "True wines of taffeta, silk, mousseline, spangled and sparkling or tranquil, dry or sweet, rejoicing hearts ere long," as Rabelais, who sang the praises of the region's wines, could have written. The 5,000 acre-area of this prestigious appellation is still rejoicing hearts with 1.32 million gallons of still wines and 2.1 million of sparkling wines.

To many drinkers, *pétillants* (semi-sparkling or crackling) is synonymous with Vouvray wines, which have a natural tendency to develop a sparkle. It is therefore easy for producers to make the wines more sparkling in mediocre vintage years by the traditional method of secondary fermentation in the bottle.

During warm, sunny years, which are ideal for overripening, the wine is vinified as semi-dry or semi-sweet, and becomes a truly legendary wine. After a two-, three- even four-decade hiatus, Vouvray is resurfacing, draped in gold and topaz, transformed into a silky smooth nectar that is vigorous, harmonious and bursting with aroma.

The Center

To try to find a common feature among the wines from the Orleanais to the Côtes du Forez would be an exercise in futility. Neither climate, nor terrain nor varietal blend has any semblance of homogeneity. Only the Loire and its tributaries like the Cher and the Allier serve as a point in common to the vineyards that are sometimes over 300 miles apart.

Sancerre

Sancerre is one of the most popular white wines among the French—crisp, spirited, fresh, fruity, and naturally vigorous with a unique flinty flavor. Sancerre is dramatically perched atop a conical hill over-looking the Loire opposite Pouilly, with some magnificent views of the slopes south and west of the town. The slopes, which can reach 980 to 1,300 feet in altitude, are among the steepest in France, and winches are sometimes required to work the vines.

Pinot Noir produces aromatic, full-bodied rosés and pleasant reds, with a nose of black currants and cherries, but the quantities produced are minimal in comparison to Sauvignon. Soft wines with a powerful bouquet that should be drunk young are produced from the hard limestone of the Kimmeridge with its stony, dry soil (called *"caillottes"* here) on the smaller hillsides. The marl-based soft limestone, or *"griottes"*—the famous white terrain rich in fossils and shells similar to that found in Chablis—produces sturdier, fuller wines that need to age to develop character. These wines keep well.

Occupying 2,500 acres in 1976, AOC Sancerre has expanded by some 4 percent annually to cover 6,000 acres, almost reaching its full potential of 7,500 acres. The vineyards span fourteen villages, and include three well-renowned crus: Bué, Champtin and Chavignol. The last is famous not only for the white Sancerre that is very fine in aroma, concentrated, sturdy, with a remarkable hint of semi-sweet in very good vintage years, but also for its fresh and dry Crottins de chèvre cheeses, which were granted the AOC rank in 1976.

Pouilly-sur-Loire and Pouilly-Fumé

Just upstream from Sancerre on the right bank of the Loire, the Nièvre *département* includes two prestigious AOC, two dry white wines produced by two grape varieties. Pouilly-sur-Loire, made from Chasselas (with or without the addition of Sauvignon), is produced on the clay- and silica-rich hills of Saint-Andelain. The vineyards are on the decline, occupying only 150 acres on the appellation area of Pouilly-Fumé. It produces soft, fine, primeur wines that are light and low in acid. Pouilly-Fumé, also known as Blanc Fumé de Pouilly, is made of a single grape variety, as Sancerre is: Sauvignon. The wine-production area of 2,375 acres spans seven communes, three of which are truly devoted to wine production: Pouilly-sur-Loire, Tracy-sur-Loire and Saint-Andelain. The flinty soil here gives Sauvignon a somewhat smoky taste, a highly mineral-like flavor which becomes more pronounced in a few years. Pouilly-Fumé is a round, extremely pleasant wine with a powerful bouquet and marked by what is usually called a "gunflint" dryness. Many prefer to drink it young, but there is a growing tendency to let it keep for a few years in the cellar. This brings out a more subtle bouquet, with a slight hint of spices. Most vignerons are opting for small yields, highly selective harvests and a low density of implantation in an effort to obtain quality that is comparable to Sancerre.

Champagne

Champagne wines are eponymous with their region and synonymous with parties and festivities. Throughout the world, Champagne is associated with celebrations, homecomings, victories, euphoria and laughter. Kings and princes drank Champagne, created by a contemporary of the Sun King Louis XIV. The Benedictine monk Dom Pierre Pérignon, cellar-master of the Abbey of Hautvillers, may not have invented Champagne's "sparkle" in the seventeenth century, but he was an excellent technician and carried out a rigorous selection of grape varieties, thus improving its quality. He refined the art of blending wines from different vineyards to obtain the best flavor, thus establishing one of the golden rules of Champagne: the blending of grapes. He was skilled at racking and clarifying wines, and perfected the means of sealing the sparkle in the bottle.

The vineyards cover 92,500 acres broken down as follows: 37.5 percent Pinot Noir, 35.5 percent Pinot Meunier and 27 percent Chardonnay. The Champagne wine trade employs approximately 30,000 people, 15,000 of them proprietors who make their own wine. Some 300 million bottles are produced annually. This is the vineyard that is closest to Paris, with some vinestocks located 42 miles from Notre-Dame.

Climate and soil

Centered around Reims and Épernay, the vineyards encompass six large areas: the Basse Montagne along the Ardre and Vesle valleys; Montagne de Reims, a vast chalky plateau overlooking the Marne; the Marne, Ay and Épernay valleys reaching to the outskirts of the Île-de-France Valley; the Côte des Blancs, from Épernay to Vertus; the Congy-Sézanne region; and 84 miles south of Épernay, the Aube vineyards near Burgundy.

Champagne is the northernmost viticultural zone in France. Paradoxically, this most northern region produces the best grapes, despite the harsh winter winds coming directly from the Atlantic, and the continental climate. Average annual temperatures never exceed 50° F, and frosts can reach -21° F, as in 1985.

Yet the many small valleys, forests and bodies of water stabilize temperatures and maintain a certain humidity. The devastating spring frosts hit the valleys and basins in particular. This is why the vines are planted halfway up the slopes and face south or southeast, except for those of Verzenay, which face north, and Côte des Blancs, east.

The vineyards thrive in Champagne as a result of the soil's composition. This huge chalky bedrock, sometimes 330 feet deep, plays a triple role: it encourages ripening through its ability to absorb humidity; reflects the sunlight onto the grapes and stores heat in the day and emits it at night. The roots penetrate deeply, sometimes reaching 30 to 65 feet into the ground, and absorb minerals which add to the wine's finesse. Huge cool caves, clean and dry, provide an ideal setting for aging Champagne, with a constant temperature of 50° F. The caves, which are generally open to the public, form a vast network of galleries some 150 miles long, for the most part beneath Reims and Épernay.

Vinification

It is impossible to mention Champagne without mentioning Dom Pérignon (1638-1715), monk and cellar-master of the Abbey of Hautvillers. He was one of the first to capitalize on the second fermentation, which takes place in the bottle during the spring. This fermentation had been seen as a disastrous event, as it caused the bottles to explode. Dom Pérignon also suggested that stronger bottles be used, as well as plugs, preferably old corks made of wood and tow, which he tied on with string. He also suggested that the wines be blended (the *coupage*) to improve quality.

He was assisted by a colleague, Dom Oudart, who was cellarer at the Abbey of

Saint-Pierre-aux-Monts in Pierry. The latter also was interested in vinification processes and pioneered experiments with corks.

The vinification process for making Champagne begins once the grapes have been pressed, with as little delay as possible after harvesting so that the clear juice avoids contact with the dark skins and discoloration is prevented. The grapes are fermented without the skins for 20 to 30 days. After this, the wine is left to stand and clarify, then is racked. The wine is blended with wines from other vineyards to obtain a harmonious, longlasting product. After being racked a second and third time, the wine is bottled (the *tirage*).

At this stage, the wine is still or nonsparkling. During the bottling process, sugar is added to the *cuvée*—the *liqueur de tirage*. The additional sugar will ferment and make the wine sparkling. This second fermentation is a slow, gradual process due to the caves' cool temperatures, which enhance the quality.

The next stage is the *remuage,* when cellarmen gently shake and twist the bottles so that the sediment gradually settles on the cork. The cork is then removed and the small amount of wine containing the sediment expelled (the *dégorgement*). The *dégorgement* nowadays is carried out by uncorking the bottle after the neck is frozen. The pressure expels the solid block of impurities, and the bottle is topped up with *liqueur d'expédition*— a mixture of sugar,

Champagne and sometimes wine spirits. Depending on the dosage of sugar, either a Brut, Semi-Dry or Sweet Champagne is produced.

The proportion of grape types used varies from site to site. The vineyards are divided into four regions:

• Montagne de Reims, where Pinot Noir is predominant, encompasses the vineyards of Ambonnay, Bouzy, Louvois, Mailly-Champagne, Sillery, Verzenay and Verzy;

• the Marne Valley, planted primarily with Pinot Meunier, includes such crus as Avenay, Ay, Mareuil-sur-Ay, Hautvillers, Damery, Boursault, Verneuil, Venteuil;

• Côte des Blancs, where Chardonnay is predominant, is where such vineyards as Avize, Cramant, Oger, and Mesnil-sur-Oger are located;

• the Aube, formerly underrated, but now beginning to produce better-quality wines.

The *méthode champenoise*

For centuries, Champagne produced primarily red wines, not sparkling wines. Champagne as we are familiar with it today was not created until the late seventeenth century by Dom Pérignon at the Abbey of Hautvillers, as described above. Since then, how has Champagne been produced? *Méthode champenoise* is the name for the process of making a still wine sparkle by allowing it to ferment a second time in the bottle. The first requirement is to carefully harvest the grapes, culling the best and eliminating any defective ones. The grapes are sorted, and quickly and carefully pressed, avoiding any delay so that the dark skins don't "stain" the clear juice. The first pressing is called the *cuvée*, the second the *taille*. The must is then racked in *pièces* (54-gallon barrels) or in vats.

A still wine with high acidity is produced. At this point, the Champagne process begins through a series of specific operations.

Making the *cuvée*

This process consists of blending different wines in special vats, in which they are mixed. Wines from the same commune or wines from distinct vineyards and grape varieties may be used; similarly, vintage wines (from the same year) can be used exclusively to create vintage Champagnes, or reserve wines made in previous years can be used in producing non-vintage Champagnes. The cellar-master aims to obtain a harmonious flavor, consistent with the established style of the house.

Bottling the wine

A cane sugar solution called the *liqueur de tirage* is added to the *cuvée* (1 ounce of sugar per quart of wine), as is yeast. After mixing, the wine is then bottled (the *tirage*). The bottles are given temporary corks and then stored in cellars on slats.

Developing the sparkle

The sugar ferments under the action of the yeasts, forming alcohol and carbon dioxide gas. As fermentation continues, the carbon dioxide builds up pressure. The sediment formed during fermentation will continue to add complexity to the wine's flavor for at least one year.

Shaking the bottles

At the end of the fermenting and ripening period, the bottles are placed in special racks or *pupitres,* which are hinged, sloping boards. The bottles, which are placed at a very slight angle, are gradually inclined so that the sediment slides down into the neck. Trained experts turn the bottles about an eighth of a turn each day, care-fully shaking the bottle. By the time the sediment is next to the cork, the bottles are standing on their heads in the racks.

Expelling the sediment

The next step involves eliminating the sediment by freezing the necks of the bottles. The neck of the upturned bottle is placed in a 24° F solution and the slug of wine containing the sediment freezes. The pressure that has been built up shoots out the slug in a frozen lump.

Sweetening the Champagne

The bottle is topped up with a *liqueur de dosage* or *liqueur d'expédition* (cane sugar and still Champagne), resulting in Cham-pagnes of varying degrees of sweetness— from Brut to Sec (Dry), Demi-sec (Semi-dry), and Doux (Sweet). The bottles are then corked, and the wire "muzzles" or cages, foil and labels put on.

Types of Champagne

Blanc de Blancs: Champagne made from white grapes only (Chardonnay), most often from the Côte des Blancs vineyards. This Champagne has greater elegance, finesse and lightness than traditional Champagnes.
Blanc de Noirs: Champagne made from black grapes only, yielding fuller-flavored, sturdier wines.
Pink Champagne: Often produced by blending white wine and a small quantity of red wine made from Pinot Noir. The result is a pleasant fruitiness.
Crémant: Champagne with less carbon dioxide and fewer bubbles produced by adding only one-half the *liqueur de tirage.*
Champagne Millésimé: Vintage Cham-pagne made only with the best quality wines from that year's grape harvest. No reserve wines are used. This Champagne ages longer than non-vintage Champagnes and cannot be marketed before three years' developing.

Cuvées Spéciales: Features a great variety of names, some of them highly prestigious. They are made of the best wines of each great Champagne house.

Champagne Brut 100 Per Cent: This is Champagne made of pure wine, without the addition of any sugar.

Champagne houses

Making Champagne is expensive, and the majority of production and marketing is run by a dozen or so large companies, led by Moët & Chandon-LVMH, which has just added Krug to its prestigious list. The most famous houses include:

- in Reims: Besserat de Bellefon, Charles Heidsieck, Mumm, Heidsieck Monopole, Henriot, Krug, Lanson, Louis Roederer, Piper-Heidsieck, Pommery, Ruinart, Taittinger, Veuve-Clicquot-Ponsardin;
- in Épernay: Moët & Chandon, Perrier-Jouët, Pol Roger, De Venoge;
- Montagne de Reims, Ay and Marne Valley: Bollinger, Canard-Duchêne, Deutz, Laurent-Perrier.

Champagne houses give their names to the wines they market. The name appears clearly on the label, which is logical given that each brand establishes a style characteristic of the house.

At the bottom of the label (in very small type) appear initials indicating the status of the producer:

- N.M., or *négociant-manipulant*. The grapes were purchased from vignerons, but the Champagne produced by the shipper.
- R.M., or *récoltant-manipulant*. Growers produce Champagne from their own vines.
- C.M., or *coopérative de manipulation*. Growers brought their grapes to a cooperative, which produced the wine.

Alsace

This region in eastern France is not only picturesque with its half-timbered houses and flower boxes. It also produces some great wines, some of which are still poorly known even to the French, although producers are working to maintain quality and promote the unique identity of Alsatian wines—with a great deal of success.

Policies to encourage mass production of cheap wine, which fluctuated as Alsace went back and forth between Germany and France in the late nineteenth and early twentieth centuries, have today given way to making quality wines of great class and distinction.

The vineyards occupy a narrow strip ranging from 1.2 to 2.4 miles in width and running along the Ill, a tributary of the Rhine River. Vines cover some 30,000 acres, from Marlenheim in the north, near Strasbourg, to Thann in the south, near Mulhouse. The vineyards are concentrated in the eastern and southern foothills of the Vosges, at an altitude of 650 to 1,300 feet, and are thus protected from the damp Atlantic winds.

The continental climate is characterized by hot summers and harsh winters, as well as exceptionally dry autumns. The low rainfall in September and October allows for the production of late-harvest wines. There is a great diversity of rocks and soils, from yellow granite, loess and marl to pink sandstone, while the best vineyards are planted on limestone-rich hillsides.

Varietal blending

The diversity of grape types used in Alsace makes for a wide variety of wines, each with a rich, powerful character. Alsatian viticulture dates back to as early as the fifteenth century, at least for the four noble grape varieties.

Gewürztraminer

Of all Alsatian grape varieties, this is the easiest to identify given its very pronounced aromas of musk and spices (*Gewürz* meaning "spice" in German). The wines are full-bodied, dry or semi-sweet in great years, and develop an exceptionally powerful fruity bouquet.

Muscat

Alsace is one of the rare regions of France where Muscat produces a dry white wine. The wine is delicately flavored, and when drunk, gives the impression of biting into

ALSACE GRAPE VARIETIES

The most noble white grapes among the Alsatian varieties are Gewürztraminer, Muscat, Pinot Gris (Tokay d'Alsace) and Riesling. Other white grapes include Pinot Blanc (Klevner), Sylvaner and Chasselas. Pinot Noir is the only red grape variety.

a fresh grape. It is subtly elegant and perfumed and is light enough to be served as an aperitif.

Pinot Gris (locally known as the Tokay d'Alsace)

Pinot Gris produces wines that are golden yellow in color, full-bodied and heady, with a powerful bouquet. In general, the wines are more opulent than subtle or elegant.

Riesling

This is the finest of Alsace's grape varieties, capable of producing wines with great breed. Riesling is a very dry wine and its pale color has a green tint. The fresh, open wines develop a remarkable bouquet, yet have a good measure of finesse.

Other grape varieties

In addition to the great aristocrats, there are some less noble varieties:

• Pinot Blanc or Klevner: Produces light, simple and clean wines that lack a certain finesse and are best drunk young and chilled.

• Sylvaner: Produces light, unpretentious white wines that are sometimes insufficiently fruity or lacking agreeable

character. To be drunk young and well-chilled.

- Chasselas: The most common grape variety in Alsace. Its sole interest lies in its light wines used in blending.
- Pinot Noir: The only red grape variety in Alsace, it is used in making rosés and light red wines.

With the exception of those made from Chasselas, Alsatian wines are named after their grape varieties. Edelzwicker wines, meaning "noble mixture," are blends of Alsatian white grape varieties.

The appellation system in Alsace

Although the system has grown more sophisticated in recent years, it remains relatively simple. The notion of "cru" or classification by vineyard, takes second place to classification by grape variety.

The following are distinguished:

- Regional appellation or Vin d'Alsace

Until 1975, indicating the grape variety, such as Riesling or Tokay, was optional. The restricted yield for these generic Alsatian wines is a generous 1,050 gallons per acre.

- Grand Cru wines

This applies exclusively to wines made from the four noble white varieties (Gewürztraminer, Muscat, Pinot Gris and Riesling) planted on specified sites. Yields are restricted to 740 gallons per acre, but the best producers intentionally do not exceed 530 or 630 gallons. There must be wine-tastings held for the Grands Crus, and the label must indicate their grape variety and vintage year.

- Communal and lieux-dits ("named places") appellations

Since 1975, the names of fifty specified sites have been authorized to appear on labels, in addition to the requirements listed above.

The commune of Bergheim with the lieu-dit of Altenberg is one example. Other examples include Ribeauvillé with Kirch-

berg or Zahnacker; Riquewihr with Sporen or Schonenburg; Guebwiller with Kitterle; and Thann with Rangen.

• Crémant d'Alsace

This is reserved for sparkling wines made from Alsatian white wines using the *méthode champenoise*. They are made mainly from Pinot Blanc.

There are also two VDQS:

• Côtes de Toul, producing light, slightly acidic reds, whites and gris.

• Moselle wine, red or white, is generally light and pale in color.

Italy

When the Greeks arrived in Italy in the eighth century B.C., they found vines flourishing throughout the land and christened the country Oenotria, meaning "land of wine."

Italy is the only place in the world where wine is produced in every region of the country. It is difficult to count the number of major wine-producing regions, since Italy looks like one vast vineyard from north to south. Each vineyard has its own colorful traditions and history—that of the legendary wine produced in Latium called Est! Est!! Est!!!, for example.

Italy not only produces and exports more wine than any other country, including France and Spain, with a yearly 2.3 billion gallons (one-quarter of world production), but Italians drink a great quantity of wine as well, with an average consumption rate of 22 gallons per year per inhabitant. There are some two thousand varieties of wine. Most of them are rather ordinary, dull or undistinguished, and they can be heady and woody; certain white wines are prone to oxidation. But every Italian wine has some interesting feature.

Fortunately, attitudes are changing, and antiquated, makeshift wine-making methods are gradually being replaced by more modern methods. The differences in continental Italy's geological and climatic conditions from north to south are so marked that Italy remains the country with the greatest diversity in wines. Dividing the peninsula roughly from north to south, Ugni Bianco and Sauvignon are predominant from the Alps region to south of Rome; next come Bombino Bianco and Montepulciano. Each grape variety has adapted to its region, some for thousands of years. Lambrusco, for example, dates back to the Etruscans, while some southern Italian wines can be traced back to the Greeks. The Italians protect their beloved wines by a very obscure system of laws and regulations that is not only burdensome but seemingly contradictory at times. Labels provide little information as to a wine's contents and origin. It may be DOC (Denominazione di Origine Controllata), DOCG (Denominazione di Origine Controllata e Garantita), Classico, Riserva or Da Tavola. They range from elite wines like Barbaresco, Barolo from the Piedmont, Brunello di Montalcino and the famous Chianti wines of Tuscany to ordinary table wines of varying quality. One piece of advice: Buy your wines from one of the reputable wine outlets which produce and market their own wines. From north to south, there are eighteen great wine-producing regions divided into administrative areas by mountains and plains. The names evoke centuries of winemaking tradition.

The village of Barolo, in the Piedmont region.

The label: a question of rank and standard

Until very recently, the DOC classification applied to only about 10 percent of Italian wines. The classification system, created in 1963, promoted both good and bad, to the point where many producers decided to apply their own quality standard criteria. Since the Goria Law was passed in 1992, however, standard rules are being enforced with greater severity.

There are two categories of wines in Italy:
- quality wines: DOCG (Denominazione di Origine Controllata e Garantita) and DOC (Denominazione di Origine Controllata)
- table wines: IGT and VdT

Quality wines

1. DOCG (Denominazione di Origine Controllata e Garantita). Only fifteen wines are entitled to this prestigious appellation. These are the best wines, and are subjected to highly restrictive regulations governing the quality of wines and the type and excellence of the *terroir*. Each bottle is marked with a seal of guarantee.

2. DOC (Denominazione di Origine Controllata). All Italian wines with a certain reputation are entitled to this classification; the list grows longer every year. Like AOC wines in France, these wines must conform to a certain number of regulations on grape varieties, delimited sites, vinification and aging.

Table wines

1. IGT (Indicazione Geografiche Tipici). This is the equivalent of Vin de Pays in France. The laws and regulations are nearly identical. The label indicates the grape variety and geographic origin.

2. VdT (Vino da Tavola). These wines may not be associated with a particular geographic region or grape variety, but some of them are marvelous. Some great wineries, disillusioned by various reforms, are turning to table wines as a last resort to maintain a certain independence, initiative and individuality.

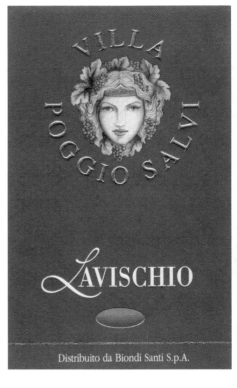

A few terms

Classico: designates wines from the best *terroirs* of the appellation before certain extensions were authorized

Riserva: applies to wines aged three years in casks

Abboccato: sweet, semi-sweet

Acerbo: young, green

Acido: acidic

Amaro: bitter

Ambrato: amber-colored

Cantina sociale: cooperative cellar

Chiaro: light

Dolce: very sweet

Fiasco: the straw-based bulbous Chianti bottle

Fruttato: fruity

Merro in bottiglia dell'origine: estate-bottled

Nero: dark red

Passante: easy to drink

Passito: strong, usually sweet wine from the concentrated musts of semidried grapes

Vino santo: wine from sundried grapes

Secco: dry

Stravecchio: very old

Vinetto: simple wine

Vino bianco: white wine

Vino da pesce: fish wine (dry, fruity white wine)

Vino frizzante: very slightly sparkling, but not enough pressure to be sparkling

Vino liquoroso: wine of high-alcohol grade, often fortified

Vino da pasto: everyday table wine

Vino rosso: red wine

Vino rosato: rosé wine

Vino spumante: sparkling wine (dry or sweet)

Vino vecchio: old wine

Vite, vitigno: vine, grape variety

ITALY'S WINE-PRODUCING REGIONS

- Tuscany
- Piedmont
- Lombardy
- Veneto
- Friuli-Venezia Giulia
- Trentino Alto-Adige
- Emilia-Romagna
- Umbria
- Marches
- Latium
- Abruzzi
- Campania
- Sardinia
- Sicily
- Basilicata
- Apulia
- Calabria
- Liguria
- Valle d'Aosta

Reading the label

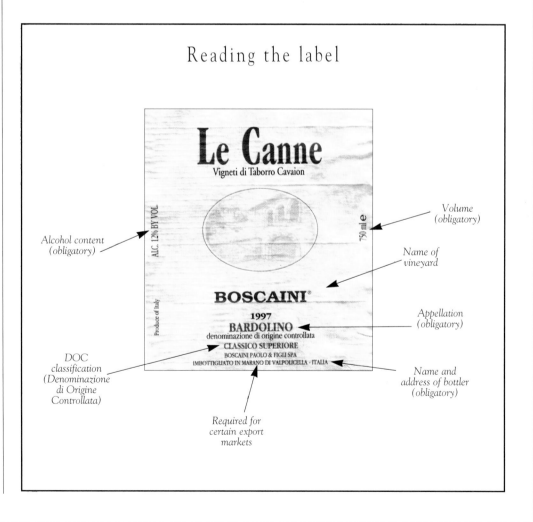

Alcohol content (obligatory)

Volume (obligatory)

Name of vineyard

Appellation (obligatory)

DOC classification (Denominazione di Origine Controllata)

Required for certain export markets

Name and address of bottler (obligatory)

Tuscany

Tuscany will be forever associated with the beauty of its landscape and the splendor of its hills, the remarkable history of such cities like Florence, Livorno, Carrara, Pisa and Siena, and for its most famous wine, Chianti. This superb region in northwestern Italy extends south to Latium and produces some 1.32 billion gallons of wine each year. It is the second-leading wine-producing region of Italy in DOC.

Chianti

What are 1.32 billion gallons compared to the oceans of Chianti that flood markets throughout the world each year? Some seven thousand producers in the seven zones of central Tuscany produce Chianti. How can true Chianti be distinguished from cheaper, insipid Chianti, produced elsewhere in Italy and the rest of the world? The answer? By its origin: it is made in a small district covering 172,900 acres between Florence and Siena. Chianti produced outside this area is not true Chianti. The origin is indicated on the label by the mention of "classico"—Chianti Classico DOCG (the highest distinction for an Italian wine). Bottles of real Chianti should have the seal of the Chianti Classico consortium (Consorzio per la Difesa del Vino Tipico di Chianti) depicting a black cockerel on a gold background encircled in red.

Chianti Classico is produced in an area of steep vine-covered hills and cypress trees, where fortified villages once served as backdrops for the rival Florentine and Sienese clans. In 1376, the Florentines created the Chianti League to defend against raiders from Siena. Today, the league could protect Chianti against the many incursions and abuses of the wine.

Chianti's particular characteristics are due to soil type. When grown carefully, Chianti is heady, tannic and powerful. The aromas of violet and licorice come from soil, a mixture of clay schist soil, layers of covering limestone and a thin top layer of pebbly sand. When young, Chianti can be *frizzante* and have a semi-sparkling bite, caused by adding the juice of late-maturing grapes after the wine is made. Chianti is traditionally composed of 80 percent of Sangiovese, which imparts body; the 5 percent of Canaiolo gives it its bouquet. Trebbiano and Malvasia lighten the intensity of the color and Colorino gives it its bright ruby-red color. There are fourteen different appellations, including Chianti Colli Aretini, Chianti Colli Fiorentini, Chianti Colli Sensei and Chianti Montalbano. These Chiantis surround true Chianti: Chianti Classico.

Cheap, crude Chianti served in pizzerias is diminishing in production (the kind served in straw-lined flasks). Making the glass flasks and covering them in straw is too costly. Good Chianti is rare and is sold exclusively in bottles; the wine ages better in bottles as well.

CHIANTI CLASSICO DOCG
The leading producers
(north of Siena between Poggibonsi and Castelnuovo Berardenga)

- Vecchie Terre di Montefili
- Querciabella
- Vignamaggio
- La Massa
- Castello dei Rampolla
- Fontodi
- Le Masse di San Leolino
- Monsanto
- Isole e Olena
- Castellare
- Rocca delle Macie
- Castello di Fonterutoli
- Castello di Volpaia
- Monte Vertine
- Badia a Coltibuono
- Riecine
- Castello di San Polo in Rosso
- Castello di Ama
- Giorgio Regni
- Rocca di Castagnoli
- Castello di Cacchiano
- Podere il Palazzino
- San Felice
- Castell'in Villa
- Pagliarese
- Felsina Berardenga

TUSCANY GRAPE VARIETIES

The best Chiantis are made from Sangiovese grapes—also called Brunello, Sangioveto and Prugnolo Gentile—with a minimum 75 to 90 percent. You can find superb Chiantis labeled Vino da Tavola, which have Cabernet Sauvignon and Merlot added to white grape varieties. The best white wines are produced from Vernaccia di San Gimignano and Trebbiano. Sauvignon and Chardonnay are gaining in popularity.

Brunello di Montalcino

With Barolo and Barbaresco, Brunello di Montalcino (DOCG)—over one hundred years old—is one of the youngest of Europe's great wines. It is produced in a hilly region of Siena with barely 2,225 acres under vine, near the small town of Montalcino. Brunello would not exist if it weren't for the Biondi-Santi. When Ferrucio Biondi-Santi, a biologist, painter and friend of Garibaldi, returned from the war, the Italian nation had just been created. It needed a wine that could rival the greatest French crus. This was what Biondi-Santi set out to do, making his Brunello solely from Sangiovese grapes.

He cultivated and refined the single grape variety for years, to obtain grapes with small pips, thick skin and a rich flavor and color. "A ruby or nearly garnet red color with intense, distinctive perfume, and a dry and warm taste, perhaps a bit tannic when young, but harmonious, full-bodied and lingering," was how Franco Biondi-Santi, Ferrucio's grandson, described it. During the grape harvest, the best grapes were picked individually by hand. The remaining grapes were used to make an honest red wine, Rosso di

Montalcino. Only the best grapes grown on the 30 acres of the family-run vineyard were used in Brunello Riserva—12,000 bottles out of the annual 60,000 produced. These were aged in cellars from ten to fifty years.

The other vines, under ten years old, produce Annata and Greppo, two more ordinary wines. Biondi-Santi serves as an example for some 138 other wine producers. All of them—from the smallest property owners to Milanese and American investors—are part of the same consortium, with the exception of the Biondi-Santi.

The two great marginals

Their names: Tignanello and Sassicaia. Affectionately referred to as the "super-Tuscans," for years, these wines disdained conforming to the highly rigid regulations and standards of the DOC classification, remaining with their Vino da Tavola classification (Sassicaia is no longer one)—although they enjoy a marvelous reputation among wine lovers.

Tignanello is produced in Chianti Classico, primarily from Sangiovese grapes.

Sassicaia, in contrast, has a more complex history. Produced on an estate located 30 miles south of Livorno, Sassicaia is no longer simply a Vino da Tavola, but a

Bolgheri Sassicaia DOC, dating from the 1994 vintage. The wine's origins can be traced to the prestigious Château Lafite in the Bordelais region: Marchese Mario Incisa had French grape varieties from the estate imported to Italy just after the Second World War.

The vineyards of Sassicaia, meaning "site of stones," are set in the upper valley region behind the Castiglion-Cello estate.

This small land mass produces an astonishing blend of Cabernet Sauvignon and Cabernet Franc. The wines are aged in small oak barrels, and require a few years in the bottle to bring out their deep bouquet and rich, velvety flavor. Sassicaia is one of the greatest crus, and wine lovers from all over the world are trying to get their hands on at least one of the precious bottles!

Other wines of Tuscany

If you are traveling to Tuscany, try to sample a traditional Vino Santo ("holy wine"), a sweet, golden-colored dessert wine with a high alcoholic content. Most of the wine is vinified from carefully dried Malvasia and Trebbiano grapes. Some growers suspend the heavy grape clusters from hooks along the rafters of a loft or attic. As the grapes dry, the sugar becomes concentrated.

After the grapes are pressed, the juice is sealed in *caratelli* (small barrels) filled about three-quarters full and stored in lofts for at least four years prior to filtering. The maderized wine takes on a lovely deep amber color similar to that of Sherry and has a wonderful nutty aroma.

During the eighteenth century, the poet Francesco Redi lauded the Vino Nobile di Montepulciano in his *Bacchus in Tuscany:* "Montepulciano, of all wines, is king." Today its fame is embodied in the DOCG classification. The Vino Nobile from Montepulciano, a hill town located 30 miles south of Siena, has been produced by a few noble families, primarily from Prugnolo Gentile (the local name for Sangioveto Grosso, a variety of Sangiovese).

The deep ruby-red wine is fairly light and is produced in the hills surrounding the town, on terrain that is rich in clay. It can be somewhat dry when young, but can become truly noble with age.

The region of Tuscany includes the Island of Elba. During his brief exile here, Napoleon encouraged viticulture. The *bianco* produced from Procanico (Trebbiano) and Canaiolo is a light wine that is straw gold in color. The *rosso,* made from Sangiovese, is more aromatic.

The Aleatico di Portoferraio, a warm, full-bodied red wine, is also worthy of mention. It can be excellent.

DOC AND DOCG APPELLATIONS

- Chianti Classico DOCG
- Chianti DOCG
- Brunello di Montalcino DOCG
- Vino Nobile di Montepulciano DOCG
- Vernaccia di San Gimignano DOCG
- Carmignano DOCG
- Montecarlo
- Pomino
- Bolgheri
- Morellino di Scansano
- Bianco di Pitigliano
- Parrina
- Elba

Piedmont

Piedmont, or "foot of the mountains," is a vast plain surrounded by the Alps to the north and west, the highest peaks of which form a huge arching border with France, Switzerland and Austria. Lake Maggiore, the Ticino River and the Po Plain lie to the east, while the Appenine Mountains begin east and run south. Vineyards are present throughout the region; 15 percent of Italian wines are produced in Piedmont, mostly in the southern part, notably in the Monferrato and Langhe hills around Alba. The Monferrato hills are relatively low yet very steep, and villages perched on high and luxurious hunting lodges built by Savoy princes can be seen amid the vines covering the countryside.

The region is noted for gastronomical delicacies such as grissini, white truffles and true gorgonzola; it also produces Italy's two best red wines: Barolo and Barbaresco (both DOCG). Turin, the capital of Piedmont, is the center of the vermouth industry as well as the automobile industry. Piedmont's quality wines are the most thoroughly categorized in Italy. Piedmont has over forty classified production zones, making it Italy's fifth-leading wine-producing region. Viticulture is most intense in the Monferrato and Langhe hills. Eighty percent of Piedmont's wines come from this area of the region. Piedmont's chief grapevine, Nebbiolo, flourishes in the clay

BAROLO AND BARBARESCO
(on each side of Alba)

The best crus

Barolo
- Brunate
- La Serra
- Rocche
- Marcenasco
- Monfalletto
- Cannubi
- Bricco Fiasco
- Villero
- Monprivato
- Bricco Rocche
- Brussia Soprana
- Marenca-Rivette
- Vigna Rionda
- Ginestra
- Cascina-Francia

Barbaresco
- Rio Sordo
- Roncagliette
- Secondine
- Asili
- Moccagatta
- Martinenga
- Rabaja
- Santo Stefano
- Basarin
- Bricco di Neive
- Serraboella
- Marcarino

PIEDMONT GRAPE VARIETIES

Nebbiolo—from *nebbia,* referring to the "fog" that often cloaks the hills of Langhe and Monferrato—is grown in northwestern Italy, particularly in the Piedmont region. It is one of the oldest red grape varieties: historians claim that the Romans planted it first in Lombardy, and then in Valle d'Aosta and Valteline. It is excellent wherever it grows, but unfortunately represents only 0.5 percent of Italian production, or 4.2 million gallons, 1.3 million of which is Barbaresco. Piedmont's limestone soil creates marvelous wines, particularly on the hills surrounding Alba, where Italy's two greatest red wines are produced: Barolo and Barbaresco. Nebbiolo yields wines that are not fruity, but have a complex of aromas and a touch of bitterness and a marvelous balance of tannin and acidity.

and limestone soil of the region, yielding marvelously complex wines that can be virtual masterpieces. The wines feature a multitude of aromas which, without being fruity, add the unusual touch of bitterness so characteristic of these wines. They are high in tannin, yet have a hint of acidity that makes for an incomparable wine.

Barolo and Barbaresco

Barolo and Barbaresco are produced in the hills adjacent to Alba, the old Piedmont city southeast of Turin. The two wines are so prestigious that they were placed among Italy's leading three red wines by a governmental ranking in 1941 and were the first to be classified as DOCG—the greatest appellation of all. Barolo is more virile and powerful, while Barbaresco is

more supple and feminine, with a slightly more harmonious touch. They are both high in tannin, but the wines become more rounded after aging two to four years in oak vats (huge Slovenian oak vats blackened with age).

As they age, they lose their harshness and become more supple in the bottle. Barbaresco is deep red in color, while Barolo looks nearly black when first served. But as soon as it hits the air, it takes on an onion skin tint. Both go very well with red meat, venison and pasta.

The Barolo apellation covers some 3,200 acres around Barolo, Castiglione, Monforte d'Alba, Falleto, Serralunga and La Morra. Some of the great wine producers include Rinaldi Francesco, Moscarello Bartolo and Renato Ratti, whose bottles are easily recognized by the blue label bearing a golden lion. The 1,235 acres of Barbaresco are located northwest of Barbaresco and the three communes of Cuneo. The label depicts the old tower of Barbaresco. Angelo Gaja is the producer who symbolizes best this wine. He has established a reputation throughout the world and is seen as the most talented wine producer of his generation in Italy. With nearly 200 acres under vine, Gaja gives priority to Barolo, Barbaresco and Alba's traditional grape varieties and *terroir*, yet he reserves 20 percent of his vineyards to wines produced essentially from French grape varieties. The Cabernet Sauvignon he produces, christened "Darmagi" ("too bad" in Piemontese), playfully recalls his grandfather's irritation over seeing his Nebbiolo grapevines replaced by Cabernet Sauvignon. Today, his wines with the somewhat austere label are exported throughout the world.

The Asti region

There has been a wide variety of names for Asti champagne since Charles Gancia returned to Canelli from France with the secret for producing it in 1860; these include Muscat champagne and Italian champagne. It is currently known through-out the world under the name Asti Spumante (the bottles are stamped with the image of Asti's patron saint, San Secondo, on horseback) or Moscato d'Asti (DOC).

Asti wines are made from very sparkling, sparkling, dry or sweet wines that are slightly fruity, from 7 to 9 % in alcohol, with a high concentration of unfermented sugar. Although still very popular (they used to be very inexpensive), they are less so than they once were. But the sparkling wine has greatly improved in quality and image; as proof, the "record" prices the Moscato (the grape variety used for Asti Spumante) fetches each year. Fifty-two communes surrounding the small village of Asti on the banks of the Tarano produce the famous wine. There is a tendency to make the wines drier; more and more Pinot and Riesling are being planted as a result and sold under the appellation Pinot Spumante, Gran Spumante, etc.

Other regions

Other Piedmont wines generally bear the name of the grape variety from which they are produced, with no indication of origin. Carema (DOC) is a tender, smooth Nebbiolo that is less bitter than Gattinara. The vines are grown on steeply terraced land between Piedmont and Valle d'Aosta. Nebbiolo flourishes in granitic soil covered with a fine layer of earth.

The Nebbiolo d'Alba (DOC) is very well known. Sometimes called Roero, it is a light red wine with a violet perfume and is a real thirst-quencher. Brachetto d'Acqui (DOC), near Alessandra and Asti, yields pale-colored wines that are slightly sweet, either very slightly sparkling (*frizzante*) or semi-sparkling. Barbera, which are powerful ruby-colored red wines, are also in this category. Although they are slightly hard when young, they tend to improve with a few years' aging.

Ghemme (DOC), a highly aromatic wine with a beautiful garnet color, is a mixture of Nebbiolo, Vespolina and Bonarda. There is a hint of bitterness to the wine, but it ages well.

Lombardy

Lombardy, stretching from the northern Alps to the banks of Lake Maggiore to the west and to Lake Garda in the east, has many wines and vines (41,990 acres of vineyards), reaching all the way to the outlying regions of Milan. The best wines come from the Valtellina area, an Alpine corner near the Swiss border, some 30 kilometers from Saint-Moritz. The vines lie on the southern slope of the upper Adda Valley, between the Grison and Bergamo Alps.

Little has changed in these stunning

WINES FROM THE TERRACED VINEYARDS

Four red wines that are quite similar to one another are made in the terraced vineyards of the Valtellina: Frascia, Sassela, Grummo, and Inferno.
Franciacorta Rosso (DOC), made from Cabernet, Barbera, Nebbiolo and Merlot, and Franciacorta Chardonnay (DOC) are from the province of Brescia.

DOC APPELLATIONS

- Oltrepò
- Oltrepò Pavese
- Franciacorta
- Lugana
- Riviera del Garda Bresciano
- Valtellina

mountainous landscapes, which are said to be haunted by werewolves. Mechanization is rare, as the slopes are very steep. The yield is limited: 712,800 gallons per year.

Four red wines are produced from Nebbiolo (called Chiavennasca here): Valgella,

Sassela, Grumello and Inferno (95 percent Nebbiolo).

These are agreeable, fresh and sometimes slightly tingling wines; Valtellina Superiore (DOC) wines, with a label that indicates place of origin, are the most tannic and warm wines. They are sometimes made from previously dried grapes, as is Sfurzat. They are aged for four years (for Riserva wines) with quite remarkable results. Farther south, between Lake Mag-

LOMBARDY GRAPE VARIETIES

Nebbiolo grows virtually everywhere in the Valtellina. It is called Chiavennasca locally. Lugana is made from Trebbiano and Vernaccia, while Frecciarossa is made from Riesling, Pinot Noir, Bonarda and Barbera grapes.

giore and Lake Como, Lugana produced from Trebbiano and Vernaccia is a light red wine or a somewhat yellow-colored white wine (which unfortunately is aged too long).

Among the DOC wines flourishing around Lake Garda, there is the Tocai di San Martino della Battaglia, an excellent white wine, as well as the Riviera del Garda Bresciano in red and rosé.

In Casteggio, near Pavia and the outskirts of Piedmont, the hillside vineyards of the Frecciarossa estate stretch across 70 continuous acres. Riesling, Pinot Noir, Bonarda and Barbera have been planted there, with an annual production of 52,800 gallons, bottled at the estate (a rarity). White wines (*bianco*), semi-sweet whites (*ambrato*), dry reds (*rosso*) and semi-dry rosés (Saint-Georges) are produced here.

In the foothills of the Brescian Alps, Lombardy produces two other AOC wines: Franciacorta Rosso and Franciacorta Chardonnay (both should be drunk young).

Rosso is a dry, very sturdy wine made from Cabernet, Barbera, Nebbiolo and Merlot. The sweet muscats and sparkling muscats called Moscato di Casteggio Spumante are worthy of mention.

Veneto

Veneto is a highly fertile region, and vines flourish between the Alps, the Po basin and Lake Garda. The wines of Veneto may not be the greatest in Italy, but they are charming and fresh enough to be appreciated by wine lovers throughout the world.

DOC APPELLATIONS

- Bardolino
- Bianco di Custoza
- Valpolicella, Recioto della Valpolicella
- Soave, Recioto di Soave
- Prosecco di Conegliano-Valdobbiadene
- Piave
- Gambellara
- Colli Berici
- Colli Euganei
- Breganze
- Lison-Pramaggiore

Veneto is considered third in importance among Italian wine districts, and has an annual production of 224 million gallons. The region's principal vineyards lie between Verona and Venice, particularly near the shores of Lake Garda. The four best-known wines produced here are Soave, a white wine that has a dry, very slightly acid taste; and three red wines: Valpolicella, Bardolino and Valpentena. These dry, light wines are best when drunk young. There are also rosés, called *chiaretto* wines.

Valpolicella

Valpolicella has a delicate bouquet and rich texture, mingling the subtlety of flowers and sourdrop candies with an unforgettable summer's eve. Valpolicella is on virtually every menu in Italy, and it is difficult to imagine how such vast quantities of the wine can possibly be produced.

Only nineteen communes produce the wine, from Corvina (40 percent to 70 percent), Rondinella (20 percent to 40 percent), Rossignola, Molinara and Negrara. The vineyards extend some 19 miles north of Verona to the shores of Lake Garda. To find the best areas, the classico and Valpantena zones, requires climbing 330 to 1,300 feet up the steep slopes of three small valleys: the Negrar, Fumane and Marano. Regulations restrict yield to 962 gallons per acre.

The famous Recioto della Valpolicella is produced in the region. Only the ripest

VENETO GRAPE VARIETIES

Valpolicella is produced from six different grape varieties: Rondinella, Molinara, Rossignola, Negrara, Corvina and Pelara. Other common grapes include Merlot and Cabernet.

grapes harvested from the upper parts of the clusters are used to make this dessert wine. The grapes are dried on wattles, a process that increases the sugar content. Classic Recioto is dark purple with garnet-red highlights.

Recioto della Valpolicella Amarone (or Amarone) is a drier red wine that is very concentrated and high in alcohol. It ages marvelously. Other Reciotos are semi-sweet, sweet and even *spumante*.

Bardolino, made from Corvina, Molinara, Negrara and Rondinella, is grown in the place of that name and in nearby territories on the southeastern shore of Lake Garda. It is a dry wine, clear ruby-red in color. The classico zone behind Bardolino has expanded considerably (the label bears the mention "classico"). Bardolino is now being fermented for much shorter periods of time than is traditional, resulting in a lighter, fresher and clearly more pleasant wine.

The 14,820-acre area of Soave (with two DOC appellations: Recioto di Soave and Soave Classico) is located between Soave and Monteforte, some 15 miles east of Verona. At its best, Soave has a light straw color with greenish highlights and is a pleasant wine.

Two other wines are worthy of mention: Prosecco di Conegliano and Prosecco di Valdobbiadene, both dry, fruity wines produced some 30 miles north of Venice, near Treviso.

Friuli-Venezia-Giulia

Friuli-Venezia Giulia has been a region with limited autonomy since 1963. The Treaty of Saint-Germain-en-Laye restored it to Italy in 1919 after a period of four centuries during which it was part of the Austro-Hungarian Empire. The Carnic Alps to the north of the region form a border with Austria; the Julian Alps and the Gulf of Trieste to the southeast form a border with Slovenia.

This small, very mountainous region has a mild climate and produces an astrono-

DOC APPELLATIONS

- Friuli Grave
- Friuli Latisana
- Friuli Aquileia
- Isonzo
- Collio
- Colli Orientali del Friuli

mical 26.4 million gallons per year. The vine-covered plains extend all the way to the Adriatic and the Gulf of Venice. Yet 40 percent of the wines produced here are entitled to a DOC appellation. (The average percentage nationally is 10 percent or less in comparison.) All grape varieties grow in the region. For reds: local varieties include Merlot, Cabernet Franc, Sauvignon and Pinot Noir; for whites (nearly two-thirds of DOC production for the entire region): Pinot Bianco, Pinot Grigio, Chardonnay, Riesling, Müller-Thurgau, Verduzzo and others.

As you leave the Po basin, the slopes are covered with vines. They follow the foothills of the Alps and gradually climb toward the Slovenian border. Here, the wines are primarily produced from a single grape variety. Stop at one of the many growers' stalls along the side of the road.

They will offer a selection of Sauvignon, Chardonnay, Pinot Grigio and Tocai, the local favorite and the most heavily planted white (not to be confused with the Tokays of Hungary and Alsace). Labels generally indicate the grape variety that is used in production.

The white wines are fresh and surprisingly lively. The reds, with the exception of Refosco, which has a typically bitter undertone, are fresh and fruity as is typical of the region (notably the Cabernet, Gamay and Merlot).

On the Adriatic coast near the Slovenian border, two DOC wines are produced: Aquileia and Collio (Goriziano), excellent white wines that benefit from the micro-

FRIULI-VENEZIA GIULIA GRAPE VARIETIES

This region is particularly known for its white wines (40 percent of production). White grape varieties are similar to those found in Austria and Slovenia: Tocai wines are very full-bodied without being overly aromatic, and have a flowery hint; Picolit, Sauvignon, Chardonnay, Pinot Bianco and Pinot Grigio, Riesling and Traminer. An indigenous grape, Ribolla, is making a comeback, and produces wines that can have an undertone of acidity.

Varieties include Merlot (one-third) for varietals, Cabernet Sauvignon and Refosco, an indigenous grape grown in France under the name Mondeuse de Savoie.

climate near Gorizia, notably in the area surrounding San Floriano and Oslavia. Latisana (DOC), an honest red wine, grows along the Tagliamento. The very famous Colli Orientali del Friuli is marketed under the name of the grape variety from which it is produced, as are other DOC wines.

Collio and Colli Orientali are among the best white wines produced in Italy. Friuli-Venezia Giulia is one of the only wine-producing regions of Italy controlled by growers, not by cooperatives or shippers. The quality of the white wines, which are rarely aged in oak barrels, brings out the fruitiness of the grape variety. In addition, the yield is low, the climate fairly mild, the soil rich in sandstone and limestone marl, the vineyards raked in terraces (called *"ronchi"* locally), and the grape varieties good. These factors all have contributed to the wine's reputation, which is by all standards excellent.

Trentino and Alto Adige

This autonomous region in northern Italy extends over the Valle di Alto-Adige, part of the Dolomites and into the southern Tyrol.

In contrast to the Austrians (right across the border), who have developed such white wines as Welschriesling, Ruländer, Pinot Blanc and Traminer and produced marvelous vintages, the some six thousand transalpine growers are satisfied with traditional red wines, which make up the majority of the 1.06 billion gallons produced yearly. Attitudes are changing, however, and thanks to new techniques, particularly in Trentino, the wines are improving. The aim is to produce wines that are comparable in quality to Austrian and Swiss wines.

Alto Adige, also known as the South Tyrol, has always been the site of territorial battles. It belonged to Austria until the Treaty of Saint-Germain-en-Laye in 1919, which gave it to Italy. With a German-speaking minority, German is an alternate language, and these Tyrolians of the south

have been entitled since 1946 to equal rights and cultural freedom. Consensus has it that the best wines (white) are produced in the most northern sector of Alto Adige above the Vale de l'Isarco near the Brenner Pass. Vines are planted on the sunniest slopes of the area between Termine and Salerno and extending to Ora; the deeper valleys are planted with fruit trees and plants. Good red wines are produced around Trento, in an extraordinary amphitheater of mountains, and along a major passage to the Dolomites, the Brenta and to the sun-drenched shores of Lake Garda.

At its best, Riesling del Trentino (DOC) of Alto Adige can achieve the quality of the best Austrian and German Rieslings (the Italians however have the bad habit of letting their wines age in barrels too long). This wine grows on the upper slopes and flourishes in a fairly cold climate. The Traminer del Trentino (DOC), which doesn't have the quality of a Riesling, is the best produced in Italy. The wine is pleasantly perfumed and lightly spicy. Among red wines, Santa Maddalena (DOC) clearly stands out as being superior. It is produced in the region surrounding Bolzano from Schiava and Lagrein grapes. The wine is round in the mouth and has a distinctive bouquet of almonds.

Caldaro (DOC), which is also known under the German name Kalterersee, derives its name from Lake Caldaro, in the Adige Valley. Such great quantities of the wine are produced that one may wonder about its provenance. True Caldaro, which

TRENTINO AND ALTO ADIGE GRAPE VARIETIES

The Austrian influence is obvious in the Riesling and Traminer, as is the French influence with Pinot, Cabernet, Merlot and Chardonnay. Schiava Grossa (Vernatsch) is the leading grape variety of Trentino-Alto-Adige. It covers some 8,645 acres. In Germany, it is called Trollinger, and is originally from Wurtemberg. It is a sturdy, fruity grape used in making Santa Maddalena, and supplies most of the local Vino da Tavola production.

Lagrein produces Lagreinkretzer, also known as Lagarino Rosato.

Teroldego and Marzemino are also found, as well as greater and greater amounts of Cabernet Sauvignon.

has a beautiful garnet color, is a harmonious and very pleasant wine to drink. Vino Santo del Trentino (DOC) resembles the sweet wines produced in Tuscany. It is made from semi-dried Malvasia and Trebbiano grapes.

Simpler wines include Val d'Adige, made on the shores of the Adige near Trento. It is produced from Schiava, Lambrusco, Pinot and Teroldego. Terlano (DOC) comes from Alto Adige and is made from Terlano—as its name indicates—and has a slightly greenish tint. The famous Lagreinkretzer (Lagarino Rosato, DOC) is a slightly sparkling rosé wine.

All of these wines, as well as Pinot Bianco (DOC) and Cabernet del Trentino (DOC), are generally fairly good and have some interesting aspect.

Excellent wines worthy of mention are the sparkling wines of Trentino, undeniably the best in Italy.

Emilia-Romagna

Emilia-Romagna is one of the most fertile plains in all Italy, extending from the broad Po valley in the north and the Apennine mountains to the south, to the Adriatic coast (the small Republic of San Marino is perched dramatically on top of a mountain soaring up from the plain).

Large chunks of vineyard are few and far between, but vines are planted everywhere throughout this vast agricultural plain, notably around Modeno, Reggio nell'Emilia and Bologna. They seem to run rampant throughout the land, clinging to walls and climbing up posts without being pruned back, tended or cultivated. But a new approach to winegrowing seems to be taking hold. Today some 124,000 acres of vineyards are being carefully cultivated, and a multitude of small crus can be found along the wine routes cutting swathes

DOC AND DOCG APPELLATIONS

- Colli Piacentini
- Gutturnio
- Lambrusco
- Colli Bolognesi
- Trebbiano di Romagna
- Albana di Romagna DOCG

through the countryside. They go extremely well with local specialties.

Emilia-Romagna is where Lambrusco, one of Italy's most popular wines (and the most exported, particularly to the United States) is produced. The grapes are vinified by huge wine cooperatives. Invariably *frizzante,* or slightly-sparkling, it is the perfect accompaniment to Bolognese cuisine, which has the reputation of being somewhat rich. Lambrusco dates back to the Etruscans and has diversified over time, and can be white, red, dry, pleasant, slightly hard, even overly sweetish. The semi-sparkling wine has a bright foam that can be somewhat disconcerting when drunk for the first time. The Lambrusco appellation includes six DOC wines from the area near Modeno and Reggio Emilia: Lambrusco, Lambrusco di Sorbara, Lambrusco di Castelvetro, Lambrusco Grasparossa, Lambrusco Salamino di Santa and Lambrusco Reggiano. Lambrusco and Albana produce the best wines, but the most common grape variety is Sangiovese, which produces 238 million gallons annually, notably Sangiovese di Romagna, a dry, strong, nearly bitter wine that has a superb ruby color. Albana di Romagna is found along the small mountainous route running from Bologna to Rimini. The wine has a golden yellow color and can be *secco*

EMILIE–ROMAGNA GRAPE VARIETIES

Emilia-Romagna is the land of Lambrusco, the famous red wine that is somewhat sweet and semi-sparkling and best when drunk young. It is produced from Lambrusco grapes.

The Etruscans named the wine Lambrusca. The grapes are trained along trellises as they were during Antiquity, and yield four DOC wines for the region. There are some sixty different varieties of Lambrusco (Piedmont, Veneto, Sicily, etc.) and it is drunk throughout the world, especially in the United States.

White grape varieties common to Emilia-Romagna include Sauvignon, Pinot Grigio, Pinot Bianco, Tocai and Riesling. Other reds include Merlot, Cabernet and Pinot Noir.

(dry) or *amabile* (semi-sweet). It is produced from an eponymous grape variety which yields pungent wines—Emilia-Romagna's sole DOCG. Galla Placidia, Regent of the Western Roman Empire (AD 435) is said to have stopped at a small town to slake her thirst. "I must drink you in gold," she exclaimed upon tasting the beverage served in a coarse mug. Hence, Bertinoro (from *bere,* to drink, and *oro,* meaning gold) has been the name of the town ever since.

Trebbiano di Romagna, a dry straw-colored wine, is produced in the area around Bologna, Forli and Ravenna; it may be vinified as a sparkling wine as well.

Another wine worthy of mention is Colli Bolognese di Monte San Pietro, red and white wines made of a single grape variety—either Pinot Bianco, Merlot or Sauvignon.

Umbria

South of Tuscany, midway between Florence and Rome, Umbria—the land of the Etruscans—runs along either side of the Tiber River. The region is partly mountainous and very rich in limestone. Of the 26.4 million gallons produced here annually on the 29,640 acres of the region, Orvieto Bianco (DOC) is the most famous wine, a limpid, pleasant wine with golden highlights. It is produced from Trebbiano Toscano and a small amount of Verdello, Grechetto, Drupeggio and Malvasia. The classico area yields one-third of the 264,000 gallons produced. Southeast of Perugia, in Umbria, is where some 2.64 million gallons of Torgiano (DOC) is

DOC AND DOCG APPELLATIONS

- Colli Altotiberini
- Colli Perugini
- Torgiano DOCG
- Montefalco
- Orvieto

produced. This fruity, red and white wine is harvested near the Torre di Giano. It is produced by one family, the Lungarottis. Two other wines are worthy of mention: Colli del Trasimeno (DOC), from the area around Lake Trasimeno, and in the upper Tiber Valley near Città di Castello, Colli Altotiberini (DOC), made from Trebbiano, Sangiovese and Merlot. In all, 660,000 gallons are produced on an 865-acre area.

Latium

Rome and all of its surrounding provinces are located in Latium. The region runs from Lake Bolsena in the north to the Tyrrhenian Sea in the southwest and the Abruzzis in the east.

Ninety percent of the wines produced in the region are dry and semi-dry whites that are fairly crisp and highly appreciated by both Romans and tourists. The most famous is the white wine of Montefiascone near Lake Bolsena in the region of Viterbo: Est! Est!! Est!! According to legend, the German Bishop Fugger made a trip to Rome in AD 1111. On his way to Rome, the bishop had the habit of dispatching his loyal servant ahead of him to taste the wines along the route and to mark on the doors of taverns whether the wine was good—"Est" (It is)—or not—"Non Est" (It is not). When the servant reached Montefiascone, he found the wine to be so extra-

CASTELLI ROMANI

Of the best dry white wines of Italy, the famous Castelli Romani wines, Frascati and Marino are the best known. The incredibly legendary Est! Est!! Est!!! of Montefiascone is either a dry or semi-dry white wine.

LATIUM GRAPE VARIETIES

Castelli Romani wines are made from Malvasia, Greco and Trebbiano, grown on soil rich in potassium and phosphorus—which gives them their characteristic hint of lightness.

ordinary that he scrawled "Est! Est!! Est!!!"
and went back to the wine cellar to await
his master.

DOC APPELLATIONS

- Est! Est!! Est!!! di Montefiascone
- Montecompatri
- Frascati
- Marino
- Colli Albani
- Colli Lanuvini
- Velletri

Castelli Romani

Stop at any trattoria in Rome and ask for a
glass of wine. You don't have to specify a
Frascati, Colonna or Colli Albani: the
owner has his own supplier, and the wine
he serves up is rarely a disappointment.
Nearly all of them come from Castelli
Romani, which produces vast quantities of
dry, sweet or semi-dry wines from Malvasia and Trebbiano.

Nearly 70 million bottles are produced
yearly from the hills surrounding Rome.

These wines are easily recognized by
their straw-yellow color. Frascati (DOC),
which can be found on virtually every
wine list in Rome, is either dry or semi-
dry. If it is sweet, it is a *cannellino*. Frascati,
which is a vigorous wine, is made from
three grape varieties: Malvasia, Greco and
Trebbiano.

There are some surprisingly good wines
south of Rome: Colli Albani (DOC), from
Albano and Aricca, is a powerful, golden-
colored wine with a delicate bouquet.
Marino, produced in the area between
Lake Albano and Rome, is a dry straw-
golden colored wine that is semi-sweet
and deliciously fruity.

Wines from Aprilia, made from Trebbiano, are straw-golden in color or rosé
and dry when made from vines planted
in Sangiovese, and garnet red when in
Merlot.

The Marches are said to have derived their
name from the period when the area served
as a frontier province in the empire of
Charlemagne. They are formed by a vast
wild mountainous zone, a sector of fertile
hills rich in clay (which produce most of
the 106 million gallons of wine annually)
and a coastal region lined with beaches.
The wines produced here are not high
enough in quality to be exported. While
passing through Ancona, the capital, try a
glass of Verdicchio dei Castelli di Jesi
(DOC); it is a light, dry or semi-dry straw-
colored white wine (the best of the
Marches). The wine can be surprisingly
high in alcohol (14 %). It is produced in the
regions of Cupramontana, Monteroberto
and Castebellino. The classico label applies
only to wines produced in the southern
area of Jesi. The best red wine is Rosso
Piceno (DOC), made from Sangiovese and
Montepulciano. Bianchello del Metauro
(DOC) is a light, dry white wine made
from Bianchello and Malvasia grapes.
The wine is interesting due to its geographical location: the Metauro Valley was
the site of one of the greatest battles of
Antiquity, when the Romans vanquished
the Carthaginians.

THE MARCHES GRAPE VARIETIES

The famous grape variety of the Marches
is Verdicchio (dei Castelli di Jesi), grown
here since the fourteenth century, particularly in the region near Ancona. The
origin of the name comes from its color:
yellow-green. It produces vigorous, acidic
wines and can make fine, bubbly wines.

DOC APPELLATIONS

- Bianchello del Metauro
- Verdicchio dei Castelli di Jesi
- Verdicchio di Matelica
- Rosso Conero
- Vernaccia di Serrapetrona
- Rosso Piceno

Abruzzi

Between the Adriatic Sea and the Apennines, there is little else but hills. The Abruzzis are arid and impoverished, the tallest being San Sano at 9,547 feet, with a thin coastal strip running along the Adriatic seaboard. Vines grow in the soft stones of the karstic hills, yielding wines which have a snappy bitterness. Montepulciano di Abruzzo is produced in great quantities in the region of Chieti, on the Adriatic seaboard; it is a robust red with an alcohol content of 12 %. It is vinified with a small amount of Sangiovese. Chieti, Aquila, Pescara and Teramo are ruby-colored wines that are slightly sweetish, and can be *cerasuolo* (with macerated must) or *vecchio* (aged for over two years). Trebbiano di Abruzzo is a dry wine of 11 %, and straw yellow in color. It is produced on fifty-seven communes of the provinces of Chieti, Aquila, Rescaro and Teramo.

DOC APPELLATIONS

- Montepulciano di Abruzzo
- Trebbiano di Abruzzo
- Biferno (in the Molise)

Campania

If one day in Naples or in any Italian restaurant somewhere in the world, someone serves you a dry white wine with golden highlights, a wine harvested on the southern slope of Vesuvius, then think of this legend, one of the most beautiful that ever existed about wine: when Lucifer fell from grace, he landed with such a thud that the land beneath him collapsed and formed the Bay of Naples, a marvelous place located at the gates of Paradise. Christ, who loved to meditate on the slopes of Vesuvius, saw that his paradise on earth had become a hell. A tear flowed down his cheek and fell onto the ground. This is where a vine sprang up called Lacrima Christi. The vineyards covering the volcanic slopes are planted with Greco and Fiano, and are a reminder to Neapolitans of the original vine. Campania is a fertile, sun-drenched region, similar to the "Campania felix" described by the Ancients: Naples, Herculaneum, Pompeii, Sorrento and the islands of Capri and Ischia. It produced the famous Falernum of Fornia, lauded by Pliny and Horace. What a disappointment the wines are today, however. It is nothing but an ordinary wine made from Falaghina for white and Aglianico for reds. It is produced in vast quantities in Capua, Campi Flegrei, Sessa Aurunca and Mondragone. On the whole, however, it is preferable to the somewhat harsh Taurasi (DOCG), which is drinkable only after a long period of aging; and to the Greco di Tufo (DOC), a dry white wine that is fairly round in the mouth and golden yellow in color; it can also be sweet or semi-sparkling.

The wines of Capri have an international reputation. They are heady, lively and dry and go very well with seafood dishes. They can also be drunk as aperitifs. Made from Greco and Falaghina, they have recently been granted DOC status. Those on the neighboring island of Ischia, however, have been entitled to it for years: Ischia Bianco or Rosso made from Forestera and Biancolella. They are pleasant wines that are straw colored and have a delicate bouquet.

CAMPANIA GRAPE VARIETIES

Vesuvio Rosso, which is harvested on volcanic soil, is made from Aglianico, Piedirosso and Olivella grapes. Greco, which is Greek in origin, may be the grape used in making the legendary Falerno wine, which was known as Falernum during Roman times. Greco di Tufo is a rich dry white wine that is golden yellow in color.

APPELLATIONS

- Taurasi DOCG
- Falerno del Massico
- Salopaca
- Greco di Tufo
- Fiano di Avellino
- Ischia
- Capri

Sardinia

Sardinia is one of the biggest islands in the Mediterranean. It is located off the coast of central Italy in the Tyrrhenian Sea. There are mountains everywhere, with an average altitude of more than 3,280 feet. This is a mysterious land: Who built the Nuraghe, the enormous cone-shaped towers? Were they tombs, look-out posts, fortresses? The answer remains a mystery even today, as does the actual origin of the Sardinians.

The island, which has become a leading tourist destination—thanks notably to the Aga Khan's considerable investments along the Costa Smeralda—is also a great wine-producing region, with some 52.8 million gallons produced annually.

Previously known for its sweet, powerful wines, Sardinia, like Sicily, launched its enological revolution in the 1960s. There were new grape varieties, early harvesting, and new vinification techniques.

The vineyards of Sella and Mosta, located north of Alghero, are recognized throughout the world as major success stories. Both vineyards belong to the Italian state, and light, perfumed, slightly snappy wines are produced from Spanish grape varieties. Vernaccia di Oristano (DOC) is the most famous Sardinian wine. The alcohol content can be as high as 16%, and it is often mistaken for Sherry, due to its lovely amber color. Vernaccia di Oristano is produced in the Valley of Tirso, near Oristano and the Gulf of Oristano. The wine can keep for up to thirty years.

In the northernmost part of the island, the region of Santa Teresa di Gallura yields a very dry wine that is straw yellow in color: Vermentino di Gallura. Cagliari is another important viticultural region, known primarily for its heady wines: Malvasia (14.5 %); Monica, a very full-bodied red wine; Moscato, which is either *dolce naturale* or *liquoroso dolce naturale*; Giro di Cagliari. Giro di Cagliari is a rare, usually sweet red from Giro grown in the Campidano north of Cagliari. It can be *secco, dolce, liquoroso secco* and *liquoroso dolce,* and the wine is used much as Port is. It has a

lovely, bright ruby color and must age at least one year in the barrel.

Nugarus (DOC), which is also produced in the region of Cagliari, is an excellent Vino da Tavola and accounts for ten percent of Sardinian wines.

Lastly, on the west coast of the island, Malvasia di Bosa (DOC) is a white wine with a slight hint of hazelnuts. It has an alcohol content of 17.5 % and must be aged at least two years in barrels.

DOC APPELLATIONS

- Throughout the island:
  – Cannonau di Sardegna
  – Vermentino di Sardegna
  – Moscato di Sardegna
  – Monica di Sardegna

- Vermentino di Gallura
- Molvasia di Bosa
- Vernaccia di Oristano
- Giro di Cagliari
- Malvasia di Cagliari
- Moscato di Cagliari
- Monica di Cagliari
- Nasco di Cagliari
- Nuragus di Cagliari

SARDINIAN GRAPE VARIETIES

In Sardinia, the Corsican equivalent of Vermentino Corse is Nugarus, introduced by the Phoenicians (the name is similar to the famous Nuraghe); Torbato, an assertive, full-bodied grape; and Nasco, which is semi-sweet with a hazelnut aroma.

Monica, which is Spanish in origin, is the most common Sardinian grape grown on the island. It yields mostly ordinary wines, with a few exceptions.

Sicily

This island, located to the southwest of the Italian peninsula and separated from Calabria by the Messina Strait, is the largest island in the Mediterranean, and owes its names to the early inhabitants, the Sicules, who were Asian in origin. Sicily is not only the largest island in the Mediterranean, but also the most beautiful. There are superb beaches, brushwood-covered heath, hills and mountains covered with olive trees and vines, and the great plain of Catania overlooking the volcanic mass of Etna. It was occupied by the Phoenicians and colonized by the Greeks beginning in the eighth century B.C. They introduced viticulture and covered the island with temples, theaters and antique cities. After the fall of Rome, Sicily passed from the Vandals to the Goths, then to the Byzantines (535). The Arabs gained a foothold in the ninth century, then were driven out during the Norman conquest of Sicily (1060–1091). It then became part of the Holy Roman Empire in 1194. The unpopular government of the French brought on the Sicilian Vespers revolt (1282). It was ceded to the Spanish, then to Austria. In the nineteenth century, Sicily became part of Italy.

The land is like a museum of European culture and, since the Greeks, has been a land of vines. Sicily's hour of glory came in 1773 when Marsala was created for the English market by John Woodhouse. The vineyard currently covers some 222,300 acres, with an annual production of 237 million gallons, of which a fair proportion is exported for blending (notably to France).

DOC APPELLATIONS

- Marsala
- Alcamo, Bianco d'Alcamo
- Faro
- Etna
- Moscato di Siracusa
- Moscato di Noto
- Cerasuolo di Vittoria
- Molvasia delle Lipari
- Moscato di Pantelleria

Sicilian viticulture has made a great comeback, saved by two measures:

- an ample reduction of Marsala, a dry, full-bodied wine with an alcohol content of up to 18 %, produced in the western part of the island from Grillo. The area has been replanted with Trebbiano, Catarratto, Inzolia for dry whites and Sangiovese for reds;

- earlier harvests, during the first part of September, to preserve the wine's fruitiness, acidity and freshness. No more long sejours in vats; bottling takes place before Christmas.

Marsala, made from Grillo, Catarratto and Inzolia, is the most famous Sicilian wine. It is a sweet wine with a stunning amber color, obtained through mutage by adding alcohol to the must.

The Marsala-producing region is strictly limited.

Depending on the glucose content, the wine can be *fino* (17 % alcohol, 5% sugar), *superiore* (18 % alcohol, 10% sugar) and *vergine* (18 % alcohol and lightly fortified; it relies on an aging system comparable to the *"solera"* system used in producing Spanish Sherry, which involves topping up the old with younger vintages; it is the most prestigious). Whether dry or sweet, it has a fairly dark color and a heady wood and caramel bouquet with a hint of dried plum. There are flavored versions as well (with egg, cream, almond and other syrups).

Mamertino is a golden white wine with a highly aromatic bouquet. The vineyards occupy the slopes near Messina. Caesar ordered the wine served during the banquet marking his Third Consulate. Corvo di Casteldaccia is a fresh dry white wine produced from Trebbiano. Faro (DOC), is a good red wine based on Nerello, grown at the island's northeastern tip around Messina. It has an alcohol content of 14 %. But the best table wines of Sicily come from the slopes of Etna; all are DOC wines and are high in alcohol. White wines are made from Carricante (*superiore*, if they are grown in the community of Milo), Catarratto and Nerello grapes; reds and rosés are made from Nerello Mascalese. Rosso is a powerful wine that needs to be

SICILIAN GRAPE VARIETIES

Nerello Mascalese is added to wines to enhance their alcohol content and color. The grape is used in making Faro, a red wine produced near Messina, as well as the wines of Etna, which generally age quite well.

For whites, the famous Marsala, dry or sweet, comes from Grillo and from Catarratto Bianco (40 percent). It dominates the island, as do Trebbiano Toscano and Grecanico, although the latter is becoming less popular.

aged a few years to give it its full perfume.

In the region of Syracuse, Moscato di Noto (DOC), a very pale yellow wine with a slight honey perfume, is worthy of mention. Farther west in the region of Ragusa, Cerasuolo di Vittoria (DOC) offers a dense cherry-red wine made from Frappato and Calabrese (Nero d'Avola) grapes. And be sure not to miss Malvasia delle Lipari (DOC), a famous sweet wine made from semi-dried grapes, grown on the Lipari or Aeolian isles north of Messina, Salina and Stromboli. The one produced on the island of Pantelleria is a superb dessert wine that has an exquisite amber color. Today eighty percent of Sicilian wines are controlled by some one hundred cooperatives: Corvo in Palermo; Settesoli near Agrigento; Villa Grande at the foot of Etna, etc. This is one of the reasons why the island's wines export so well. Sicily has remained true and faithful to its original grapes; wines ranked DOC represent only three percent of total production.

Other wine-producing regions

Basilicata

Basilicata, formerly Lucania, is one of the poorest regions in southern Italy, as well as the wildest and most mountainous. The slopes of Mount Vulture produce a warm red wine, Aglianico del Vulture (DOC), which has a hint of the volcanic soil it grows in. The wine ages very well; after three years of being barrel-aged, it becomes *vecchio* (old) and after five years *riserva*. The Muscat and Malvoisie grapes are also abundant in the area of Mount Vulture, and produce excellent dessert wines thanks to what Italians call *passito*—strong, usually sweet wine from the concentrated musts of semi-dried grapes.

BASILICATA GRAPE VARIETIES

Aglianico del Vulture, a sturdy warm wine with a slight strawberry and raspberry taste, comes from Aglianico—famous for having been the grape of ancient Falernum. The wine picks up a tang from the volcanic soil, and requires a long period of bottle-aging.

Muscat and Malvasia vines also are common in the region.

Apulia

Apulia, formerly Apuglia, lies farther east, in the heel of the boot between the Appenines and the Adriatic. This region consists of a series of plains and plateaus interspersed with valleys. Wheat grows in the most fertile areas, and olive trees and vines

---

DOC APPELLATION (Basilicata)

- Aglianico del Vulture

DOC APPELLATIONS (Apulia)

- Throughout the region :
  – Aleatico di Puglia

- San Severo
- Moscato di Trani
- Castel del Monte
- Locorotondo
- Primitivo di Manduria

---

are scattered everywhere. Under a leaden sun, Apulia produces over 290 million gallons of wine per year, most of the country's ordinary wines, the remainder used to make vermouth. This is the largest wine-producing region of southern Italy. It runs for nearly 250 miles along the Adriatic and produces approximately 17 percent of Italian wines. Among the most pleasant is Locorotondo, near Bari, a pale, straw-green subtly fruity wine made from Verdeca and

APULIA GRAPE VARIETIES

Sangiovese and Trebbiano in the north of the region near San Severo produce a good one-third of DOC wines. Uva di Troia is the basic grape used in making Castel del Monte in central Apulia, while farther south, in the Salentino peninsula, Negroauraro yields deep-colored, bitter wines.

Bianco d'Alessano grapes. As you wait for the boat to Greece in Brindisi, try some Martina Franca, which is served iced. Near Bari, Castel del Monte (DOC), named after the octagonal castle of Emperor Friedrich II von Hohenstaufen, is a bestselling *rosato* made mainly from Bombino Nero, while Moscato di Trani (DOC) is a rich, golden dessert wine.

Matino (DOC) is the southernmost DOC of Salento. Matino's *rosso* and *rosato* are based on Negroamaro grapes.

DOC APPELLATIONS (Calabria)
- Ciró
- Donnici
- Savuto

DOC APPELLATIONS (Liguria)
- Rossese di Dolceacqua
- Cinqueterre

DOC APPELLATION (Valle d'Aosta)
- Valle d'Aosta

Calabria

While Apulia is the heel of the boot, Calabria is the foot. It is a very poor mountainous region, and a land rich with legends and bandits.

Tourists flock to the coast, which is lined with orange, lemon and olive trees. But Calabria, with its volcanic soil, is also a leading wine-producing region. The wines are somewhat ordinary for the most part, but there are some surprising exceptions, such as Ciro di Calabria (DOC), produced east of Cosenza. The whites are straw-colored and made from Greco di Bianco and Trebbiano. The powerful and warm reds and rosés are made from Gaglioppo, Greco and Trebbiano. Greco di Gerace, named after a small town in the Appenines, is a rare, expensive wine that dates

CALABRIAN GRAPE VARIETIES

In Calabria, Gaglioppo occupies 60 percent of the vineyard. It is believed to be Greek in origin and produces Ciró di Calabria, a very heady red wine that requires aging. For white wines, Greco di Gerace is a sweet yellow wine that is very high in alcohol and famous for its floral bouquet.

back to Antiquity and was highly appreciated by the Romans. Today, the superb golden-colored wine (called Greco di Bianco) has an aromatic bouquet and can be one of Italy's outstanding dessert wines.

Liguria

Liguria is the Italian extension of the French Riviera and features a series of beach resorts along the Gulf of Genoa, with the Alps in the background.

Some 10.6 million gallons of wine are produced yearly under difficult conditions (in some places, the vines are inaccessible to machines). Most of it is somewhat questionable in quality, with two exceptions: Rossese di Dolceacqua (DOC), a pleasant, perfumed wine that resembles Beaujolais (according to legend, it was one of Napoleon's favorites); and Cinqueterre ("Five Lands"), the best wine in Liguria, made from Bosco and Vernaccia.

Cinqueterre is a white wine with a beautiful amber color and, as its name indicates, comes from five "lands": the villages of Vernazza, Corniglia, Monterosso, Riomaggiore and Manarola. It may be dry or semi-dry.

Seek out the Rossese, Pigato, Vermentino and Ormeasco wines for their roundness, ample structure and aromas. The

quality of the wines can be quite surprising.

Sciacchetrà (DOC) is a dessert version of Cinqueterre made from the same grapes, semi-dried. With an alcohol content of least 17 %, the wine is quite rare.

Valle d'Aosta

Valle d'Aosta is Italy's smallest and least populous region. It shares a border on the north with Switzerland, and on the west with France and with Piedmont to the east and south.

The Valle d'Aoste appellation encompasses fifteen different wines, including the two famous DOCs, Donnaz and Enfer d'Arvier. The Gamay and Nebbiolo wines are interesting and Moscato can be surprisingly good.

Most vines grow over pergolas on narrow stone terraces. They produce sweet wines from Nebbiolo that have a garnet-red color and are called Picotener locally,

VALLE D'AOSTA GRAPE VARIETIES

Donnaz and Enfer d'Arvier are the two best-known wines here, made from Nebbiolo (called Picotener) and Petit Rouge.

grown around Donnaz, on the communes of Paloz, Bord and Pont-Saint-Martin.

Enfer d'Arvier is also a red wine made from Petit Rouge and a small amount of Vien de Nus, Negret and Dolcetto. It ages very well in barrels and is easily recognizable by its sharp, bitter grape flavor that softens with age.

Spain

Until recently, world-famous Sherry and a few other appellations seemed to eclipse other Spanish wines. Wines produced in Spain were generally associated with excess sunshine and high alcohol content, with a greater emphasis on quantity over quality. Such oversimplifications need to be redressed, however—and quickly!

The global amount of wine currently produced in Spain is still much lower than what the country has the capacity to produce. In terms of quantity of wine produced, Spain ranks third among European countries, whereas it ranks first in terms of land surface under vine. This gap is explained as much by the excessive aridness of the soil as by the fact that the country lags behind many other countries in terms of modern winemaking techniques and mechanization. Yet wineries are grouping together to form a greater number of wine cooperatives, and the leading bodegas, where the wines are stored, now rely on modern equipment. Stainless steel vats, controlled temperatures during fermentation and other modern equipment have contributed a great deal to improving overall quality levels, and permit more careful, methodical vinification processes. The more rigorous selection of grape varieties currently being carried out in many regions is also part of a general trend toward improving quality. The wines produced in Rioja in northern Spain best reflect these new efforts.

Above: Sherry is stored in cool areas in the bodegas.
Left: Working the vineyards in Andalusia.

The label: a question of rank and standard

Like wines produced in other European countries, Spanish wines fall into two categories:

- quality wines: VCPRD (Vino de Calidad Producido en Región Demarcada)
- table wines (Vino de Mesa)

1. Quality wines
- Denominación de Origen (DO). These are the equivalent of the French AOC wines. Some forty wines are subjected to extremely strict rules governing grape varieties, yields, and production conditions.
- Denominación de Origen Calificada (DOC). This category was established in 1991. It applies to one region only, Rioja. The regulations are much stricter and the wines subjected to rigorous taste tests.

2. Table wines
- Vino de la Tierra (VdlT). Wines which have not acquired DO status but come from specified sites. They must have certain characteristics that are typical of the category.
- Vino Comarcal (VC). No specific criteria here, only the indication of origin. Some thirty wine-producing zones have been established.
- Vino de Mesa (VdM). No indication of origin, year or grape variety. Wines that conform to European regulations.

Spain's great winegrowing areas (DO and DOC wines)

- Rioja and Navarre
  - Rioja
  - Navarra

- Catalonia
  - Costers del Segre
  - Terra Alta
  - Tarragona
  - Priorato
  - Conca de Barberá

- Penedés
- Alella
- Ampurdán-Costa Brava

- Galicia
  - Rias Baiscas
  - Ribeiro
  - Valdeorrar

- Andalusia
  - Montilla-Moriles
  - Málaga
  - Jerez-Xeres-Sherry and Manzanilla-Sanlúcar de Barrameda
  - Condado de Hueva

- Alicante and Valencia
  - Valencia
  - Utiel-Requena
  - Alicante

- Basque country
  - Chacoli de Bizkaia
  - Chacoli de Getaria

- Old Castile y Léon
  - Bierzo
  - Cigales
  - Toro
  - Rueda
  - Ribera del Duero

A FEW TERMS

Abocado: sweet
Afrutado: fruity
Bodega: cellar
Bodega cooperative: cooperative cellar
Cepa: grape variety
Cosecha (or vendimia): harvest, the year a wine was harvested
Dulce: very sweet
Fino: fine, for dry Sherry
Maduro: ripe
Sabroso: pleasant
Vinillo: ordinary wine
Vino blanco: white wine
Vino de mesa: table wine
Vino de postre: dessert wine
Vino con aguja: very slightly sparkling wine
Vino envejecido: old wine
Vin espumoso: sparkling wine
Vino mosado, vino aluque, vino ojo de gallo: rosé wine
Vino tinto: red wine
Vino de uvas pasificadas or asolcado: straw wine
Vina, vinedo: vine, vineyard

- New Castile and La Mancha
  • Almansa
  • Valdepeñas
  • La Mancha
  • Méntrida

- Madrid
  • Vinos de Madrid

- Balearic Islands
  • Binissalem

- Canary Islands
  • La Palma
  • Lanzarote
  • Ycoden-Dante-Isora
  • Tacoronte-Acentejo

- Aragon
  • Campo de Borja
  • Calatayud
  • Cariñena
  • Somontano

- Murcia
  • Vecla
  • Jumilla
  • Bullas

How to read a label

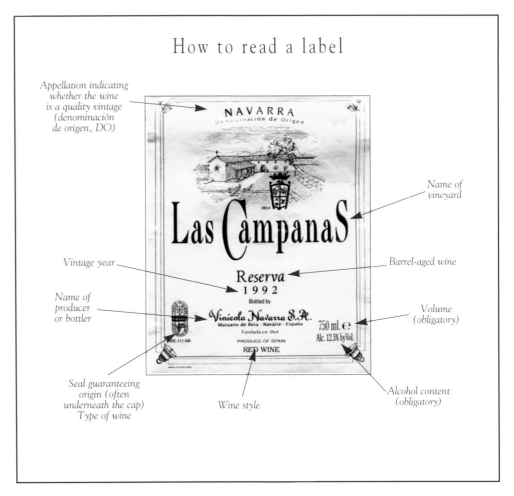

Appellation indicating whether the wine is a quality vintage (denominación de origen, DO)

Name of vineyard

Vintage year

Barrel-aged wine

Name of producer or bottler

Volume (obligatory)

Seal guaranteeing origin (often underneath the cap) Type of wine

Wine style

Alcohol content (obligatory)

Rioja

No other wine-producing region in Spain has as stellar a reputation as Rioja has throughout the world.

Rioja wines have been awarded a series of prizes in several recent international wine competitions. Rioja exports its wines to over sixty different countries, including Great Britain, its leading customer. The viticultural tradition of the region began to flourish in the late nineteenth century under the auspices of the first great modern bodegas. The bodegas not only seized upon the temporary commercial decline in Bordelais wine production, but skillfully drew upon the French region's winemaking methods. They prefigured the enormous bodegas active today which, with the backing of major financiers, introduced cutting-edge equipment into the wineries.

It's not surprising then that Rioja was the first region in Spain to introduce a system of quality control. As early as 1926, a Consejo Regulador was set up to oversee and implement a series of stringent regulations and to ensure that they were applied.

The Rioja winegrowing region in northern Spain includes just over 111,000 acres on both banks of the Ebro River and is approximately 75 miles long and 25 miles wide. The soil of the region is composed of a mixture of limestone, ferruginous clay and alluvium deposits.

The region has a temperate climate with hot, although not torrid, summers and mild winters.

For years, the one outstanding feature of all Rioja wines has been a powerful oak-like aroma due to the wines' being aged for many years in oak barrels. Wineries today, however, tend to adapt the wines more to international tastes. Few wine-producing regions throughout the world have used as much oak in the winemaking process as this one has. There are nearly 600,000 barrels in the bodegas, generally American oak casks of 58 gallons (*barricas bordelesas* or Bordeaux barrels), which impart aromas of vanilla and fresh butter

to the wines. Aging the wine in bottles is becoming the preferred method, allowing a richer, more complex aroma to develop as opposed to the sometimes invasive wood aromas.

The range of wines and their grape varieties

All Rioja wines, whether they are red, white or rosé, are produced by assemblages, or blending wines by mixing and marrying them.

White Rioja

The predominant grape variety (90 percent) for whites is Viura, known elsewhere as Macabeo. Its success stems primarily from its generous yield. In addition, its fairly fruity juice has the extra advantage of being somewhat impervious to oxidation. Although Viura overshadows nearly all other white grapes, the best wineries continue to add a small amount of Malvasía, which gives the wines a greater measure of flavor and subtlety. Some bodegas also use small amounts of Garnacha Blanca, which increases the wine's alcohol content.

Red Rioja

Reds are produced primarily from Tempranillo, which is the noblest grape in Rioja. Professional tasters often draw comparisons with the French noble grape Pinot Noir de Bourgogne. Tempranillo yields wines that are deep in color, which do not alter even long periods of aging. The grape has a good yield, yet a slight trace of acidity. It is therefore necessary to add other grapes such as Garnacha, Mazuelo or Graciano. The latter grape, the most aromatic of Rioja red grape varieties, imparts a rich, delicate flavor to the wines. There are two types of red wines: once very common, *clarete* (a light-colored wine) is gradually giving way to *tinto,* which is a deep-colored, more robust wine. It is also fruitier and has an excellent capacity to age and a fine, velvety texture. White wines are generally very dry and have a maximum alcohol content of

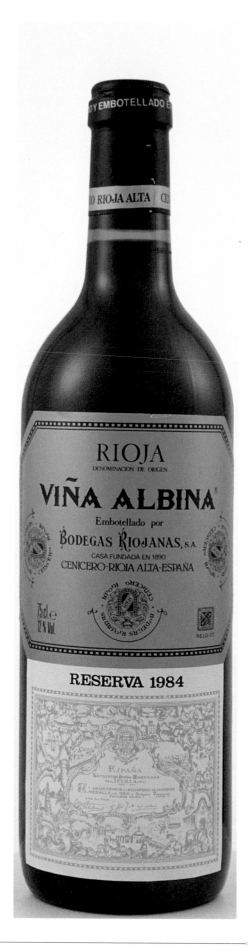

RIOJA GRAPE VARIETIES

For whites, Viura (also called Macabeo) is predominant, with small amounts of Malvasía and Garnacha Blanca added.

Tempranillo is the predominant grape for red wines. Small amounts of Garnacha (Alicante), Mazuelo (Carignan) and the highly aromatic Graciano may be added. Cabernet Sauvignon is becoming more popular as well.

11 percent. Most wineries have cut down on aging periods in oak vats, and some have done away with aging altogether to allow the rudimentary aromas to develop. This is particularly true with Recentie, which must be drunk during the year of vintage, while others generally improve with a few years' bottle-aging.

Rioja's wine-producing districts

The region is divided into three distinct districts:

• Rioja Alta. This zone runs south of the Ebro River, where some thirty bodegas are active with approximately 42,000 acres under vine. Nearly one-half of these companies are clustered around the small town of Haro, while the others are scattered between Cenicero, Fuenmayor and Navarrete. The high altitude of the vineyards, the ferruginous clay soil and adequate humidity are the three factors behind Rioja Alta's success. The wines—the best in the entire region—have a rich bouquet, solid robustness and excellent capacity to age for long periods of time.

• Rioja Alavesa. This is the northernmost zone, running north of the Ebro for nearly

133

17,300 acres, where the hillside vineyards are planted in a predominantly limestone soil. The main bodegas are located in the communes of Abala, Elciego, Labastida, Laguardia, Oyon and Villabuena. The bodegas produce primarily light, supple red wines with a powerful aroma.

• Rioja Baja. Nearly 49,500 acres of vineyards are under vine. The percentage of Garnacha is too high to obtain the same measure of finesse that their neighbors acquire. Sturdy and high in alcohol, they are used primarily for blending in the two other Rioja districts.

Navarre

In the days of Antiquity, Navarre was the leading wine-producing region of Spain. Its wines were also quite famous during the eleventh century, but the phylloxera blight that hit Europe in the late nineteenth century was devastating here. This large region, which is located south of Pamplona, is known throughout the world for its annual San Fermín Festival and the running of the bulls each July. The vineyards in the area along the upper Ebro River run along the southwest border of Rioja. There are four distinct zones, three of which benefit from the relatively cool air of the Pyrenees (Baja Montana, Valdizarbe and Tierra Estrella). Experiments conducted here to plant Cabernet Sauvignon and Chardonnay grapes have had some very encouraging results. But Navarre is particularly known for its rosé wines, made of Grenache (80 percent of the vineyards), and for its hearty reds, which are heavier than the red wines produced in Rioja. Tempranillo is becoming more and more popular as well. One experimental cellar in Olite—the largest in Europe—best reflects Navarre's dynamic approach to wine-making, which is part of a general effort to boost the quality of the wines, as well as the region's reputation.

Galicia

Galicia, located in northwest Spain just above Portugal, is a lush region with a relatively high degree of humidity. It borders on the Atlantic, and has a series of inlets along the coast, known as *rías*, which bear an uncanny resemblance to the fjords of Norway.

Galicia is unlike other regions of Spain. It is relatively isolated, dominated by Cabo Finisterre and cut off from the rest of the country by the Catabriques Mountains. Galicia bears a striking resemblance to Brittany or Scotland, and even claims to have been inhabited by the Celts.

Only the two most southern regions of Pontevedra and Orense produce major quantities of wine. Yet Galicia has the highest wine consumption per capita in all of Spain—more than 37 gallons consumed annually per habitant on average, or three times the amount drunk in other areas of Spain. But if Galicia ranks first in terms of quantity, it comes nowhere close to first in terms of quality. The climatic conditions, granitic soil and viticultural methods are similar to those in northern Portugal. On the banks of the Miño River, the varietal blends are identical as well, with Albarino (which produces very dry white wines) capping the list, as well as Treixadura. These two predominant grape varieties yield wines that are fairly satisfying in terms of quality only in the regions of Pontevedra, notably in the DO of Val de Salnes, Candado de Salvatierra and El Rosal, at the mouth of the Miño. Some good, very slightly sparkling wines are produced here, although they pale somewhat in comparison with Portugal's Vinho Verde. One drawback is that the few existing wine cooperatives are poorly equipped, and are gradually being replaced by a few

Old Castile y Léon

small wine estate owners who rely on artisanal methods for wine production. In the province of Orense, three DO wines are found: in the eastern section, Valdeorras produces a white wine from Palomino and a deeply-colored red wine made primarily from Garnacha. Both are simple and rustic wines. Mencia, a grape variety that is somewhat similar to Cabernet Franc, produces a surprisingly good wine. But it is difficult to find wines made solely from Mencia, given that it is frequently blended with other varieties.

The landlocked vineyards in the center of the region must withstand torrid summers. Most of them are in the Sil River valley, where what little water there is is most plentiful.

Ribeiro, in the western area surrounding Ribadavia, produces finer-quality reds and whites. The largest wine cooperative in Galicia is located here, and the local grapes Godello (whites) and the aromatic Sonson (reds) are used in winemaking. The vineyards are often terraced on the hillsides of the Miño, the Avia and the Arnoya. Monterrey, on the border with Portugal, produces mostly robust red wines with a high alcohol content, due in part to the leaden sunshine baking the area.

The rest of regional production is used mostly for blending purposes, or is sold to the neighboring region of Asturias, where wineries cannot produce sufficient amounts of wine to meet demand.

Old Castile, along with the former kingdom of Léon, represents one of the largest winegrowing regions of Spain. The land is arid, and the area subjected to harsh winters and torrid summers.

In light of these conditions, the presence of the Douro River plays a key role in wine production. The two DO wines, Ribera del Duero and Ribera de Rueda, are produced along the banks of the river. In general, virtually all of the major viticultural districts—although not officially specified sites—are located near the river or near one of its tributaries. Old Castile produces a highly diversified range of wines, and its reputation is growing, primarily as a result of its red wines, which can compete with some of the best produced in Rioja.

Ribera del Duero

This is the heart of Castile in the Douro Valley, which cuts across the provinces of Burgos, Valladolid and Soria. The vineyards are planted at high altitudes, and can therefore benefit from the cool nights. Bordering the Douro from northwest of Valladolid to Penafel and extending into the province of Burgos, Ribera del Duero reds are made primarily from Tinto Fino or Tinto Aragones. These fruity, robust wines can age admirably in oak barrels, which improve their depth and richness. Vega Sicilia stands out for its remarkable quality.

OLD CASTILE APPELLATIONS (DO)

- Bierzo
- Toro
- Rueda
- Cigales
- Ribera del Duero

Vega Sicilia: a legendary wine

Vega Sicilia was a favorite with Winston Churchill and King Alfonso XIII: "An exceptional, expensive wine produced on the banks of the Douro, not far from Valladolid, with an astonishing finesse, it ages well and is difficult to find." This is how the wine is described in the prestigious *Encyclopedia of Wine* by the American Frank Schoonmaker. The wine's exceptional quality is due to the microclimate of the production area. Yet it is difficult for vines to flourish in Ribera del Duero. When Eloy Lecauda founded his estate here in 1864, he was aware that the conditions were exceptional and were quite similar to those of the Bordeaux region in France, with more optimal sunshine. In addition, he established a harmonious balance of grape varieties—Tinto Fino, Cabernet Sauvignon, Merlot and Malbec—and a unique method of aging the wines in oak barrels. The result: a wine with excellent breed, on a par with the greatest Rioja wines. Production is limited to between 40,000 to 100,000 bottles per year; prices range from 60 and 100 U.S. dollars.

Farther north, leaving from Atanda del Duero, Ribera de Burgos, which extends the appellation, produces mainly good quality *claretes*, albeit with slightly less structure and amplitude.

Rueda

Southeast of Valladolid, the second DO of Old Castile is found in the area surrounding the commune of Rueda. The soil is rich in chalk and clay and produces a remarkable amber-colored wine from Verdejo. This white grape is capable of developing flor, the microscopic yeasty flowers that form a scum on the wine, and the flor is as abundant as that found in the best Sherries. But it soon may be overshadowed by a newcomer: a dry, robust assertive white wine that shows great promise, made with new vinification methods. Several wine-producing districts of Old Castile, which are not yet entitled to DO status, are also worthy of mention:

• Toro, between the communes of Rueda and Zamora, produces a dark red wine that is extremely powerful and very popular with the Spanish, when it is not used for blending.

• Cigales, north of Valladolid, owes its reputation to its *claretes,* made from a mixture of red and white grapes.

• El Bierzo and Valdevimbre, in the province of Léon, produce well-balanced light reds and deep-colored rosés.

Catalonia

Although Catalonia ranks fifth in terms of the land surface of its winegrowing region, it is the second greatest in terms of quality. This best sums up the wine-production activities of the region.

In the northeastern part of the country, Catalonia forms a triangle bordered by the Pyrenees on the north and the Mediterranean on the east. Mountain vineyards are terraced at altitudes up to 2,295 feet. Throughout the entire region, the winters are mild and the constant summer heat is tempered by the winds that blow in from the coast.

CATALONIA APPELLATIONS

- Ampurdán - Costa Brava
- Alella
- Coster del Segre
- Conca de Barberá
- Penedés
- Priorato
- Tarragona
- Terra Alta

A great many growers are clustered around wine cooperatives to which certain bodegas supply wines destined to be used in blending. The varietal blends are highly diversified. As in Rioja, Macabeo is predominant for white wines, although small amounts of Malvasía and Garnacha Blanca are also used, as well as two local grapes, Parellada and Xarello, which furnish a degree of acidity that is lacking. Likewise, for reds, there is Tempranillo, called Ull de Llebre here, as well as Garnacha, Monastrell and Cariñena, appreciated for its high yield. In addition to the many grape varieties, Catalonia has a variety of soil types, resulting in the widest range of wines of any region of Spain—reds, rosés, and dry, sparkling and richly sweet white wines.

The diversity of Catalonian wines is reflected in the region's seven DO wines that are produced on officially delimited sites.

Alella

The vineyards of this coastal zone, which are located north of Barcelona, are suffering somewhat from the increasing urbanization of the area. Ten years ago, the wine-producing area occupied 3,700 acres, but the area has now been reduced to 1,235.

Wine estate owners are persevering in their winemaking, with a majority of white wines being produced, some of them dry with a good measure of acidity, others semi-sweet and more subtly alluring.

CATALONIA GRAPE VARIETIES

Macabeo is the leading grape used in making white wines, as well as Malvasía, Garnacha Blanca and Parellada and Xarello, which add a certain measure of acidity.

Newer grape varieties are being introduced. White wines are now being made from Riesling, Muscat, Chardonnay, Gewürztraminer and Sauvignon.

Ull de Llebre (Tempranillo) is the predominant grape variety used to produce red wines, in addition to Garnacha Tinta (Alicante), Cariñena and especially Monastrell. Yet Pinot Noir, Merlot and especially Cabernet Sauvignon are becoming more and more popular.

Ampurdán - Costa Brava

This zone, sufficiently removed from the coast and tourist havens, is the northernmost area. It recently acquired its appellation.

Between the Pyrenees and the Mediterranean, swept by the mistral and the tramontane winds, these 12,350 acres of vineyards produce rosés and reds from Grenache and Carignan. White wines are produced from Macabeo and Xarello. The region recently has introduced a new light red wine that has been modeled after the Beaujolais Primeur.

Conca de Barberá

This DO, the most recent, occupies 24,700 acres of hillside vineyards which, using Macabeo and Parellada, produce a widely popular white wine. The most acidic is added to Penedés to make sparkling wines.

Another unusual feature of this DO is that it was here that Bodega Torres successfully began to experiment with introducing the French noble grape varieties of Cabernet Sauvignon and Pinot Noir.

Penedés

Midway along the coast, Penedés occupies an area between Barcelona and Tarragona. Some 61,750 acres are under vine on the limestone slopes that reach altitudes of 2,295 feet. Penedés is best known for its dry white wines. The most acidic ones

yield some good sparkling wines, produced according to the *méthode champenoise*. Most of the bodegas are clustered around the communes of Vilafranca de Penedés and San Sadurni de Noya.

Sparkling Penedés wines fall into two categories:

• *cavas*, which are produced by a second fermentation in the bottle; these are the finer-quality wines.

• *granvás*, which are naturally sparkling wines, produced by a second fermentation in large pressurized vats.

The quality of *cavas* should not overshadow the fine reds produced in the

region. Some are full-bodied and fruity and rival Rioja's best vintages. These include such wines as Marqués de Riscal and Marqués de Murieta.

Priorato

This DO, which is produced in the largest appellation area of Tarragona, is an enclave occupying 9,140 acres of vineyards growing along the hillsides. The volcanic soil, which is planted with a high percentage of the Garnacha grape, yields a wine that is nearly black in color, intensely robust and high in alcohol. In addition, a golden-colored white wine is found here, which has the characteristic tang and heavy presence of a rancio, as a result of oxidation.

Tarragona

The wine cooperatives active in this 61,750-acre vineyard—the largest DO in Catalonia—produce a robust red wine that is high in alcohol, used primarily for blending. Tarragona thus stands out because of its sweet wines, which are aged in *solera* (see box above).

Terra Alta

Some 39,520 acres of vineyards flourishing along the hillsides make up this recent DO, the center of which is the town of Gandesa, in southern Catalonia. The area produces sturdy red and white wines, which are used primarily for blending.

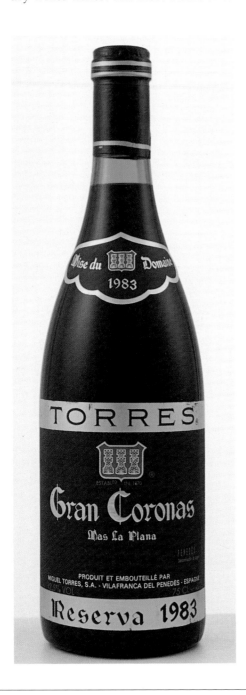

Valencia

The area of Valencia that runs along the coast of the Mediterranean is a rich coastal land and one of Spain's most active wine-producing regions. Although no prestigious vintages are made here, the area does encompass five DO wines. The Mediterranean climate produces very sturdy, generous wines. Monastrell is the predominant grape for reds, which relies on Alicante Bouschet to impart color to the wines.

VALENCIA APPELLATIONS

The five DO wines of Valencia are making great leaps in quality, and are particularly noteworthy. They include:
- Alicante
- Valencia
- Utiel-Requena
- Jumilla
- Yecla

Valencia

The city of Valencia is a good starting point for a visit of the region. The immense vineyards of the region are near Valencia, formerly called Cheste. The area produces a rustic white wine with a high alcohol content, made from the Merseguera grape.

Although the wines produced in this region are relatively uninteresting—with perhaps the exception of the richly sweet wine made from Moscatel—the bodegas in Valencia are by far the most modern and productive in all of Spain.

Utiel-Requena

West of Valencia and nearly an extension of it, this hillside vineyard is planted almost entirely with dark-skinned grapes. The leading grape is Bobal, which yields a dark inky wine. Not enough Cencibel and Garnacha grapes are grown here to lighten the wine. After the grape skins have been macerated for long periods of time, the wines have a very intense dark color as well as high levels of tannin. These

are the characteristics of the typical Vino de Doble Pasta. The term "doble" is derived from the fact that the quantity of grape skins which are left to macerate is doubled. As a result, the juice remains in contact with the skins for only very brief periods of time; this juice is used to make a pleasant light rosé.

Alicante

The appellation area is divided into two sections, each corresponding to particular types of wines. The coastal region, where the vineyards are planted with Moscatel, produces a superb sweet wine. The hillsides farther inland are planted primarily with Monastrell, which yields a very rich deep-colored Vino de Doble Pasta as well as a light rosé. A few white wines are produced, from the Verdil grape as well.

Jumilla

This DO is produced south of Alicante in the province of Murcia, in an area where the soil is very chalky. Wineries here are working to produce wines from Monastrell that are lighter in color and have a lower alcohol content.

Yecla

This zone, neighboring on Jumilla, inevitably yields wines that are very similar to the sturdy dark wines produced in Jumilla.

Andalusia

Andalusia, located in southern Spain, boasts a variety of very famous wines. Sherry is the most renowned of them all, with Montilla-Moriles and Málaga being fine examples of the high-quality Sherry produced in the region.

Sherry

Sherry, which takes its name from the Latin *Xeres* and the Arabian *Sherrisch*, became extremely popular with the English toward the end of the fifteenth century. They boosted its reputation and ensured its commercial success. Even today, the United Kingdom is the leading market for Sherry, and it is just as popular with the English now as it was back then. The name Bristol itself—once the biggest trading center for Sherry—still appears on some labels as a seal of quality.

The Sherry vineyards, which occupy 37,050 acres, lie inland from the Bay of Cadiz between the Guadalquivir River to the north and the Guadalete River to the south. The three main wine-producing centers are Jerez de la Frontera, the coastal town of Puerto de Santa María and Sanlúcar de Barrameda, at the mouth of the Guadalquivir.

There is intense sunshine throughout the entire region all year round, with very little rainfall on average. All wines produced in the region share certain characteristics as a result of these climatic conditions, regardless of differences in soil composition. There are three different soil types.

The finest soil type is albariza, a soil rich in clay with a high percentage of white chalk (between 60 percent and 80 percent), found primarily in the northern and western regions of Andalusia. This type of soil is very high in calcium, and is as white as snow during the summer.

Barro is less chalky, and does not retain humidity as well, while the sandy soil type known as arena is used less and less. Chalky soils are reserved for Sherry's noblest grape, the Palomino, which gives 90 percent of Sherry and can have a productive yield of 855 gallons per acre.

There are other varieties of grape, namely Pedro Ximenez and a small amount of Moscatel. The quality of the wines produced from Palomino is average, underscoring the importance of the blending and aging

ANDALUSIAN APPELLATIONS

Appellations include Jerez-Xeres-Sherry, Manzanilla-Sanlúcar de Barrameda, Condado de Huelva, Málaga, Montilla-Moriles.

processes, which can turn a mediocre wine into an excellent vintage.

Making Sherry

Sherry wines are not stored according to traditional methods in airtight barrels. Sherry thrives on air, which imparts its characteristic taste, and the bodegas are open to the passage of air. The best Sherries quickly develop a thick coat of whitish yeast that forms on the surface of the wine.

ANDALUSIAN GRAPE VARIETIES

Palomino is by far the predominant grape used in the vineyards of Jerez, while Pedro Ximenez is the leading grape for Montilla-Moriles. There is currently very little Moscatel used.

This is flor, which plays a major role in preventing the wine from oxidizing. It transforms the wine into what are called Finos, thicker on a must going into Fino than on one going to Oloroso, which is more rustic and higher in alcohol. Raya is incapable of producing flor.

But there is more. The different wines produced by this kind of maceration are virtually never sold at this point in the vinification process. Bodegas carry out blending, not only to obtain specific characteristics for each label, but also to sweeten the wine, which is initially very dry. To do this, sweetening wines like Dulce Pasa and Dulce Apagado or pure amounts of Moscatel, obtained from sun-dried grapes with concentrated amounts of sugar, are used. *Arrope,* or grape juice boiled to a concentrate, may also be added as sweeteners.

For blending, bodegas rely on the solera system, which progressively mixes younger wines with older, finer wines. The leading wine producers never use Raya for blending purposes; it is unfortunate for Sherry's fine reputation that some wineries sometimes yield to this temptation.

Different types of Sherry

Other Sherries, besides the two main types, Fino and Oloroso, include:

• Amontillado. Originally a Fino, but much more generous and concentrated, as it is aged after the flor is eliminated. Fino-Amontillado is merely a Fino with certain aspects characteristic of Amontillado.

• Manzanilla. This is the name of Sherry

stored in the bodegas of the seacoast town of Sanlúcar de Barramedo. The sea gives it a tangy bitterness.

• Cream Sherry. A dessert wine which is most often a heavily sweetened Oloroso. Pale Cream Sherry is usually Fino with Dulce Apagado added.

Montilla-Moriles

An independent DO since 1993 but still very close to the Jerez vineyard, Montilla-Moriles produces wines south of Córdoba which are similar to Sherry. Despite a more intense heat, it has the same very chalky soil, the only two major differences being that Pedro Ximenez is the predominant grape here, and earthenware jars are often used for fermenting the wines. Like Sherry, the wines produce varying amounts of flor. The Finos are just as good, and are dry yet semi-sweet.

Málaga

The vineyards cover the sun-drenched hillsides in the back country of the Costa del Sol, where Moscatel and Pedro Ximenez are planted in virtually the same amounts. It is planted in part on the coast surrounding Estepona and Málaga, where the climate is milder. But most of the vineyards are farther inland, in the warm soil of the undulating plateau of Antequera. Cement vats as opposed to earthenware jugs are used in fermenting the wines here. Moscatel yields the most aromatic wines which, when blended in solera, can become excellent in quality. The top quality is found in the *lágrima* (literally "teardrop" of the grapes), obtained by a very gentle pressing by hand. On the other hand, the most ordinary quality is typical of Dulce Color, which contains a fair amount of *arrope*.

New Castile and La Mancha

The arid region of New Castile in central Spain includes the huge area of La Mancha, immortalized by Don Quixote, running across the central and southern parts. The climate is very dry, with torrid summers and glacial winters. These factors lie behind the very high alcohol content of the wines produced here. Irrigation, however, is illegal here. The vineyards, which are owned by a great number of growers clustered together in over four hundred wine cooperatives, seem to be scattered across the entire region. La Mancha is planted predominantly with the Airen grape variety, a white grape that is valued for its incredible vigor. Although the grape produces essentially white wines, it is often blended with Cencibel, which makes the darker wines slightly lighter and headier. On the whole, New Castile wines are far from superb in terms of quality, but the region does produce five DO wines.

Méntrida

In the province of Toledo, southwest of Madrid, this 79,040-acre vineyard produces essentially a robust red wine that is very high in alcohol, and is generally used in blending.

La Mancha

The appellation area runs across an immense limestone plateau in the central and southern parts of the region. Some 1.24 million acres are under vine, planted

NEW CASTILE APPELLATIONS

Although the wines of New Castile are somewhat average for the most part, there are five regional DOC wines: Mentrida, La Mancha, Valdepeñas, Manchuela and Almansa.

NEW CASTILE GRAPE VARIETIES

Airen is the predominant white grape variety. Red wines come from Garnacha Tinta and Monastrell, as well as from Cencibel, which is so dark that it must be blended with Airen.

primarily with Airen, which produces a very strong white wine that is somewhat lacking in fruitiness. Modern vinification methods that are currently being introduced to the region are improving the wine to a great extent.

Valdepeñas

This southern DO appellation, located in the province of Ciudad Real, has the unusual feature of producing mainly red wines, although the predominant variety grown here is the white grape Airen. It is mixed with Cencibel, which is so dark that only a mere 10 percent is necessary for darkening the white juice. The light ruby-colored wine obtained is called Aloque, which is somewhat lacking in structure and acidity.

Almansa

This 24,700-acre vineyard, located east of Albacete, is mainly planted with Monastrell and Garnacha Tinta grapes, which produce heavy reds that are very deep in color and are most frequently used in blending.

Manchuela

This vineyard, located east of La Mancha and south of Cuenca, produces little else than *claretes* and extremely heavy red wines that are sold in bulk.

Portugal

Located on the western region of the Iberian Peninsula, Portugal (*Portus Calle,* from the Roman name for the city of Porto) has always been synonymous with vines and vineyards. Well before the Roman occupation, vineyards were cultivated along the Douro and Miño valleys, flourishing in the sandy soil and the temperate climate due to the proximity of the Atlantic Ocean.

In the twelfth century, Henry of Burgundy, count of Portugal, died, leaving a territory that was to become the independent kingdom of Portugal under his son Alfonso I. The fifteenth and sixteenth centuries were the Golden Age of Portugal. Vasco da Gama circled the Cape of Good Hope, and a fabulous empire was built from Brazil to Africa. The Portuguese planted their vines wherever they went.

At the time, the country exported its wines to England. Commercial treaties and accords linked the two countries to each other for many years—English wool in exchange for Portuguese wine. England played a major role in maintaining the quality and trade of Portuguese wines. In 1765, Porto established its identity and became officially protected. It was the first vineyard in the world to set legal limits on yield. Wine consumption per capita is very high, an average 25 gallons per year. Some 865,000 acres are under vine, for an annual production of over 264 million gallons (one-fifth of which is exported). Red wines account for 75 percent of production.

Very stringent regulations govern the eighteen winegrowing regions that produce three categories of wine: fortified wines, including the ultrafamous Port and Madeira (7.39 million gallons and 2.1 million gallons); wines produced on specified sites, notably the famous Vinhos Verdes (79.2 million gallons); and ordinary wines.

After five years of aging, a kind of crust forms on the barrel, and Port's ruby color begins to grow lighter.

Classification of Portuguese wines

When Portugal joined the European Community in 1986, its wine regulations had to be brought into compliance with the standards in force throughout the other EC countries. There are currently four separate categories of quality:

1. Denominaçao de Origen Controlada (DOC), the equivalent of the French AOC. This replaced what used to be the Região Demarcada (RD) until 1990. There are currently some twenty DOCs.

2. Indicaçao de Proveniênca Regulamentada (IPR), also called Vinho de Qualidade Produzido en Região Determinada (VQPRD): some thirty regions, the wines being similar in ranking to French VDQS wines, nearly all of which aspire to DOC status.

3. Vinho Regional (VR). These are Vins de Pays, found notably in the south. The grape varieties and vintages may appear on the label.

4. Vinho de Mesa: ordinary table wines.

Great wine-producing regions of Portugal (DOC)

- Vinhos Verdes
- Porto Douro
- Dão
- Bairrada
- Bucelas
- Colares
- Carcavelos
- Setúbal
- Portalegre
- Borba
- Redondo
- Reguengos
- Vidigueira
- Lagos
- Portimão
- Lagoa
- Tavina
- Madeira

Upper Douro

Port

It's hard not to wax lyrical when describing the extraordinary history of Port. How did this hard, bitter wine produced in the Upper Douro region of Portugal become one of the greatest fortified wines ever, drunk and appreciated throughout the world?

The answer is in the superb alchemy created by nature and man. Three factors lie behind the wine's success: an exceptional climate, a certain type of rock called schist and methods of treatment worked out over a long period of time. But Port is also a consequence of British enterprise and climate, and of the British palate as well. In 1703, England banned imports of all wines produced in the region of Aquitaine, and Portugal became the main supplier of wines as a result.

The Englishman Baron of Forrester first had the idea of transporting the barrels from the Upper Douro to Porto.

As the wines did not travel well, he decided to add more alcohol to them—and Port was born. This is one of the first regions in the world to limit its production zone to ensure quality control and oversee production of the wines. The result reflects these efforts on maintaining quality control.

Imagine vines growing on thousands of stepped and terraced levels on the cliffs of the Douro, baking in the sun. Port takes its characteristics from the schistous soil found here. The gorges of the Upper Douro are a spectacular sight, which generations have transformed and shaped from the smallest plot of land. Each vineyard plot is ranked according to a classification system ranging from A, for the best sites, to E. Criteria include such factors as altitude, soil type and angle of the slope.

Some twenty grape varieties are grown here (Port is actually a blend). The highly meticulous harvesting begins in late September or early October.

Rapid fermentation must be avoided at all costs. The grapes are no longer pressed in treading-troughs as they once were, although there are a few *quintas,* or wine estates, which still use *lagares,* or treading-troughs that are large, shallow, open tanks usually made of concrete or granite slabs. Today, most of the grapes are pressed by mechanized crushers. Just as fermentation has reached the proper moment, 170 proof brandy is added: one part brandy for five parts juice. The degree of sweetness

depends on when the brandy is introduced, or on how long the juice is left to ferment. It also depends on the blending processes carried out at a later point.

The must is then stored in cool sections of the huge wine cellars. In springtime, the crude Port is barreled and shipped to the

PORT GRAPE VARIETIES

Nine great grapes must make up at least 60 percent of a blended Red Port.

These include:
- Touriga Nacional, the best grape variety, with small berries and few grapes per cluster. It yields a dark, powerful wine with a hint of black raspberry.
- Touriga Francesca, highly appreciated for Port; it is light, has a productive yield and imparts a powerful aroma.
- Tinto Barroca is used primarily to sweeten Port blends.

At least six grapes varieties make up a minimum 60 percent of White Ports: Verdelho, which gives it a good alcohol content; Esgana-Cão, which is somewhat acidic; Rabigato, one of the best grapes of the Douro Valley; Folgozão, which is fairly flat; Malvasia Fina and Viosinho.

winemaking plants—not in *rabelos*, the legendary single-sail flat-bottom boats which once traveled down the rapids of the Douro to the mouth of the river, but in trucks to warehouses in Vila Nova de Gaia (opposite Oporto).

In good years, winemakers will reserve the best of their wine to produce Vintage Port. It may be used to make blends, such as Tawny Port, which matures in oak for three years. Each Port has its own classification. White Port can be very dry or dry, red Port can be semi-dry or sweet.

A young "Full Retinto" will be dark red, a "Tinto Aloirado" ruby-red in color, "Aloirado" a tannish brown, and "Aloirado Claro," light brown. The range of colors for white Ports is infinite—from off-white, straw-colored, golden and onion-skin to golden blond. It takes from between twenty and thirty years for a Vintage Port to reach perfection. It is best drunk as a digestif, either with cheese or dessert.

Very dry, chilled white Ports can be drunk as aperitifs.

All about Port

- Place: Douro Valley (northern region of Portugal) and its tributaries (from the Spanish border to 93 miles from Porto).
- Land mass: 617,500 acres (including 10 percent terraced vineyards above the river).
- Climate: torrid, dry summers and cold, damp winters.
- Soil composition: schistous. Vines often find their way at least 6 feet deep into the ground to secure moisture.
- Grape varieties: see box page 153.
- Harvest: late September to early October.
- *Lagares:* huge granite troughs where the grapes are placed after they are selected and stalked. They can hold up to 4,620 gallons of must.
- Mutage: fermentation after two to three days is interrupted by the addition of alcohol, or mutage. The degree of alcohol added depends on the desired sweetness of the Port (dry, semi-dry or sweet).
- Tuns, hogsheads, large casks: the wine is placed in large casks for transport to warehouses in Vila Nova de Gaia opposite Oporto.
- Blending: once tested, Port is then blended with other crus of various quality and age, depending on its quality and ability to age.
- The different kinds of Port:
• Ruby Port: the lightest Port. It is wood-aged and has a ruby color.
• Tawny Port: the most powerful and concentrated Port. It ages for longer periods of time.
Indication of age: ten, twenty, thirty or more. This is always an average, because Tawny Port is a blend of several different vintages.
• Vintage Port: during exceptional years, blending is carried out using a single harvest. Port is bottled after two years' aging. The vintage year is indicated, as is the qualification "vintage." The bottles keep for several decades.

THE BEST QUINTAS

Quinta da Água Alta
Quinta da Boa Vista
Quinta da Cavadinha
Quinta da Côrte
Quinta da Foz
Quinta da Roêda
Quinta das Lages
Quinta de la Rosa
Quinta de Nápoles
Quinta de São Luiz
Quinta de Sto António
Quinta de Terra Feita
Quinta de Vargellas
Quinta do Bomfim
Quinta do Bom Retiro
Quinta do Cruzeiro
Quinta do Noval
Quinta do Panascal
Quinta do Passadouro
Quinta do Porto
Quinta dos Canaïs
Quinta do Seixo
Quinta dos Malvedos
Quinta do Vesúvio

• LBV Port (late-bottled vintages): in general, LBV Port is aged in cellars four to six years longer than other Ports (in casks).
• White Port: dry Port made exclusively from white grapes. It is served chilled (46 to 50 °F), in contrast to red Port, which is drunk at room temperature or lightly chilled.

Vinhos Verdes

Vinhos Verdes are very well-known and are called "green" wines because they are young, not because they are green in color. They are produced in northwestern Portugal, between the Douro and the Miño, which has a pleasant climate due to the proximity of the Atlantic Ocean. The vines grow freely along the trees, which protect them from the sun and the heat. Will the picturesque pergolas that can be found along pathways or on the outskirts of fields soon disappear?

They are gradually being replaced by *cruzetas*, tall cross-shaped struts, or by vines strung up on wire.

The grapes are harvested early, before the grape is fully ripe. The wine is fresh, fruity and light with a hint of a sparkle

resulting from a slight fermentation in the bottle. The white wines are best. They are drunk during the year, served chilled as an aperitif or as an accompaniment to fish. The reds, which are fairly tannic and have a slight bitterness, are less popular. Monção, which is sold in brown bottles, Agulha, Gatão and Lagosta are wines that are found easily on foreign markets.

RED GRAPE VARIETIES

Mourisco Tinto, a very popular grape in the Douro, yields a pleasant, invigorating wine. Tinta Amarella has a very beautiful color and a very productive yield. Baga is the most common red grape in Portugal; it is a thick-skinned grape with a productive yield. It has a lovely color, but lacks a certain measure of finesse. Ramisco, which grows in the sandy soil of southern Portugal, produces an excellent wine that ages very well.

WHITE GRAPE VARIETIES

Alvarinho, the sole grape used in making Vinho Verde, can grow only in the region of Monçao. Its high alcohol content and aroma make it a more attractive wine than other vintages from the Minho region. Toward Braga, in the Lima and Cavado valleys, a livelier, lighter Vinho Verde with a hint of Muscat is made from Loureiro.

Dão

The red wines of Dão are produced in a triangle formed by the towns of Viseu, Guarda and Coimbra, in central Portugal—one of the wildest and most mountainous areas in the country. The vines are grown in terraces on granitic, schistous soil. They grow on poles or along trees, which allows for crops to be planted in the soil that they would otherwise take up. The wines of Dão are somewhat reminiscent of Côtes du Rhone wines: a trace of tannin and a good measure of suppleness and smoothness. They keep a few years in the cellar. In the last few years, however, this region has been undergoing a quiet revolution, and the vines are flourishing in the granitic soil surrounded by pine and eucalyptus trees. A leading producer, Sogrape, spearheaded this metamorphosis by using a noble grape, Touriga Nacional—undoubtedly the best of Dão—which now grows alongside Tinta Pinheira and Bastardo.

Bairrada

This rather flat winegrowing region, relatively close to the Atlantic, is located in the area surrounding Anadia, between the Caramulo Mountains and the coast. Baga is the predominant grape of this region, producing incredibly tannic red wines with a slightly tangy taste. A few years' cellar-aging is therefore necessary to yield a smooth wine, which goes very well with Leitão, or milk-fed pig, the local specialty. Other wines worthy of note include the slightly sparkling rosés and spirited whites, most of which are marketed in the United Kingdom.

Douro

Vines have gained the upper hand over mother nature in this magnificent, wild region that is traversed by the Douro, Portugal's second-largest river after the Tagus. Some of the best Port is produced here. But it shouldn't overshadow the other wines that come from the region. Red wines made from Tinta Amarella, Tinta Barroca and Mourisco Tinto grapes for the most part are tannic, robust and keep well. The Lafoes vineyard between Dão and Douro is worth mentioning as it produces a highly unusual vinho verde based on Arinto and Jampal or Dona Branca—one of the least noble grapes of the Douro.

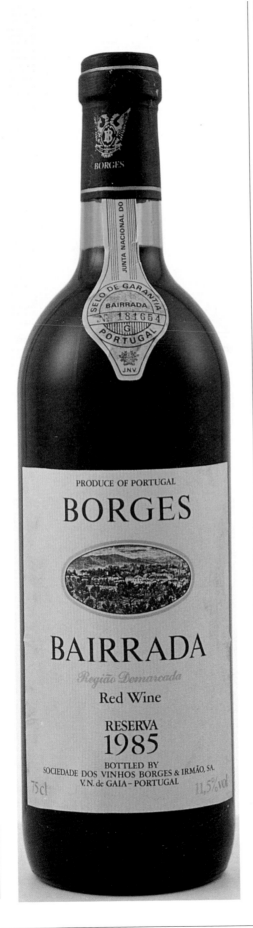

Colares

The wines of Colares, just northwest of Lisbon, are wines of the dunes. The vines, sheltered by low walls of dry stone, grow in sandy soil (which protects them from phylloxera), from the ocean up to Cintra. Byron was crazy about these wines. They are one of the best red wines produced in Portugal, a wine made from Ramisco that can be laid down for years.

The region has been described as the eighth wonder of the world, and rightly so. Made from Ramisco, the wines are powerful and slow to mature, with a rich bouquet. The best Colares wines can age fourteen years in enormous mahogany or sequoia casks.

Bucelas

The wine-producing area is located north of Lisbon, on one of the banks of the Tagus estuary. The wines were greatly appreciated by the English—from Wellington to Dickens, at a time when the wine was sweet and amber-colored. Today Bucelas are dry and light, straw-colored wines to be served well chilled.

They can also be slightly acidic and assertive and, with age, give off a pronounced lemony taste. They are made primarily from the Arinto grape.

Island of Madeira

The island of Madeira, lying under its eternal halo of clouds, is part of a vast volcanic archipelago located 310 miles west of Morocco. When the sailors of Prince Henry the Navigator discovered the island 500 years ago, it was nicknamed Madeira ("Isle of Trees"), because the forest covering it was so dense that pathways had to be burned through it. It is said that the fire raged for seven years. Malvoisie vines imported from Cyprus were planted in the ashes, and the lush oasis of Madeira sprang up in the middle of the Atlantic.

During the eighteenth century, someone came up with the brilliant idea of adding "a bucket of brandy to each barrel of wine" before shipping it.

MADEIRA GRAPE VARIETIES

Jacquet is the most common hybrid grown on Madeira, having replaced the vines devastated by phylloxera. It has a very average yield, but is high in sugar and has a superb deep-red color.

There are three main white grapes: Verdelho, which imparts alcoholic strength to Madeira, as well as its characteristic color; Bual, which is becoming increasingly rare; and Sercial, a late-ripening grape that is very popular. It gives Madeira its subtle aromas and splendid sheen. It is one of the richest Madeiras and is highly prized.

Madeira displayed an unusual characteristic: it became more refined as it traveled. It became famous wherever it went.

Some say that it is the only wine that will never die. Americans loved it: all boats destined for the United States traditionally made a stopover at Funchal to replenish food and water supplies and to fill their casks with Madeira. The tradition continued until disaster hit in 1852, when oïdium and phylloxera devastated the vineyards. Since then, Madeira has never fully recovered.

Terraced vineyards on the mountainsides

The island, which has a subtropical climate, is very propitious for vine growing. The wine-producing region covers some 4,940 acres split up among four thousand estate owners. The average winegrowing area is 1.24 acres. The vines are planted on pergolas on tiny terraces on the mountainsides, called *poios*. Toward 655 feet in

altitude, Bual and Malvoisie are predominant grapes; toward 1,640 feet, Verdelho; and up to 2,625 feet, the Sercial grape is predominant. The best vines lie in the southern regions of the island, in the areas of Campanario, Ponta de Pargo, Camara de Lobos and Etreito. A faire share of the wines of Madeira are today produced by the Madeira Wine Company, which controls half of all exports.

The French market plays a major role in production: a highly unusual Madeira, used primarily in cooking, is made from Tinta Negra Mole and fortified with brandy which is gradually heated in an *estufa* (a large store with central heating in which pipes of wine are placed) to temperatures of 104° F to 122° F—a process repeated for at least three months.

The result is a Madeira that is fairly rustic and very much disputed—and has little to do with real Madeira, produced from the four great grapes: Sercial, Bual, Malvoisie and Verdelho. The great Madeiras age very slowly as they bake in the heat of the island sunshine. They are then stored in *canteiros* in wooden vats in the eaves of the cellars of Funchal, the capital.

Types of Madeira

There are many medicore Madeira wines today; very little is truly exceptional in quality. *Seco* (dry), *meio seco* (semi-dry), *meio doce* (semi-sweet) and *doce* (richly sweet) are indicated on the bottles. The best of the Madeiras is Sercial, which is sometimes pale, at times golden. It is the driest as well (it is produced from Riesling from the Rhine). It always has an incredible nose and a hint of a bite (and is best drunk as an aperitif).

Verdelho is similar to Sercial but is sweeter and softer, and slightly more supple.

Malmsey. From the Malvoisie grape. It is extremely rich, luscious and fruity, with good body and a superb dark brown color. It is good with dessert.

Rainwater. A more ordinary blend that is paler and lighter. Like Port, a good Madeira must always be decanted.

Germany

Germany was hardly predisposed to becoming a major wine-producing country, given its northern geographical position and its cold climate, with late frosts and rainy autumns. Yet Germans persisted in cultivating vines —and these weren't just any ordinary vines, but the great Riesling, the prolific Sylvaner, the highly resistant Müller-Thurgau, the aromatic Gewürztraminer and the Ruländer and Pinot Gris. For over two thousand years, winegrowing sites have been meticulously selected and geared toward a particular microclimate, notably the slopes with the best exposure to the sun along the Rhine and the Moselle and their tributaries, as the rivers capture the heat. The goal was to produce top-quality vintages. Over the centuries, Germans honed their wine-making skills, focusing in particular on dry or richly sweet white wines that are fairly low in alcohol (10% to 11%), fruity and refreshing, with just the right dose of acidity. The limpid color, aroma and distinction of these wines have made them truly legendary.

The 247,000 acres under vine in Germany—a total of 1 percent of all agricultural land—are situated in the southwestern region of the country, between Lake Constance (Bodensee, to Germans) and Bonn, the former capital. Of the 238 million gallons of wine produced in Germany each year, 85 percent are white wines. Germany's international reputation is based essentially on these wines, which English-speaking countries have nicknamed "Hocks." These are generally produced in the Rhine Valley, an area of myth and legend, where the steep vineyards are dominated by fairytale castles. Yet the Rhine is only one of the ten wine-producing regions of Germany.

There are currently some ninety thousand winegrowers, most operating part-time, because German vineyards have been tiny in size and parceled out like a maze of plots since Napoleonic rule in the early nineteenth century. The average size of each plot rarely exceeds 2.5 acres, which forces growers to deliver their grapes or must to wine cooperatives.

The history of German wine is linked closely to the Rhine and the Moselle rivers. The Romans left a deep imprint here, notably by instilling the tradition of winemaking. At the fall of the Roman Empire, monasteries took charge of wine production. By the eighteenth century, fine quality wines were being produced. The first campaigns to uproot certain grape varieties in the Rheingau and Moselle and replant Riesling grapes in their place were carried out. It was customary at the time to store specially reserved wines in small cellars—the famous Cabinet Keller *(Kabinett),* today known as the "Prädikat Kabinett"—that included any fine growth to which a proprietor chooses to give this name *(Kabinettwein).*

Rüdesheim am Rhein.

163

The first official *Kabinettwein* was Schloss Vollrads, dating back to 1728.

Another key date, 1775, marks the first late harvest *(Spätlese)*. According to legend, these left-on-the-vine wines originated when the Bishop of Fulda forgot to order the grapes to be picked one year when harvest time came around. By the time it dawned on him, the grapes were nearly rotten and were thrown to the peasants—who produced one of the most delicious wines known to man.

In the late eighteenth century, wine began to be estate-bottled; following Aloys Senefedler's invention of lithography, each bottle could be easily distinguished from the others by its label. In 1803, Napoleon, who occupied Germany at the time, revolutionized the viticultural industry when he secularized the vineyards, which were still Church property at the time. In addition, the Napoleonic code decreed that estates were not to be passed down intact to a single heir, but split equally among all descendants. The result was thirty thousand different crus, which were later grouped together and reduced to 2,600 in 1971.

During the nineteenth century, wine cooperatives sprang up and regions were grouped together to market their "natural" not chaptalized wines, which were sold at auctions. In 1910, the "Verband Deutscher Prädikats und Qualitätsweingüter," or VDP was created, a guarantee of quality for natural wines sold at auction. A law passed in 1971 established the Prädikat system. Today, the association of German Prädikat estates and quality wines counts 171 members, which adhere to highly stringent regulations, thus ensuring the reputation of German wines throughout the world. The decision to add sugar to the wines, a highly regulated process, depends largely on the climatic conditions. In poorer years, growers rely on the Gall Process. Gallization is the addition of sugar to supplement a natural lack of sugar or alcohol or to counterbalance a natural excess of acid. The sugar is added to the must prior to fermentation.

It is sometimes preferable to leave the grapes on the rootstocks after they are fully ripe to let them reach noble rot, as is done in France to produce the great Sauternes and in Germany with the marvelous Trockenbeerenauslesen and Beerenauslesen wines. At this stage, each grape is picked individually and selected with great care. In light of this, it is easy to see why prices for these wines are so high.

The twelve regions in which quality wines are produced *(Gebiet)*:

• Moselle-Saar-Ruwer (31,615 acres): on both banks of the Moselle and its tributaries.
• Ahr (1,285 acres): along the Ahr, before it flows into the Rhine, south of Bonn.
• Middle Rhine (1,730 acres): from the mouth of the Nahe River and on both shores of the Rhine extending to Siebengebirge mountains.
• Nahe (11,610 acres): a tributary of the Rhine, in the area surrounding Bad-Kreuznach.
• Rheingau (7,730 acres): the right banks of the Main and Rhine rivers, from Mainz to Lorch.
• Rheinhessen (61,750 acres): left bank of the Rhine between Worms, Mainz, Bingen and Alsheim.
• Palatinate (or Pfalz, 56,810 acres): a northern extension of Alsace.
• Hessische Bergstrasse: steep hills opposite Heidelberg.
• Franconia (Franken, 14,820 acres): the banks of the Main between Steigerwald and Spessart.
• Württemberg (24,700 acres): along the shores of the Neckar between Stuttgart and Heidelberg.
• Baden (37,050 acres): the right bank of the Rhine between Lake Constance and Heidelberg.
• Saale-Unstrut (965 acres) and Sachsen (740 acres): the only two winegrowing districts that were part of the former East Germany, along the Saal, the Unstrut and the Sachsen, along the Elbe Valley.

Regulations, classifications and labels

Everything depends on the degree of sugar concentrated in the must, while the winery that has produced the wine is secondary in importance. What matters is the degree of ripeness of the grape, the degree of sugar and the origin of the grape. The geographic origin of the vintage supercedes this hierarchy. Where are wines produced?
• *Einzellage* (single site): under 5.5 acres.
• *Grosslage* (a collection of vineyards): can encompass several communes.
• *Bereich*: wine-producing subdistrict.
• *Anbaugebiet*: region in which quality wines are produced; Germany has thirteen such regions.

Classifying wines

• Deutscher Tafelwein: German table wine with no indication of origin.
• Landwein: special table wine named after one of the nineteen Landwein regions of Germany.
• Qualitätswein bestimmter Anbaugebiete (QbA): quality wine produced from a delimited winegrowing region. It is indicated on the label, generally with the name of the grape variety.

MOSEL·SAAR·RUWER

halbtrocken

Abfüller:
J. KOLL & CIE.
D-56812 Cochem/Mosel

ANNO 1744

KOLL RIESLING

1995 RIESLING-HOCHGEWÄCHS

QUALITÄTSWEIN

A. P. Nr.
1 907 115 06 96

10,5% vol

0,75 L

GERMANY

1996
Ilbesheimer Herrlich Qualitätswein
MORIO-MUSKAT
A. P. Nr. 5 907 115 02 97
Abfüller J. KOLL & CIE., Weinkellerei, D-56812 Cochem/Mosel Germany
9,5% vol   PFALZ   750 ml

• Qualtätswein mit Prädikat (QmP): quality wine that come in six levels according to the degree of ripeness of the grapes:
- *Kabinett:* perfectly ripe grapes, minimum 7 % alcohol at harvest, generally light wines.
- *Spätlese:* literally means "late harvest." Wines of superior quality made from remaining grapes harvested after a normal harvest (minimum seven days after harvest).
- *Auslese:* harvest of selected, very ripe bunches; dry and richly sweet.
- *Beerenauslese:* harvest of individually selected, overripe berries with a high concentration of sugar; rich, sweet dessert wines.
- *Trockenbeerenauslese:* harvest of individually selected, overripe berries that are dried up almost like raisins; rich, sweet honey-like wines.
- *Eiswein:* wine made from grapes harvested and pressed while frozen (at least 19° F) to concentrate sugar, acidity and extract.

None of these wines can be chaptalized.
• Qualitätswein garantierten Ursprungs (QbU): since 1994, a new regulation authorizing regions to stipulate which assemblages, as well as which type of wines (dry or semi-dry, for example) are best.

How to read a label

The first obligatory mention is the region (*Anbaugebiet*), for example, Rheingau, Ahr or Nahe. If the mention *"Einzellage"* (single site) or *"Grosslage"* (winegrowing area) is indicated, the commune in which the wine was produced must appear.

The grape variety is generally indicated, as well as the quality level of the grape (*Kabinett, Spätlese, Auslese,* etc.), if the wine is a Qualitätswein mit Prädikat (QmP).
• AP, followed by a reference number, is the official tasting number and authenticates the wine.
• The sugar concentration is also indicated:
- *Trocken* (dry): less than 1/3 ounce per quart of residual sugar.
- *Halbtrocken* (semi-dry): less than 2/3 ounce per quart of residual sugar.
- *Sekt:* sparkling wine.
- *Perlwein:* slightly sparkling wine.

How to read a label

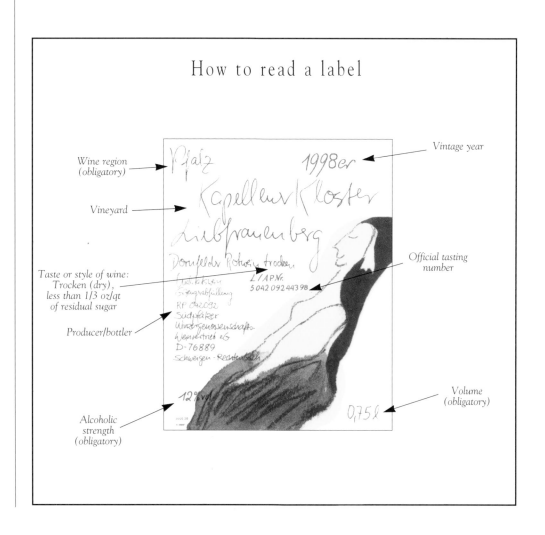

165

Moselle-Saar-Ruwer

A few VDQS wines are produced in Lorraine, France, near the Moselle River, which runs from the French Vosges Mountains to the Rhine, forming a border between Luxembourg and the state of Rhine-Palatinate. The wines produced here are surprisingly generous and fresh (see Luxembourg). But the Moselle wine-producing area that is most famous lies north of the ancient Roman city of Trier, and along the Moselle's two tributaries, the Ruwer and the Saar, just before reaching Koblenz.

To any wine lover, the white wines produced near the Moselle are incomparable. They are fruity and delicate, elegant, richly fragrant and ever so slightly piquant. Wine specialists consider Riesling wines from the Moselle to be the best in the world. The secret lies in the association between the grape and the slate found in the soil. The slaty soil imparts a distinctive taste to Moselle wines, from fine-fruity to earthy or flinty.

Vines flourish in the valley. During prehistoric times, the Devonian Sea covered the area. When the sea disappeared, the marine life fossilized and formed a kind of slate, which is widespread today.

Over the millennia, the Moselle carved out its own riverbed, creating a series of microclimates sheltered from the winds and which absorbed the energy of the sun to be diffused during cold spells. Wine has been produced here since the Roman times, although not from Riesling grapes—which had not yet come into existence—but from a grape variety very similar to what currently is known as Elbling. The grape yields light white wines that are highly acidic, used notably in making sparkling wines (Sekt). It was not obligatory to plant Riesling until 1787, following a decree by Prince-Bishop Clemens Wenceslaus of Trier.

The fourth-leading winegrowing region of Germany, with 31,615 acres, is the Mosel-Saar-Ruwer (as it appears on German wine labels), which produces only Riesling white wines on the steepest slate-rich (57 percent) hillsides. The Müller-Thurgau grape (23 percent) is planted on the flattest areas of the region. Eleven thousand wine producers work the vines (the average wine estate is just under 2.5 acres). Half of the production is marketed by companies; one-fourth goes to wine cooperatives, which count five thousand members (Moselland Cooperative); the remainder is sold directly to growers.

In Moselle, the *Fuder* is a 1,000-liter (264-gallon) oak barrel containing the equivalent of 1,333 bottles. Each grower has its own *Fuder*, in which the superior wines are aged.

In general, the vineyards run along the Moselle Valley from Trier. The heart of the winegrowing area is Mittelmosel (Middle Moselle) from Trittenheim to Traven-Trarbach, which includes the communes of Piesport, Bernkastel, Graach, Wehlen, Zeltingen and Brauneberg. There are four officially recognized wine districts (*Bereiche*): Zell (Untermosel, or Lower Moselle), which runs from Koblenz to the village of Zell, known for its Schwarze Katz or Black Cat vineyards; Bernkastel (Mittelmosel), the most famous; Saar and Ruwer, encompassing the vineyards surrounding Trier, and Obermosel and Moseltor.

Bereich Bernkastel (Mittelmosel)

It is important to note that the inner side of a river bend, which is formed by the river encountering very hard shale, is steep. The outside is a low promontory of earth deposited by the eddy of the river. Wines produced on the former are dryer and have a greater measure of breed; vintages made on the side with the alluvial deposits are more full-bodied and less lively.

Deferring to the most noble of all, the Trockenbeerenauslese, the German Sau-

ternes, tops the list. This delicious golden wine is unbelievably rich, with a high concentration of the various aromas of Moselle wines. Each grape that goes into its making is individually selected just as it reaches the perfect degree of overripeness (hence its price).

Bernkastel, founded in the twelfth century by Frederick Barbarossa, is a small town that draws massive crowds every first weekend of September for its annual grape harvest festival. The vineyards are some of the best in Germany. Bernkasteler Doktor, located southwest, dominates the city. The wine's exceptional quality is due to the slaty soil, which imparts a hint of flint and spices and a slightly smoky taste. The full southern exposure gives the wine its roundness and richness. In poor years, Bernkasteler Doktor is sold under the appellation Badstube.

Opposite Bernkasteler, the vineyards of Kues are located on the exterior of the river bend, and the soil composition much richer in river deposits as a result. The appellations Kardinalsberg and Rosenberg unfortunately lack the kind of elegance which slate imparts to wines. The Braunberg hillsides ("brown hill") on the other bank yield pleasant, fruity wines (Grosslage Kurfürstlay; the superior crus are Juffer and Juffer-Sonnenuhr, Kammer).

The Erden slope is called Moselle's Mountain of Gold, producing fruity wines with great breed, some of which attain Premier Cru quality. The region's inhabitants maintain that Erden wines are more *Bube* (boy) and that those produced in Wehlen are more *Mädel* (girl). The best crus are Bussley and Herrenberg. Wehlener Sonnenuhr, a wine with legendary measures of finesse and elegance, is produced in Wehlen; some consider it to be superior to Bernkasteler Doktor. The high terraced vineyards here rise up to 656 feet above the Moselle. Opposite the township of Wehlen lies the vineyard of Sonnenuhr, which is owned by the Prüm family. The name Johann Joseph Prüm still appears on the estate's labels; he was the one who launched the reputation of this prestigious house in the late nineteenth century. A sundial *(Sonnenuhr)* also

appears on the label. There is also a sundial in the middle of the vines, where the rock and the slate soil meet.

The vineyards of Wehlen date back to 1084. Until they were secularized by Napoleon (1802), they belonged to the Cistercian abbey of Kloster Machem. Graach, of the Grosslage Münzlay, has a southwestern exposure. The vineyards running around the hillsides are made up of rocky soil (Graach comes from the Gallic word meaning "gravel"), a mixture of slate and clay which gives the wine a good measure of body and roundness. In poor years, Graach produces exceptional wines (Himmelreich, Domprobst, Josefshöfer). Moreover, Josefshöfer is one of the only German wines, along with Schloss Vollrads and Schloss Johannisberg, that is marketed without any mention of origin.

In Moselle, the wines of Piesport (Goldtröpfchen, Günterslay, Falkenberg, Grafenberg, Schubertslay, etc.) have a great deal of distinction and are remarkably balanced, highly fragrant and delicate. In great years, they are masterpieces.

Ürzig (Grosslage Schwarzlay) has two crus—Goldwingert and Würzgarten (garden of spices)—which are fruitier and

BEREICH BERNKASTEL
Best vineyards
(from northeast to southwest)

- Erdener Treppchen
- Erdener Prälat
- Ürziger Würzgarten
- Zeltinger Schlossberg
- Zeltinger Sonnenuhr
- Wehlener Sonnenuhr
- Josefshöfer
- Graacher Himmelreich
- Graacher Domprobst
- Bernkasteler Doktor
- Bernkasteler Bratenhöfchen
- Bernkasteler Lay
- Bernkasteler Graben
- Bernkasteler Alte Badstube am Doktorberg
- Lieserer Niebderberg-Helden
- Brauneberger Juffer
- Brauneberger Juffer-Sonnenuhr
- Wintricher Ohligsberg
- Piesporter Domherr
- Piesporter Goldtröpfchen
- Trittenheimer Apotheke
- Trittenheimer Leiterchen
- Trittenheimer Felsenkopf
- Dhroner Hofberger

spicier than other wines. This is determined by the sheer drop of the vineyards, which grow in deep-strata volcanic soil of mixed slate and croppings of sandstone that have a full southern exposure.

Bereich Zell-Mosel (Lower Moselle)

This section runs from Zell to Koblenz, where the Moselle runs into the Rhine. It produces wines which, without obtaining the quality of those made in Bereich Bernkastel, are fairly pleasant and quite honest.

Schwarze Katz in Zell supplies Germany with its most popular wines: Schwartz Katz, or Black Cat, for according to legend it was a black cat that determined which *Fuder* contained the most superior wine by catnapping on top of it.

Leaving Zell, there is a great place to walk to the village of Alf, Belstein and Breurm, which has the steepest vineyards of Europe. The picturesque setting of medieval villages, in a landscape of hillsides covered with vineyards, is sumptuous.

Bereich Obermosel Bereich Moseltor (Upper Moselle)

This sector, upriver from Trier, is a prime growing area for Elbling (related closely to the variety imported by the Romans two thousand years earlier) and Ruländer grapes. The soil is not slaty but of chalk substance. The wines, without being great, have a certain charm. In addition, the prices are lower than those of other Moselle wines.

Bereich Saar-Ruwer

The wines harvested around Trier (the most important town of northern Europe under the Roman Empire), on the banks of the Saar and the Ruwer, have just the right balance of acidity and fruitiness. In very good years, Moselle wines tend to be overrated. They are slow maturing wines, which allow them to develop their charac-

teristic elegance. Their bouquet is reminiscent of black currants with a slight taste of Muscat—a bouquet found nowhere else outside Germany (the villages of Avelsbach, Eitelsbach, Kasel, Mertesdorf in the Ruhr, Ayl, Filzen, Kanzen and Ockfent in the Saar). Before leaving the gentle valleys bordering the Ruhr, stop at the vineyards of Herrenberg.

The estate of Maximin Grünhaus is so well known that his name alone can appear on the label—a rare honor in Germany. Riesling is the predominant grape variety here, flourishing in the reddish slaty soil which is very crumbly. The estate consists of a single slope, and is sheltered in a valley and surrounded by a forest which acts as a windbreak. The vineyard overlooks a manor house, the residence of the von Schubert family, who has owned the estate since 1882. There are three sections of this single slope: the Bruderberg, whose wines date back to the monks of the Saint-Maximin Abbey; the Herrenberg, reserved for the fathers and the lords; and the Abtsberg, featuring ten different wines, reserved for the abbot. Today over twenty different wines are produced, most of which keep very well. The top wines come from late harvests requiring up to six different pickings in the vineyard. The result: an Abtsberg Kabinett Trocken that is unbeatable.

BEREICH SAAR-RUWER
Best vineyards (north to south)

- Waldracher Hubertusberg
- Kaseler Kehrnagel
- Kaseler Nies'chen
- Maximin Grühauser Herrenberg
- Maximin Grühauser Abtsberg
- Eitelsbacher Karlhaüserhofberg
- Avelsbacher Altenberg
- Oberemmeler Hütte
- Wiltinger Braune Kupp
- Wiltinger Hölle
- Scharzhofberg
- Kanzerner Altenberg
- Filzener Pulchen
- Wawerner Herrenberg
- Ockfener Bockstein
- Ayler Kupp
- Saarburger Rausch

Rheingau

This small region of Hesse produces the best white Riesling wines in the world (along with those produced in Moselle). It is believed that Riesling originated in the Rheingau. The planting of the grape has been nearly mandatory since the seventeenth century; it currently represents some 80 percent of the vineyard.

The Rheingau is located along the Rhine

Valley, between Wiesbaden and Bingen, in the extension of the Taunus Mountains, an area 28 miles long and 5 miles wide, located 19 miles from Frankfurt. The vines opposite the Rhine grow in a prime location at the foot of the Taunus, a schistous range over 2,885 feet high. At this spot, the Rhine, which is 2,625 feet wide, forms a curve running east to west, affording the vines full southern exposure. Sheltered from the cold winds by the hills, the Riesling absorbs the heat from the sun, which the waters of the Rhine reflect during cold spells, providing the vines with the humidity and mildness required for late-ripening grapes.

The grape harvests occur late in the season in the Rheingau, during the last two weeks of October, and often extends into November. The late harvests impart a certain elegance and freshness characteristic of very fine Rieslings. Each autumn, wine festivals take place throughout the villages, with many wine-tasting stalls—an ideal time to take a trip along the Riesling Route (Rheingauer Riesling Route), which links the twenty-four winegrowing villages of the Rheingau along a 44-mile route, from Hochheim to Lorchhausen. The winegrowing history of the Rheingau dates back to the Romans. But according to legend, it was Charlemagne who, from his palace in Ingelheim on the opposite bank of the Rhine (in the Rheinhessen), interpreted the early melting of the snows on Johannisberg as a good omen for the vines. They didn't actually prosper until much later during the Middle Ages, under the auspices of the bishops of Mainz and the monks of the monasteries of Johannisberg and Eberbach.

The Rheingau is synonymous with Riesling. It was first mentioned on March 13, 1435, on a bill for the Klaus Kleinfish company concerning a certain delivery of Riesling to the fortress of Rüsselsheim. In the seventeenth century, the first campaigns to uproot the red-wine vine Spätburgunder (Pinot Noir), imported from Burgundy by

Cistercian monks in the twelfth century to replant the area with Riesling grapes, were carried out. By chance, the late harvests were discovered during the exact same period. In 1736, the first Cabinet Keller was established at Kloster Eberbach (a small cellar in which special reserves were stored), later called *Kabinettwein*. In the ear-ly nineteenth century, the international reputation of Riesling wines from the Rheingau began to be established.

Today the Rheingau has 7,410 acres under vine and produces 5.28 million gallons of wine each year (80 percent of which is Riesling). The some 1,500 growers own an average 5 acres of vineyard, which forces them to market the wine directly. The great wine estates (some one hundred or so) auction off their wines each year through an intermediary brokers' guild dating back to the fourteenth century. In addition, there are a dozen major wine cooperatives and an association of thirty-three estates formed by the Vereinigung Rheingauer Weingüter, considered to be the elite of Riesling producers.

Bereich Johannisberg

In the Rheingau, Riesling has the potential to develop a wide range of nuances determined by soil type, terrain and exposure of the vineyards to the sun. The precipitous hillsides of Rüdesheim, in the middle of the Rheingau, extending to the hillsides of Assmannshausen and Lorch, at the bend of the river, produce wines that can be either piquant, acidic or smooth, but they always have a great measure of breed. Vineyards growing on graduated slopes generally yield wines that are fruitier and more robust. Geologically speaking, the central and northern Rheingau, notably in Erbach, Markobrunn and Kiedrich, have soil rich in marl and clay, with a mixture of sand and gravel covered in a layer of loess. Warmer soil rich in limestone, loess and loam is found in the upper Rheingau, notably in Geisenheim, Östrich, Eltville and Hattenheim. In the western regions, there is a great deal of clayey slate, sandstone and quartz.

If a classification needed to be established to determine a good year, according to experts, the best crus are the following: Rauenthal of the famous Erbach-Hattenheim-Hallgarten triangle; Johannisberg (Schloss Vollrads), Winkel, Rüdesheim, Oestrich and Hattenheim. The Rheingau appellation applies to the vineyards of Hochheim, to the extreme east of the area, where the Mainz flows into the Rhine. Here the terrain is flat and the climate is exceptional; as a result, the grapes ripen two to three weeks earlier than they do elsewhere. This represents a considerable advantage in producing fruity, highly fragrant Rieslings, which are classified as being the best from the Rheingau (Kirchenstück and Domdechaney). Riesling from Hochheim, nicknamed Hock (used in England for the Rheingau wines, sometimes for all wines of the Rhine area), has been the preferred German wine of the British ever since Queen Victoria visited in 1850. In honor of the royal visit, a vineyard has been named Königin-Victoriaberg (Grosslage Daubhaus).

In the far western section of the Rheingau, Assmannshausen is famous for its red wines, which are among the best produced in Germany (the best cru: Höllenberg). The red-wine vine growing in bluish-red shale is the Spätburgunder (Pinot Noir), which was transplanted here from Burgundy in the twelfth century by Cistercian monks. A slightly lighter version than its Burgundian ancestor, it is a velvety smooth wine with a subtle hint of almonds. Not far from here, the incredibly steep slaty hillsides of Lorch yield Rieslings that have a very good measure of breed and are sufficiently acidic to be very slightly sparkling (*spritzig*).

Among the best crus: Bodenthalsteinberg, Kapellenberg, Pfaffenwies and Krone

---

RHEINGAU GRAPE VARIETIES

Rheingau produces the best Rieslings in the world. The percentage of Riesling grown here is the highest in Germany (80 percent), with 6 percent of Müller-Thurgau, 5 percent of Spätburgunder, 3 percent of Ehrenfelser and 2 percent of Kerner.

(Grosslage Burgweg). But the biggest wineries of the Rheingau are located south of Wiesbaden, where the Rhine veers west. Rauenthal, located on the upper regions of the Taunus, with its terraced vineyards and steep hillsides, yields the best wines in Germany in warm years—incomparable Rieslings that are fruity and spicy, with a great capacity to age.

The best cru is Bailken (Grosslage Steinmacher). Gehrn, Wülfen and Rothenberg are also worthy of mention.

Past Eltville, a major wine-producing center along the Rhine where Gutenberg once stayed in the fifteenth century, is the the small town of Markobrunn ("spring of Saint Mark"), halfway between Erbach and Hattenheim. The wines produced here

(Grosslage Deutelsberg and a few Grands Crus: Rheinhell, Siegelsberg and Hohenrain) are among the best produced in the Rheingau. Slightly more full-bodied than Rauenthaler wines, they are splendid, generous Rieslings with wonderful bouquets. The wines are internationally renowned as a result of Thomas Jefferson's visit here in 1788: He preferred this wine to all other Rheingaus.

The village of Hattenheim, which is next along the way, is associated with two famous institutions: Kloster Eberbach, the Cistercian abbey, and the legendary Steinberg vineyard, which produces one of the leading Grands Crus of the Rheingau region—a wine that is extraordinarily fresh and delicate. The 79-acre vineyard was planted by the monks of Eberbach during the twelfth century. Following the example of Clos de Vougeot in Burgundy, the area was fully enclosed by a wall. Today Kloster Eberbach belongs to the state and has become the cultural viticultural center of the Rheingau, where the German Wine Academy and the Rheingau Wine Society are located. Classical concerts are held in the superb Romanesque basilica, as is the Erntedankfest, each first Sunday in December during which four thousand bottles of Riesling are auctioned off for charity.

The "Cabinet Keller" originated in Eberbach, dating back to a bill written in 1773 for some carpentry work carried out at Kloster Eberbach in the Cabinet Keller. Certain documents reveal that the first bottles laid down in this small cellar date from the grape harvest of 1712 (at least the best).

Schloss Johannisberg

Farther west, the historic castle and vineyard of Johannisberg overlooking the town is a surprising site. The terrace, which offers a superb view, runs along the 50th latitude, the same latitude as Labrador and Mongolia.

The cellars of the castle are some of the largest in the world. They date back to the eleventh century and are steeped in history. Louis the Pious, the son of Charlemagne, recounts that the 817 grape harvest yielded 1,585 gallons of wine. Schloss Johannisberg was originally a Benedictine monastery built in honor of John the Baptist. Following Napoleon's secularization of the vineyards in 1803, the vineyard became the property first of the Prince of Orange, then Napoleon, and then the Emperor of Austria, who gave it to Metternich in 1816 in exchange for services rendered during the 1814 Vienna Congress. It currently belongs to the Metternich family. (Note the large casks dedicated to Prince Metternich in the vaulted cellars of the castle.)

The vineyards are just as historic. Riesling became the sole grape variety as early as 1720. According to legend, in the year 1775, the growers dependent on the Abbey of Fulda awaited the order for the grapes to be harvested. They waited for such a long period of time, however, that when the order finally arrived it was too late. What happened to these left-on-the-vine wines is quite well known: The grapes were harvested, and much to the amazement of everyone, produced an excellent wine. The late harvests, or *Spätlese,* had been born.

The greatest estates include Hölle, Hansenberg and notably Schloss Vollrads, an exquisite wine that is fruity, elegant, slightly piquant and reminiscent of Steinberg and Schloss Johannisberg.

Vollrads wines date back to 1291. The current proprietor, Erwein, Graf Matuschka-Greiffenclau, still lives in the superb baroque palace built by his family in the seventeenth century.

The last stop on our journey through the Rheingau is Geisenheim, located between Rüdesheim and Johannisberg, a well-known name, as it is the seat of the Institute of Research for Viticulture and Enology. Dr. Herman Müller von Thurgau created the highly resistant grape variety that bears his name by crossing Riesling and Sylvaner grapes here in 1882.

BEREICH JOHANNISBERG
Best vineyards
(west to east)

- Lorcher Kapellenberg
- Assmannshaüser Höllenberg
- Rüdesheimer Berg Schlossberg
- Rüdesheimer Berg Roseneck
- Rüdesheimer Berg Rottland
- Geisenheimer Rothenberg
- Geisenheimer Kläuserweg
- Schloss Johannisberg
- Johannisberg Klauss
- Winkeler Jesuitengarten
- Winkeler Hasensprung
- Schloss Vollrads
- Hallgartener Schönhell
- Oestricher Lenchen
- Oestricher Doosberg
- Hattenheimer Nussbrunnen
- Hattenheimer Wisselbrunnen
- Steinberg
- Erbacher Marcobrunn
- Erbacher Siegelsberg
- Kiedricher Sandgrub
- Kiedricher Gräfenberg
- Rauenthaler Baïken
- Eltviller Sonnerberg
- Wallufer Walkenberg

173

Palatinate (Pfalz)

This province (Pfalz), which is part of the state of Rhineland-Palatinate (Rheinland Pfalz), is the second-leading winegrowing region of Germany with 64,220 acres under vine. It is the leading region in terms of production. Located west of the Rhine, it is bordered on the north by Rheinessen and by Alsace to the south. The leading advantage of this region is its southern-style climate with 1,800 hours of sunlight per year and an average temperature of 52° F. Winters are extremely mild. The Palatinate owes its sunny climate to the Haardt Mountains, a sandstone massif that is a northern extension of the Vosges Mountains. Reaching altitudes of 2,254 feet, the mountains shelter the vineyards from cold winds and rain.

Its name is derived from Palatine, the seven hills of the ancient city of Rome on which Augustus had his palace ("palatium") built. The term was then generalized to refer to all imperial palaces. "Palatinate" came from the office known as count palatine (Pfalzgraf), a title used in the Holy Roman Empire to designate the secular prince who ruled a region in absence of the Holy Roman Emperor.

Some 150 million rootstocks currently occupy the slopes of the smaller hills, from the Haardt Mountains to the fertile plains of the Rhine. The vineyards occupy 58 square miles here and there along the 50-mile-long German Wine Route (Deutsche Weinstrasse), established in 1934. The southern region of the wine route, Bereich Mittelhaardt Deutsche Weinstrasse, between Bad Dürkheim and Neustadt, is world famous. The 11,500 winegrowers located in the Palatinate, with the wine estates averaging 7.5 acres, produce 66 million gallons of wine each year. Forty percent among them produce their own wine, which they market directly. The stone gateway of Schweigen (Deutsches Weintor) marks the beginning of the wine route, with the Alsatian wine route running just along the opposite side. Advancing north, you find yourself in a hilly landscape filled with orchards, vineyards and picturesque villages.

Bereich Mittelhaardt-Deutsche Weinstrasse

The wine route begins after the town of Grünstadt in the northern part of the Palatinate, with Dackenheim, Herxheim and Freinsheim, a small fortified town with a Gothic church and half-timbered houses that is very popular with tourists. Honest white wines are produced here. A few good red wines produced from Portugieser and Spätburgunder grapes are worthy of mention.

The best sector of the vineyards begins after Kallstadt, namely with Ungstein, Bad Dürkheim, Wachenheim and Forst. Saumagen, a district in Kallstadt, is worthy of mention, not only for its full-bodied, round wines, but also for its local culinary specialty: sow bellies stuffed with spiced meat and potatoes. The next village is Ungstein, which produces sweet wines that are tasty and have the reputation of rousing the dead (Ungstein's motto).

Bad Dürkheim is certainly the most popular village in the Palatinate, famous for its unique crus—Spielberg, Michelsberg, Fronhof, Abtsfronhof, Fuchsmantel—and for its collective crus: Feuerberg (a semi-sweet, heady red wine), Hochmess and Schenkenböhl. Once a year, in September, the Dürkheim Wurstmarkt, or Sausage Fair, is held—a misnomer, given that it is Germany's biggest wine festival. Another tourist attraction is the gigantic barrel of Dürkheim, which has been converted into a restaurant.

The wines of Wachenheim (Rechbächel, Goldbächel, Gerümpel and Luginsland) have the solid reputation for being rich, heady and full-bodied yet very fine. Don't miss the excellent Sekt made from Riesling grapes that has been produced by Schloss Wachenheim since 1888.

For generations, Forst and Deidesheim have been competing to rank as the city producing the best wines of the Palatinate. In Forst, the soil is rich in volcanic basalt, which absorbs and stores sunlight very

PALATINATE GRAPE VARIETIES

White grape varieties. Rieslings, which represent 14 percent of the Palatinate vineyard, are generally of very good quality: elegant, full-bodied and superb. Sylvaners, which are diminishing in popularity, occupy only 9 percent of the growing area (compared to 40 percent in the early 1960s). The predominant grape of the Palatinate is Müller-Thurgau (the crossing of Riesling and Sylvaner), with 24 percent of the vineyard. Palatinate wines, 40 percent of which are dry, have the reputation for being very honest wines that are easy to drink and harmonious.

Red grape varieties. Practically all of the red wine comes from the Blauer Portugieser variety, with small amounts of Domfelder and Pinot Noir.

well. As a result, the grape harvests take place later in the season here than they do elsewhere. Another characteristic of the soil is that is rich in clay, which makes the soil heavy. This allows for the soil to retain moisture, which protects the vines during dry periods.

The best crus are found in Kirchenstück, Jesuitengarten and wines marketed under the appellation Grosslage Mariengarten.

In Deidesheim, the soil is lighter, yielding wines that are fruitier and more elegant. The best crus include Hohenmorgen, Leinhöhle, Kieselberg and Herrgottsacker. Deidesheim has one of the oldest inns in Germany, the Gasthaus Zur Kanne, founded in 1160. It is also the seat of the "Three Bs"-the three largest winegrowing estates in the Palatinate: Dr. Bürklin-Wolf, Reichrat von Buhl and Bassermann-Jordan. The association of eight villages located around Neustadt, which is right in the center of Mittelhaardt, has created the largest viticultural commune in Germany with some 4,940 acres under vine.

Each year, an autumn festival is organized during which the wine queen is crowned. The best crus include Erkenbrecht, Monchgarten and Grain.

South of Neustadt and Donnersberg, where the Haardt Mountains are highest, the southern winegrowing districts (Südliche Weinstrasse) begin, featuring a picturesque landscape with steep vineyards: Maikammer, Edesheim and Rhodt Unter Rietburg, which is well-known for its famous Traminer vineyard that is well over three hundred years old. Ludwig II of Bavaria's residence, the Schloss Ludwigshöre, overlooks the city.

While the Mittelhaart groups together the larger winegrowing estates, here the average vineyard rarely exceeds 2.5 acres. This district furnishes nearly half of the total amount of Liebfraumilch produced, the remainder coming primarily from Rheinhessen.

Rheinhessen

The 61,750 acres that are under vine in the Rheinhessen are divided among 160 vineyards. The Rheinhessen, located in the state of Rhineland-Palatinate, is the largest winegrowing area of Germany. It is a hilly region bordered on the east and north by the Rhine, on the west by the Nahe Valley and on the south the Palatinate. The vines were introduced to the region by Roman legions. After the fall of the Roman Empire, Rhine wines did not make a comeback until the eighth century. Hesse, which became the grand duchy of Hesse, later annexed by the Prussians, marketed its wines and its Hessian troops of mercenaries (notably to the Hanoverian kings of England) as its major source of income. The Rheinhessen is divided into three *Bereiche,* or wine-producing districts: from Bingen to Mainz in the west; in the south, the district of Wonnegau, around the city of Worms; and the Rhine riverfront with its terraced vineyards, and the famous village of Nierstein.

Two factors play a major role in Rheinhessen wine production: a mild climate with dry autumns, few late frosts, and a soil type composed of marl, quartz and limestone. As in Moselle, there is also slaty soil in Bingen, along the Rhine River, and a kind of red limestone deposited during the Ice Age between Nierstein and Nackenheim. Rheinhessen wines are generally soft, sweet and supple, but are not wines to lay down (except for Beerenauslese). Rieslings and Sylvaners produced along the Rhine are fruity, distinguished and expansive, comparable to the best vintages produced in Rheingau.

Bereich Bingen

Bingen, located on the left bank of the Rhine, is a crossroads of four great districts: the Rheinhessen, the Nahe Valley, the middle sector of the Rhine, and the Rheingau. The reputation of the district as a wine-producing area dates back to the Romans, with the vineyards of Bingen-Dempten and Bingen-Büdesheim. Today

RHEINHESSEN GRAPE VARIETIES

Müller-Thurgau is predominant in the region, at 24 percent. Yet the grape presence is diminishing (compared to 33 percent in 1964). Sylvaner is dwindling as well, currently occupying 14 percent of the vineyard (twenty years ago it occupied 47 percent). Next in line comes a cross between Sylvaner and Riesling called Scheurebe (10 percent), then Kerner, a cross between Trollinger and Riesling (7 percent). Riesling represents 5 percent. Rheinhessen is one of the rare regions of Germany to produce quality red wines, especially from Ingelheim, which are often confused with white wines. They are fruity, with a good measure of acidity, and low in tannin. They come from two grape varieties: Spätburgunder (Pinot Noir) and Blauer Portugieser (Portuguese Blue), and represent barely 4 percent of varietal blends.

the best crus come from Schlossberg, Rosengarten, Schwëtzerchen, Kirchberg and Osterberg. Don't be surprised if you ask to borrow a pencil in Bingen and someone hands you a corkscrew. This is the famous Bingen pencil, which dates back to a certain legend. One day when a past Bishop of Mainz, while addressing the Bingen clergy, asked to borrow a pencil, the clergy member reached under their cassocks and pulled out not a pencil, but a corkscrew—hence the "Bingen pencil."

Bereich Nierstein

South of Mainz begins one of the most marvelous spots in Germany: the terraces along the Rhine. Nackenheim is the first

stop. Dramatically overlooking the Rhine, its baroque church stands in the midst of vine-covered slopes. The soil is composed of a reddish argilous sandstone, and the wines produced here (Rothenberg, Engelsberg, Schmitts-Kapelle)—although very similar to those produced in Nierstein— were used for blending for many years. Who hasn't heard of Niersteiner—the elegant, full-bodied Riesling with a superbly complex bouquet? Glöck, Orbel, Hipping, Kranzberg, Brückchen, Bildstock, Schwabsburg, Heiligenbaum and Pettenthal are only some of the most prestigious names. From the time of the Romans, Nierstein marked the division between Frankish and German territories. Today many winegrowers cultivate vines that are well over one hundred years old. In Oppenheim, the wines are fuller and softer than those made in Nierstein; in very good years, they can even surpass them in terms of quality (best crus: Paterhof, Herrengarten, Daubhaus, Kreuz, Herrenberg). Slightly farther south, the flat vineyards of Ockenheim and Gau-Algesheim yield excellent Müller-Thurgau wines in good years. Gau-Algesheim was famous in the Middle Ages for the vast wine fair held there every year. Today there

is a fair for new vintages (the second weekend in October). Not far away, the limestone soil of the village of Ingelheim is ideal for producing light red wines that are fruity and low in tannin. This district, which is planted predominantly with Spätburgunder and Portugieser, is nicknamed the islet of red wine. Legend has it that Charlemagne, who built a fortress here, looked across from his palace and noticed that the snow melted earlier on one of the nearby slopes than on the surrounding countryside. He ordained that the vines be planted there, currently called Schloss Johannisberg. Thus begins the story of Johannisberg (see the section on the Rheingau).

Bereich Wonnegau

North of Worms, the southern vineyards of Guntersblum, Alsheim and Osthofen are made up of gently sloping hills and a soil rich in loess, which yields fruity, harmonious wines. Don't miss taking a visit to Guntersblurm to see the Kellerweg, or wine cellar route, where all of the wine cellars of the city seem clustered around the foot of the vines for nearly three-quarters of a mile.

Liebfraumilch

Worms is famous for more than one attraction—its cathedral where Martin Luther was condemned as a heretic in 1521. Near Worms is the Liebfrauenkirche, a church surrounded by the vineyards which gave its name to the area's noted white wine, Liebfraumilch-Kirchenbück (Qualitätswein), one of the most popular German wines of the region.

The Liebfraumilch appellation has applied since 1910 to all quality wines (QbA) produced in one of the three *Bereiche* of the Rheinhenen, the Rheinhessen, Palatinate, Nahe or the Rheingau, on condition that it be produced from at least 70 percent Riesling, Müller-Thurgau, Sylvaner or Kerner grapes, without any indication of the grape variety on the label. It must have between 2/3 ounce to $1\frac{1}{3}$ ounce of residual sugar per quart.

Baden

The Baden vineyard, located in the state of Baden-Württemberg, is the third-leading wine-producing region of Germany, with 37,050 acres under vine.

The area begins along the southern shore of Lake Constance (the famous Bodensee), runs along the slopes of the Black Forest, juts briefly into France and Switzerland, then continues northward along the Rhine River, running parallel to the Alsatian vineyards to Heidelberg.

The history of the region's viticultural activity is exemplary. In the 1860s, before phylloxera devastated one-half of the vineyards, the grand duchy of Baden was the leading wine producer in Germany. Just as Baden was beginning to recover from the catastrophe, a 1938–40 law decreed that all hybrid vines had to be uprooted. Although the effect was catastrophic in the short run, the long-term impact of the law has been a great improvement in the quality of the wines produced here (the introduction of cutting-edge equipment has also helped). Nearly all of the wines are vinified in cooperative cellars. White grape varieties are predominant (77 percent), notably Müller-Thurgau, which represents 40 percent of the vineyard. The wines produced in Baden are currently the most widely consumed in Germany, particularly the more ordinary wines from the region.

Bereich Bodensee

Our trip through Baden begins on the shores of Lake Constance, where you can discover the famous Seeweine (Lake Wines) made from Spätburgunder (Pinot Noir), Rülander and Gewürztraminer grapes. The Föhn, a warm wind typical of the alpine area, has a disturbing effect on man and beast, and even causes milk to sour, but it also speeds up the ripening of the grapes. Meersburg is the seat of a castle that is over thirteen hundred years old, and has one of the largest vineyards of Bodensee.

Bereich Markgrëflerland

Following southwest along the Rhine to the border with France and Switzerland, Bereich Markgräflerland was planted with Gutedel (Chasselas) grapes as early as the late eighteenth century. The grapes were brought from Vevey in Switzerland. Today, however, the Müller-Thurgau grape is predominant throughout the entire region. Farther north and opposite Alsace, toward Freibourg in Brisgau, is a kind of cone-shaped volcanic islet covered with vines: the Kaiserstuhl. The soil is a mixture of volcanic soil and clay, which is ideal for Müller-Thurgau (which yields white wines that are a deep amber color), Spätburgunder and Rülander.

Bereich Breisgau

Bereich Breisgau, slightly farther north, produces lighter wines. Weissherbst, near Freiburg, is one of the best Baden vintages. The area which produces very good quality wines is Bereich Ortenau, notably a narrow strip of land located between the Rhine and the mountainous massif which prolongs the Black Forest of Offenburg to Baden-Baden. The soil is rich in decomposed granite, and the best Rieslings, Traminers and Spätburgunders of the state are produced here.

Each village has some interesting feature: Dunbach, Ortenburg, Neuweir. The Bocksbeutel, a flat, flask-shaped wine bottle typically found in Franconia, is used to bottle the wine.

There is little to say about Bereich Bergstrasse-Kraichgau, south of Heidelberg, or the Bereiche in the state of Baden-Württemburg, major suppliers of Müller-Thurgau.

Other European countries

The vast Balkan Peninsula extending from the eastern Alps, Greece and the Transylvanian Alps to the Balkans has been a major crossroads of European and Asian civilizations for centuries. The area, part of the former Ottoman Empire, has been the site of some of the most turbulent religious wars and nationalistic battles. The vineyards, like silent witnesses of history, stand as a symbol of new hope and reconciliation.

The Danube, 1,770 miles long, is the great river of central and southeastern Europe. Austrians call it the Donau, and the land surrounding it produces excellent white wines from Riesling, Müller-Thurgau, Sylvaner, Gewürztraminer and local grape varieties such as Rotgipfler and Grüner Veltliner. From Austria, it flows through the Czech Republic and Slovakia (where it is called the Dunaj), Hungary (Duna), Croatia and Serbia (Dunav), Romania (Dunàrea) and Bulgaria (Dunà), then enters the Black Sea west of Odessa. The Chardonnay grape is widely planted in Georgia, Moldavia and the Ukraine, and gradually is replacing more of the traditional grape varieties, Rka-Ziteli and Saperavi.

It is somewhat unfair to devote only a few pages to these vast vineyards (larger than those of France and Italy combined), but the wines produced here have a relatively low profile. Bulgaria is adopting the same approach to wine production as in Georgia and the Ukraine; Cabernet Sauvignon and Merlot gradually are eclipsing Melnik, Pamid and Mavrud grapes. In contrast, the Hungarians have succeeded brilliantly in maintaining the supremacy of the famous Tokay grape, the noted Furmint, popular throughout eastern Europe, as well as the Hàrslevelü, Kéknyelü and Kardarka grapes, the latter being a red variety originally from Albania which represents 17 percent of the Hungarian vineyards.

But before exploring Austria and the Balkan Peninsula, let's go west for a brief detour to the vineyards of Luxembourg, Switzerland and the United Kingdom.

Luxembourg

This small state, wedged between Belgium to the west, France to the south and Germany to the east, produces white wines that are little known outside the Benelux Union. The light, fruity wines resemble those produced in Alsace. Most of the Luxembourg vineyards are located along the left bank of the Moselle River, which forms a border with Germany. They are ideally positioned to receive the early morning sunshine, yet are sheltered from westerly winds by the dense forest on the upper hillsides. The Grand Duchy consumes some 70 percent of its wine production, a total of 4.5 million per year produced along a 3,000-acre strip of land. Very little of this is exported.

The founding of the Government Viticultural Station at Remich along the Moselle, which paid out premiums for uprooting second-class vineyards, marked a step toward promoting quality over quantity. One of the station's main responsibilities is to supervise the laws governing place-names on bottle labels. Like Alsatian wines, Luxembourg wines (primarily whites) are varietals, named after the grape variety. The wines that bear the national seal on the label offer proof of quality control. There are some thirty winemaking areas, including Schengen (of the famous Schengen Treaty), Remerschen and Wormeldange.

REGULATIONS

In addition to European regulations governing wine, Luxembourg established its own Marque Nationale in 1935. The seal is affixed to the neck of certified bottles. The wines are tested and controlled by government civil servants. Appellation Côntrolée labels must indicate locality, vineyard site and grape variety. Fine wines must also include vintage year, along with the name and address of the grower, for both Premier Cru and Grand Cru wines.

LUXEMBOURG GRAPE VARIETIES

Müller-Thurgau (or Rivaner), yielding a light wine with a remarkable Muscat taste; Auxerrois, Pinot Blanc and Ruländer are grown in southern parts of the country, where the soil is very marly. Table wines are produced from Elbling, a grape variety indigenous to the Moselle Valley. It produces dry table wines with bitter undertones. Riesling and Sylvaner yield more elegant vintages, with a hint of acidity typical of Moselle wines.

The best vineyards are planted with Riesling and have chalky soil with stone and a marly subsoil; these include Remich, Grevenmacher and Ehnen. They yield wines that are very similar to German Moselle wines—elegant, with a touch of acidity during rainy years. These are wines to lay down. The other grape varieties, notably Ruländer (Pinot Gris), Pinot Blanc and Auxerrois, produce heartier, more full-bodied wines which lack a certain bouquet; these are produced at Wellenstein, Remerschen and Schengen. The vineyards of Ahn and Wellemstein also yield excellent Traminer wines that are velvety and have a characteristic spicy perfume and taste.

United Kingdom

Wine was most likely made in Britain as early as Roman times. During the ninth century, the wine lobby was so powerful that a decree by Alfred the Great compensated grape growers for damage inflicted on the vines. During the Norman conquest, vines carpeted the area around monasteries and extended into Lincolnshire. But winemaking suffered after Eleanor of Aquitaine's marriage to Henri II. By annexing the Aquitaine lands, the English discovered Bordeaux wines, and it was the beginning of a longlasting love affair. Until the Second World War, vines were used mainly for ornamental purposes, and it was fashionable to dress up a sun-drenched wall with a few rootstocks. In 1952, Sir Guy Salisbury-Jones of Hambledon (Hampshire) restored the past glory of the British vine.

Other efforts to revive British wine production followed, and the Association of English Vineyards was created in 1967. There are currently some thirty wine-producing communes, located mainly in the southern counties and in East Anglia; these cover 1,112 acres with an average 1.24 acres per grower and over four hundred wine producers in all. During the 1990s, large companies like Harvest Wine sprang up, each controlling several vineyards. Most grape varieties are white, selected for their early ripening. One-sixth of the English vineyard is occupied by Müller-Thurgau, followed by the very early maturing Reichensteiner, Bacchus and Schönburger. Chardonnay is still rare, and is used primarily in producing effervescent wines. For reds, Thames Valley is making great strides with Pinot Noir in vinifying reds and rosés, as well as Beenleigh Manor in Devon, for its experimental plantations of Merlot and Cabernet Sauvignon.

ENGLISH GRAPE VARIETIES

There are very few red grape varieties, mainly Pinot Noir. The climate imposes certain white grapes that are able to ripen in the conditions of the country. The most common are Müller-Thurgau and Reichensteiner. Seyval Blanc, a highly robust French hybrid, has yielded excellent results since it was introduced by Sir Guy Salisbury-Jones in 1952. He was the one to supply still and sparkling wines that are among the best produced in the country. Yet the wines are controversial, given that European regulations stipulate that no hybrids be used in making quality wines.

Chardonnay is also grown here, as well as Austrian Schönburger and Triomphe d'Alsace. In all, some thirty various grape varieties are found, including a majority of German crossings.

REGULATIONS

Note: the mention "British wine" (to be distinguished from English wine, which is natural and 11.5% proof alcohol) applies to wines that are 15% proof and made from dry grapes and grape juice imported from abroad but vinified in Great Britain.

THE BEST VINEYARDS

– Sussex
- Carr Taylor, near Hastings
- Leeford
- Sedlescombe
- Hidden Spring
- Barkham Manor
- Breaky Bottom
- Chapel Down
- Nutbourne Manor
- Rock Lodge

– Kent
- Staple Vineyard
- Tenterden
- Biddenden
- Lamberhurst
- Penshurst
- Headcorn
- High Weald Winery

– Essex
- East Mersea
- New Hall

– Suffolk
- Bruisyard
- Shawgate

– Norfolk
- Elmham Park (the northernmost)
- Pulham

– Hampshire
- Wickham
- Meon Valley
- Hambledon Wines

– Isle of Wight
- Adgestone

– Surrey
- Denbies

– Berkshire, Oxfordshire and Buckinghamshire
- Cane End
- Chiltern Valley
- Thames Valley (known for its slightly sparkling Gamay Blanc and excellent Pinot Noir)

– Somerset
- Oatley
- Moorlynch
- Pilton Manor
- Wootton

– Devon
- Sharpham
- Beenleigh Manor

– Worcestershire and Gloucestershire
- Astley
- Bodenham
- Three Choirs

Switzerland

Switzerland, a confederation of cantons since the late thirteenth century, is in the highly unusual position of being surrounded by four great wine-producing nations—France, Italy, Germany and Austria. Swiss winegrowing regions tend to follow the linguistic breakdown; in other words, there are three distinct regions.

To the east lies German-speaking Switzerland (Ostschweiz); to the west, French Switzerland (Suisse Romande); and to the south, Italian Switzerland in the Ticino. Of the total 36,555 acres of vineyards, French Switzerland occupies 27,170 acres, German Switzerland occupies 7,410 and Italian Switzerland 1,975 acres. Together they produce 26.4 million gallons of wine annually, three-quarters of which is white.

Vines flourish in most Swiss cantons; these descended from the great medieval vineyards which were in part devastated by various epidemics during the eighteenth and nineteenth centuries. Only a few barrels of wine are exported, and Swiss wines remain something of a curiosity as a result. They are rare, of exceptional quality and infinitely diverse. Look at the incredible difference between the Dézaley or Grand Vaux produced on the sunny slopes above Lake Geneva and the Vispertminen wines harvested on vineyards in the Valais that grow at altitudes of 3,600 feet above sea level, for example.

French Switzerland

This is by far Switzerland's leading vineyard, with 27,170 acres under vine. Half of the vineyards are located in the Valais, and vines flourish around Lake Geneva and Lake Neuchâtel and along the terraced shores of the Upper Rhône. The white grape Chasselas Doré is predominant; it is a neutral grape, and its unique flavor depends on the terroir. In certain cantons, the wines have generic appellations, such as Fendant wines produced in Valais. Fendant, the

most well-known Swiss wine, is generous and has a great measure of breed. Near Geneva, it is called Perlan, and Neuchâtel in Neuchâtel. In the area surrounding Lake Geneva, in the canton of Vaud, it is found under its appellation of origin, along with the prestigious name of such villages as Mont-sur-Rolle, Féchy, Bonvillars, Épesses, Saint-Saphorin and Dézaley.

Valais

Any self-respecting inhabitant of Valais owns a plot of land under vine. The 12,350 acres of land on the steep slopes of the Rhône Valley are divided up among some 20,000 winegrowers. Most Valais wines take their names from the grape, not the place, the exception being the famous Sion wines. There are twelve regions of local production, with a definite preference for developing certain red grapes, including Gamay and Pinot Noir. Dôle is undeniably the best red wine produced in Switzerland. Pinot Noir imparts the wine's vigor, bouquet and striking ruby color; Gamay gives it its freshness and fruitiness. Marvelous Dôle wines are produced in the chalky soil of Sierre. The third-leading grape variety of the Valais canton is Johannisberg, from Sylvaner, which is stronger in alcohol than Fendant. It is pleasant, fine and semi-sweet and is quite abundant in the lower Valais. In addition, there are varieties that date back to earlier periods of time, including Arvine, for example, which yields a white wine to be laid down. Proud and virile, with a fruity, well-balanced bouquet, it is best served chilled as an aperitif. Amigne yields wines that have a brilliant golden color and make wonderful dessert wines. Malvoisie, from Pinot Gris, produces wines that have an alcohol content of 14%. Païen, in the upper Valais, is a dry, pleasantly acidic wine harvested on very steep terraced vineyards 3,600 feet above sea level near Vispertminen. Rèze, another specialty of the Valais, grows in high altitudes as well. This little-known grape is used in making the extremely rare Vin du Glacier, an ample, generous wine that has a stunning amber color. Oeil du Perdrix is a powerful, full-bodied rosé

SWISS GRAPE VARIETIES

Of the 34,580 acres of the Swiss vineyard, 14,820 are planted with Chasselas. The grape has an amazing history. Originally from south Lebanon, it was probably the first vine cultivated by mankind (representations of its characteristic leaf can be found on the walls of Luxor temples). It was believed to have been introduced to Europe by the Phoenicians. It is well-documented, however, that a general under Louis XV named Courtin transplanted the vine to the Valais canton. The Chasselas grape, called Fendant in the Valais, is supple, dry and fruity, with only a trace of aroma, yet has a lively, slightly crackling taste. The grape is called Dorin in the canton of Vaud, where it is planted between Lausanne and Vevey. Here, it takes on a good measure of finesse and has a hint of a smoky taste. In Geneva it is called Perlan (indeed it is very slightly sparkling, or *perlant*). Chasselas—which has a high yield—ripens just after Sylvaner, which is reserved for the best *terroirs*. Local grape varieties include Amigne, Arvine, Humagne and Rèze. Pinot Noir and Gamay are predominant among red grapes.

from the Valais, made from Pinot Noir. Again, these special wines can be surprisingly good, yet are rare and hard to find.

Vaud

Vaud is the second-leading wine-producing canton of Switzerland, after Valais. It is divided into three sections: Chablais, between Martigny and Montreux; Lavaux, between Montreux and Lausanne on the shores of Lake Geneva; and La Côte, which extends from Orbe in the north to Neu-

châtel as the Jura Mountains gradually run into the snowy Alps.

The wines are sprightly, light and often slightly sparkling. The rolling landscape is dotted with wine estates and castles. The wine route takes you past Féchy, Mont-sur-Rolle, Vinzel and Luins. In the foothills of the Alps, near Aigle, the Chablais region of Vaud yields heady wines with the gun-flint taste that is typical of the area. Lavaux is known for its terraced vineyards and its wines that bear such illustrious names as Lutry, Villette, Dézaley, Vevy, Montreux, Saint-Saphorin and Épesses.

The vineyards climb up from the shore in a progression of steep terraces, and the grapes ripen exceptionally well in the sunlight, which is intensified by the reflection off the water. Chasselas, which is called Dorin, thrives here, producing dry, fruity wines that have a lovely golden color and are among the best produced in Switzerland. Dézaley is the best by far, produced on a vineyard established by Cistercian monks in the thirteenth century. It is full-bodied and generous with aromas of almond and toasted bread and hints of honey and tea.

Red wines, called Solvagnins, come from Pinot Noir and Gamay.

Geneva

The vineyards growing in this gently sloping region lie on the outskirts of the city. Mandement, a dry, light white wine with a hint of hazelnut in the bouquet, is by far the most well known. Chasselas, called Perlan in Geneva, is the predominant grape variety and is naturally slightly sparkling. The increasingly popular Gamay is used to produce red wines called Clef d'Or, or rosés, called Rosette de Genève. In addition, there is Pinot Noir (Camerier), Müller-Thurgau (Goût du Prieur) and Sylvaner (Clavendier).

Neuchâtel

Neuchâtel, farther north, is where the Jura lakes of Neuchâtel, Bienne and Morat are located. The highly partitioned vineyards are hit periodically by frosts. Chasselas is the predominant grape, while Pinot Noir—

the only authorized red variety—is becoming fashionable. Neuchâtel wine is produced on eighteen viticultural communes; the name of the commune always appears on labels. Only three Neuchâtel crus are entitled to an appellation: Château Vaumarcus, Domaine de Champréveyres and Hôpital Pourtalès. Oeil du Perdrix is another regional specialty; it is a delicate rosé wine made from Pinot Noir.

German Switzerland

The eastern region of Switzerland, with 7,410 acres under vine, groups the German-speaking cantons of Zurich, Schaffhausen, Aargau, Thurgau, Saint Gall and the Graubünden (Grisons) along the Rhine Valley. Demand for wine far exceeds supply; in addition, the wines of German Switzerland are much sought after. They are light, fruity wines that are skillfully vinified. Pinot Noir (Klevner) is believed to have been introduced into the Graubünden by the Duc de Rohan during the Thirty Years' War. This region of the Bündner Herschaft, located on the Upper Rhine, is called the "little Burgundy of the Alps."

SWITZERLAND'S MAJOR VITICULTURAL REGIONS

- **Valais**
- **Jura**
- **Neuchâtel**
- **Vaud**
- Bonvillars
- Côtes de l'Orbe
- Vully
- La Côte
- Lavaux
- Chablais
- **Geneva**
- Mandement
- Arve-et-Rhône
- Arve-et-Lac
- **Ticino**
- Sottoceneri
- Sopraceneri
- **Graubünden (Grisons)**
- Misox
- Herrschaft
- **Saint-Gall**
- Oberland
- Rheintal
- **Thurgovie**
- Thurtal
- Untersee
- **Zurich**
- Weinland
- Lake Zurich
- Limmettal
- Unterland
- **Schaffhouse**
- Klettgau
- **Basel**
- **Bern**
- **Aargau**
- Lac de Thoune
- Bielersee
- **Fribourg**
- Wully
- Broye

Ticino (Italian Switzerland)

In 1900, some 17,000 acres were under vine; today the vineyards occupy only 1,975 acres. Yet the Ticino seems to have been blessed by the gods. The climate is mild and the slopes receive excellent exposure from the sun. Grapes traditionally were either indigenous (Bondola) or from the Piedmont region of Italy. Since the Second World War, the red Bordelais grape of Merlot has been producing some of Switzerland's best wines: the superb Merlot di Ticino, which is velvety and fruity. It bears the "Viti" label, a government seal of quality.

Austria

Austria possesses one of the most beautiful European vineyards, which dates back to the Austro-Hungarian Empire. It extends from the northeast, where the famous Blue Danube flows, into the eastern section of the country, where the Great Hungarian Plain begins. In the tenth century, Otto I ordered the replanting of the Austrian vineyards which, as in Bavaria, were tended primarily by monks. It was the first revival of the vine since the departure of the Romans. In the late eighteenth century, Empress Maria Theresa revised the wine taxes, and wine producers were entitled to market their own wine free of tax. When a grower wanted to announced that he was selling his new wine, or Heurige, he hung branches on the door of his home. *Heurige,* more generally known as May wine, is still drunk today and *aushängen,* meaning "to hang out," is the origin of the Hengelweine.

There are officially four major viticultural regions of Austria: Lower Austria, with the very famous areas of Wachau, Kamptal-Donauland and Wienviertel; the Vienna vineyard, on the outskirts of Vienna; Burgenland, near the Hungarian border; and

MAJOR VITICULTURAL REGIONS OF AUSTRIA
(Quality wines)

– Lower Austria
(Niederösterreich)
• Wachau
• Kremstal
• Kamptal
• Weinviertel
• Donauland
• Carnuntum
– Vienna
(Wien)
• Wien
– Burgenland
• Neusiedlersee
• Neusiedlersee-Hügelland
• Mittelburgenland
• Südburgenland
– Styria
(Steiermark)
• Süd-Oststeiermark
• Südsteiermark
• Weststeiermark

Styria to the south, near Slovenia. There are 56,000 wine-producing businesses spread over 143,260 acres, few of which exceed 5 acres. The annual wine production is 79.2 million gallons, 80 percent of which are good quality white wines. The Austrian vineyard barely meets national demand, which has an average per capita consumption rate of 10 gallons per year. Red wine is imported primarily from France and Italy.

Lower Austria

Lower Austria (Niederösterreich), the granary of Austria with cornfields, market gardens and vines, is home to three-quarters of the country's vineyards. Grüner Veltliner, the local white grape, is used in making 40 percent of Austrian wines. The mild climate of the Danube, Kamp and Strasser valleys, as well as the soil, which is rich in loess, provide ideal conditions for wines. Wachau, which stretches from Melk to Mautern, is considered by many to be one of the most beautiful valleys in the world. Terraced vineyards grow along the steep slopes of the Danube. Wachau wines, notably Kremser and Dürnsteiner, stand out for their freshness and fruitiness; they

can be laid down for many years in wine cellars. Slightly farther north, in Kamp Valley (Kamptal-Donauland) is Langenlois, Austria's biggest wine-producing center, where Heiligenstein, one of the region's finest crus, is produced. Near Vienna, in Klosterneuburg, Augustine prelates have been cultivating the vineyards for nine hundred years. They started up the oldest

viticulture school in the world. Am Wagram vineyards grow in terraces plots near the village where one of Napoleon's great military victories took place. The region of Weinviertel, north of the Danube, includes the "Brünnerstrasse" area, on both sides of the old main road between Vienna and Brünn. It is one of the most productive regions in Austria. Veltliner gives light, palatable wines that leave a slightly spicy taste in the mouth and a very refreshing touch of acidity (great vintage wines). The Thermes viticultural district (Thermen) is one of the warmest in Austria. The stony limestone soil produces the famous Gumpoldskirchen, a sweet wine made from late-harvested grapes. In the area around Bad Vöslau, the red Portugieser grape yields excellent Vöslauer.

Burgenland

Seventy-five percent of the wines produced in this former Hungarian province, which is still inhabited by Magyars and Croats, are red wines. The Lake district bordering the Neusiedlersee, set in the midst of the Puszta, a kind of steppe, has a particular climate that produces full-bodied white wines from Welsch-Riesling and Muscat-Ottonel grapes. The Wenzel family estate, occupying 25 acres, reserves its choice land plots to making sweet and richly sweet wines, including the extremely rare Ausbruch, produced uniquely in 50 centiliter (16.9-ounce) bottles. The pleasant red wines which are also produced were delivered to the Imperial Court for years (Pottelsdorf and Oggauer Blanfän Kischer).

Styria

Located in southeastern Austria near the Slovenian border, Styria is nicknamed the Austrian Tuscany. It has a Mediterranean-type climate and volcanic soil in parts. The vineyards, between 820 and 2,130 feet above sea level, produce a famous rosé wine with a tangy acidity called Schilder, made from Blauer Wildbacher. The southern region of

AUSTRIAN GRAPE VARIETIES

Among the 200 grape varieties grown, thirty are used in producing "quality wines." Among them, Grüner Veltliner represents one-third of all production. It yields an Austrian wine par excellence— fruity, very slightly sparkling, with a slight trace of spice and pepper in great vintage years. Neuburger has a slightly nutty taste and a delicate bouquet. It is found primarily on the chalky soil of Lower Austria. Riesling and Gewürztraminer are two light, fruity grapes that are very common in Styria and Burgenland. Zierfandler, associated with Rotgipfler, produces the famous Gumpoldskircher. It is an assertive, full-bodied wine with a good measure of breed and is one of Austria's best. In addition, grape varieties include Welsch-Riesling, which ripens late, and Müller-Thurgau, which gives sweet wines with a Muscat taste that are quite common throughout Austria.

Styria, around Leibniz, specializes in Chardonnay (called Morillon here), Gelber Muskateller and Sauvignon.

Vienna

Vienna, the capital, is surrounded by the Vienna Woods, on the slopes of which the vines grow. They yield a charming, slightly tangy "new" wine, *Heurige,* often served up in carafes in outdoor cafes in the Grinzing district. *Heurige* refers to the new wine and to the winegrower's inn (Buschenschenken). To end on a historical note, it was from these same vine-covered hills— two in particular, Kahlenberg and Leopoldsberg—that the Turks were driven back from western Europe in 1529.

Slovakia and the Czech Republic

It is generally assumed that wine was made in Bohemia as early as the eleventh century. Emperor Charles IV imported and planted Burgundian vines in the latter half of the fourteenth century, making Prague a highly prosperous viticultural center. It remained so until the havoc wreaked during the Thirty Years' War.

Since then, few countries have had such a turbulent viticultural policy. The vineyards were planted and replanted time and time again until the late nineteenth century, when phylloxera destroyed all of the vineyards.

Of the three regions that made up the former Czechoslovakia—Bohemia, Moravia and Slovakia (there are currently only two, since the division of the country into two countries)—Slovakia supplies two-thirds of the wine, occupying 76,570 acres; Moravia produces slightly less than the remaining one-third. The Czechs have their own specialty: beer.

Bohemia

The Bohemian vineyard is like a small-scale version of Germany's (it is on the same latitude as Rheingau).

It is therefore not surprising to find Riesling, Traminer and Sylvaner, as well as a majority of Blauer Burgunder for red wines, around Prague.

The best quality zone is found north of Prague, in Mělnik, on the Elbe River, and slightly farther west in Velké Zernoseky and Brezanky.

Moravia

Most Moravian wine comes from the area south of Brno, where tributaries of the Danube (Svratka, Moravia and Dyje) provide good winegrowing conditions. The zone extends west to Znojmo and north-east via Mikulov and Hustopeče, on the Austrian border, near the Viennese vineyards of Weinviertel.

Veltliner grapes are abundant here, as they are in Austria, along with Rhine Riesling and Welsch-Riesling (20 percent of the land area). The white wines produced here are fresh, light and aromatic, with a dash of pepper (they are similar to the wines made from Austrian Grüner Veltliner). Don't miss sampling two wines made from little-known grapes: Polava, a white wine, and Saint-Laurent, a red.

Slovakia

At the far eastern end of the country, opposite Hungary and its legendary Tokay wines, Tokájská produces one of Slovakia's best wines, similar in quality to its prestigious neighbor. The same grape varieties that grow in Hungary are found here and there along the border: Furmint, Lipovina and Muscat, but the results are not the same. Most of Slovakia's wines are best in the Carpathian foothills and the Tatra Mountains, near Bratislava, with production concentrated in Modra and Pezinok.

VITICULTURAL REGIONS

Czech Republic

– **Bohemia**
– **Moravia**
• Znojmo-Mikulov
• Hustopeče-Hodonin
• Bzenec-Stražnice

Slovakia
(from the Czech Border to the Ukraine)

• Shalika-Zahorie
• Lesser Carpatians (Bratislava region)
• Danube
• Hlohovec-Trnava
• Nitra
• Eastern Slovakia (extreme east), encompassing a parcel of Tokay (Tokájská).

Hungary

Hungary and Tokay are closely associated, the latter being one of the rare wines in the world to be truly legendary. *Vinum regum, rex vinorum:* the wine of kings, the king of wines. Yet Hungarians boast of producing a variety of excellent wines. The Hungarian vineyard is the largest of Eastern Europe.

Total production is 132 million gallons, with 296,400 acres under vine. Sixty percent of the vineyard is planted with Welsch-Riesling, which gives a white wine with a complex bouquet that is high in alcohol content. The four major wine-producing regions follow the country's natural borders. A quick glance at a map shows that the Danube divides Hungary in two. There are two regions in the western sector: the Kisalföld (Little Plain) in the north, and the Transdanubian region in the south. The eastern sector includes the Alföld (Great Hungarian Plain, or famous Hungarian Puszta) between the Danube and the Tisza extending to the Romanian border, and in the far north, toward the Carpathians, the region of Eger and Tokay. The Kisalföld, better known as Sopron, lies on the Austrian border in Hungarian Burgenland. This is a major red wine-producing area, primarily from Gamay Noir grapes. Note one name: Soproni Kékfrankos, a kind of local Beaujolais that is drunk young and chilled. Transdanubia is a hilly region (Badacsony) on the northern shore of Lake Balaton (the largest lake in Hungary).

During the Roman occupation, the imperial wine cellars of Rome were filled with wines from Hungary. A variety of factors contribute to the excellent quality of these wines, including the microclimate around the lake, and the basaltic soil with a layer of loess. The terraced vines produce primarily French-derived Pinot Gris, which gives the golden Badacsonyi Szürkebarát (Gray Friar) and Kéknyelü (Blue Stem). Olaszrizling (Italian Riesling), Traminer, Sylvaner and Muscat flourish on the neighboring slopes of Balatonfüred Csopak. Furmint yields a delicious full-bodied dessert wine that is as reputable as Tokay. The wine was a favorite with the Habsburgs for its genetic properties. The region of Szekszárd, located northeast of Pécs, is known for its Fleuré of Pécs, its Riesling and the red wines of Kadarka, which age remarkably well. Farther south, on the

Croatian border, Kékfrankos produces one of Hungary's best red wines, Villány-Siklós, which is reminiscent of Burgundy reds. The Great Hungarian Plain east of the Danube produces 65 percent of Hungarian wines made from Kadarka for reds and from Olaszrizling for whites.

This former desert, which the Magyars transformed into arable land, is where the great wine estates are found. Kecskemét, 50 miles southeast of Budapest, is famous for its excellent apricot brandy (Barack Pálinka), as well as its Leanyka, a very honest white wine, and a few good reds. Toward the north, the viticultural zone of Gyöngyös, located in the mountainous regions, produces white wines from Chas-

HUNGARIAN GRAPE VARIETIES

Many white grape varieties flourish in Hungary. The most famous, which is associated with Tokay, is Furmint, which has a golden straw-yellow color. It is a robust grape and imparts a tangy zest to Tokay wines. This characteristic touch of acidity is tempered by the Hárslevelü (known as *lindenblättriger,* or "linden leaf"), the other grape variety used in making Tokays. It adds a spicy taste to the wine. The most widely grown red grape is Kadarka, originally from the Middle East. It occupies 17 percent of the Hungarian vineyard, primarily in the Great Plain.

REGULATIONS

Hungary has the most rigorous winemaking standards of any Eastern European country. The place-name classification system governing place of origin and grape variety was established in 1893. Classified wines are either First Great Growths or Great Growths.

selas grapes that are as soft and sweet as honey. Farther east, the very beautiful city of Eger produces Hungary's two best red wines: Egri Kadarka and the legendary Egri Bikavér (Bull's Blood of Eger). The latter is a hearty, semi-sweet wine to lay down, which gets much of its character from the soil (a mixture of clay and volcanic rock). The extraordinary Tokay wines are produced in northeastern Hungary, near the river town of Tokaj, where the Bodgrog and Hernád rush from the Carpathian Mountains and flow into the Danube.

Tokay (Tokaj)

The winegrowing region of Tokaj-Hegyalja (meaning "spur" in Hungarian) lies in the Carpathian foothills at the fork of the Bodgrog and Tisza. The vineyard occupies 14,820 acres, divided among 15,000 property owners which produce 5.3 million gallons of wine per year. No one really knows how long vines have been here, although they were present when the Magyar tribes arrived over one thousand years ago.

To Hungarians, Tokay is a national symbol, a festive wine, and is believed to have therapeutic properties.

Its reputation dates to the Council of Trent in 1562; but it was Louis XV's famous remark when offering Madame de Pompadour a glass of Tokay Aszú that confirmed its reputation: "Madame, it is the king of wines, and the wine of kings."

During the forty-year Communist regime, most of the vineyards were nationalized and became a state monopoly. Emphasis was placed on producing greater and greater amounts of wine, often at the expense of quality. As a result, white wines that were somewhat ordinary were produced, destined primarily for the Russian market.

Since 1990, the Hungarian state has been gradually privatizing part of the vineyards. Former landowners whose property had been confiscated sought to get their land back, while foreign investors, primarily French, British and Spanish, have teamed up with Hungarians in joint ventures, bringing winemaking skills and marketing expertise. There are currently some fifteen owners or companies whose vineyard estates cover between 125 and 250 acres. Following in the tradition of the Rákóczi princes' ancient chateau of Sarospatak, the estates are named Château Disnoko, Pajzos, Hetzolo, Meyger and Messzelato, or Royal Tokaji Wine Company and Bodegas Oremus. To restore Tokay's prestige and former glory, companies with foreign investors have created an association called Tokaji Renaissance.

Everything here is magical: the Furmint and Hárslevelü (Lindenblättriger), its two principal grape varieties; the volcanic soil containing feldspar, porcelain clay and porphyry, and the climate, which features dry, sunny autumns ideal for drying the grapes on straw beds. The grape harvests are late, from late October to early December, allowing the grape to obtain its maximum sugar content. The overripe grapes then achieve the condition of *Botrytis cinerea*. The dried, extra-rich berries (hence the name *aszú*, meaning "dried") are prepared. The must is stored in small barrels called Gönci as soon as fermentation sets in; the barrels are then placed in the famous cellars that are covered with a layer of black fungus, *Cladosporium cellare,* and the Tokay wine is aged slowly. Only the underground cellars produce great Tokay. Dating back to the thirteenth century, the cellars were originally dug as shelters against Turkish invasions, and can be found in such townships as Sarospatak, Tokay, Mad and Tolsva.

It is bottled five to fifteen years later (in traditional 0.5-l/17.6-ounce) bottles with long throats. Tokay Szamorodni is obtained, sold as Edes (sweet) or Szaraz (dry), with 13.8% alcohol content.

Tokay Aszú is altogether different: a marvelously sweet wine with incomparable bouquet, it is a Premier Cru unlike any other. It is rare and expensive, and it is easy to see why. Late harvesting allows noble rot to achieve maximum concentration. The grapes, nearly candied at this point, are crushed to form a thick paste. Buckets (called *puttonyos* in Hungarian) of the paste are added to the dry white base wine made from non-botrytized grapes. The number of *puttonyos* determines Tokay Aszú's sugar level (maximum six *puttonyos* and 15% alcohol content). The more *puttonyos,* the better the Tokay. The best comes from the small commune of Tallya. Its delicate bouquet, unforgettable flavor and golden color make it one of the greatest wines ever.

MAJOR WINE-PRODUCING REGIONS OF HUNGARY

– From the western border to the Danube (north to south)
- Sopron (next to Austrian Burgenland))
- Pannonhalma-Sokoróalja
- Ászar-Neszmély
- Etyek
- Mór
- Somlo

– Around Lake Balaton
- Balatonfüred-Csopak
- Badacsony
- Balatonmellék
- Dél-Dél-Balaton

– North of Croatia
- Vilány-Siklos
- Mecsekalja
- Szekszárd

– Between the Danube and Tisza
- Hajós-Vaskut
- Kiskunság
- Csongrád

– South of Slovakia
- Eger
- Mátraalja
- Bükkalja

– Toward the Carpathians and the Ukraine
- Tokajhegyalja

West of the Balkan Peninsula

What used to be called Yugoslavia is located at the northwestern part of the Balkan Peninsula. It is on the same latitude as Italy, from which it is separated by the Adriatic. Vines are scattered throughout the region, occupying 617,500 acres and producing 185 million gallons of wine each year—making the region Europe's seventh-leading wine producer. The former provinces of the former Austro-Hungarian Empire today form five states: Slovenia, Croatia, Bosnia-Herzogovina, Macedonia and the Federal Republic of Yugoslavia, comprising Serbia, with Vojvodina in the north and Kosovo in the south, bordered on the west by Montenegro. There are four official languages and two alphabets. The history of this region is both Mediterranean and Balkan. Its viticultural tradition came from Thrace after crossing the mountains of Macedonia four thousand years ago. The many Greek amphoras and artefacts found here reveal that wine was being produced in Dalmatia and Istria under the Greek occupation (and in Slovenia during the Roman occupation). The vocabulary concerning wine is derived from Greek and Latin. After developing considerably during the Middle Ages, there was a long hiatus in wine production during the Ottoman occupation. Today, Serbia and Croatia alone produce two-thirds of the wines of the region, while Macedonia produces 20 percent, Sovenia, 8 percent and Bosnia-Herzegovina, 3 percent.

In Serbia, the wine is made primarily from Prokupac, a local grape variety which gradually is being replaced by such European grapes as Gamay and Cabernet. Most of the vines grow in the Danube and Morava valleys, as well as farther south on the slopes of Vojvodina (bordering on Hungary and Romania). The greatest vineyards are in Fruska Gora, with large amounts of a fairly good white wine produced from Welsch-Riesling, Sémillon and Sauvignon. Red wine is also produced, in memory of the famous Carlowitz (karlovice rothwein). Between the Danube and the Tisza, Suboticka Pescara is a sandy extension of the Great Hungarian Plain. In addition to Hungarian grape varieties, there is a local white grape grown called Kevedinka.

VARIOUS VITICULTURAL REGIONS

Slovenia (northwest between Italy, Austria and Hungary)
– Drava Valley
• Ljutomer-Ormoz
• Maribor
• Haloze
• Slovenske-Gorice
• Radgona-Kapela
• Prekmurje
– Sava Valley
• Bela Krajina
• Dolenjska
• Bizeljsko-Sremič

Croatia (along the Adriatic)
• Istric
• Hrvatsko Primorje
• Islands Kvarner
• Dalmatia
• Dalmatinska Zagora
• Danube Valley, Save Valley, Drave Valley
• Plješivica
• Zagorje-Medimurje
• Prigorje
• Moslavina
• Kupa

Vojvodina (northern Serbia)
• Banat
• Truska Gora

Serbia (between Romania and Albania)
– Morava and Nišava
• Čacăk
• Kruševac
• Aleksinac
• Toplica
• Niš
• Leskovac
• Vranje
• Mlava
• Oplenac
• Jagodina
– Timok Valley (on Romanian and Bulgarian border)
• Krajina
• Knjazevac

BALKAN PENINSULA GRAPE VARIETIES

This geographical sector is inundated with Riesling, Merlot, Cabernet and Chardonnay, yet Plavác, whether it be *beli* (white) or *zuti* (yellow), manages to stand its ground. Like Marastina, it is grown in Slovenia on the sandy soil of the islands off the Dalmatian coast and around Dubrovnik. It lacks aroma, however, and must be associated with Welsch-Riesling.

Plavác Mali, the equivalent of the preceding grape but in red, produces a good wine to lay down, which is tannic and rich. It is grown along the Dalmatian coast. Prokupac, which is more rustic, is the most abundant red grape in the region and is used in most wines produced here.

Kosovo, bordering on Albania and Macedonia, is particularly known for the quality of its red wines made from Cabernet and Pinot Noir. Toward the center, the winegrowing zone of Zupa, around Aleksandrovac on the Morava, and that of Vencac-Oplenac, yield simple, robust red wines from Prokupac. Oplenac is a very popular rosé produced in the same region.

In Croatia, two sectors are clearly delimited: the vast Danube plain that extends to Zagreb, between the Drave and the Save. Pleasant, light wines are produced here, such as Plješivica, Vinica and Varazdin. The north is much more Austrian in terms of grapes, and Traminer, Riesling, Sauvignon and Sémillon are abundant. The second sector covers the former Italian province of Istria, as well as the famous Dalmatian coast.

Along the Adriatic, the borra, a wind that blows in from the sea, sweeps the slopes on which tannic, full-bodied and hearty red wines are produced. They are so rich that Dalmatians have taken to diluting them with water or, worse, soda. A local grape, Plavác Mali (Little Plavác), which thrives in sandy soil, produces such wines as Peljesac, Vis (island), Brela, Lastovo and Dingac. The rosé wines, which are also excellent, are sold under the appellation Opol. The

APPELLATIONS

There are some three hundred grape varieties. Quality, enhanced by Gamays and Cabernets, is becoming a greater priority. Vintage year means nothing here, since nearly all wines are blends. Vinification and marketing of wines is carried out by large cooperatives. Quality and provenance are becoming better regulated as a result of recent legislation. The label must indicate the grape variety and place of origin (required for export).

preferred white wine is Grk (pronounced "gerk"), a dry wine with an amber color that comes from Split and the island of Korcula. Also note a white wine made from Bogdanusa, a specialty of the island of Hvar; and two other reputable wines: Red Blatina and White Zilavka. Both are dry, hearty wines harvested in the region of Mostar. There are no great vineyards here, but plots of land wedged between two rocks; no wine cooperatives, but independent growers who make their own wine.

Istria, which is very near to Italy, mixes its vines with other crops. Its best vintage is Malvazyä (Malvasia).

The famous Ljutomer wine (better known as Lutomer), produced in the wine-growing district of Slovenia's Drave Valley, is found on tables throughout the world. The wine comes from Riesling, Sylvaner and Sauvignon, as well as a local grape called Sipon (the label indicates the grape variety). Its color, depending on the grapes used, ranges from gold to green. It is full-bodied and bursting with spice; the bouquet, at least for the best vintages, is superb.

The Ancient Illyrians cultivated the vines in Macedonia. Since the Second World War, this region, with 74,100 acres, has become a major production zone. The vineyard, straddling the Mediterranean and central Europe, yields an excellent red wine, Vranac, which is heavy, rich and semi-sweet, as well as two white wines from Zilavartea and Smederevka.

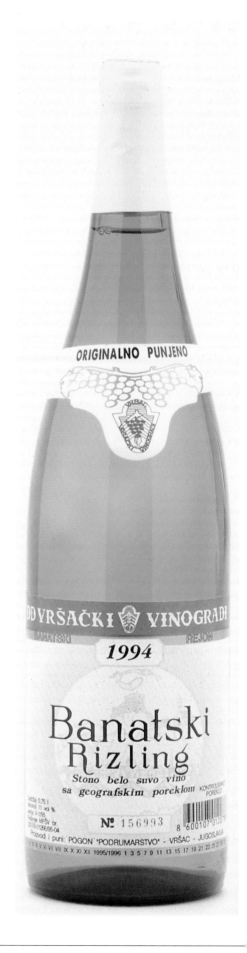

Romania

Romania, once the Roman province of Dacia, has preserved its Latinate speech over the centuries, as well as its long wine-making tradition. Wine has always been harvested in the foothills of the Carpathians, well before the Greeks colonized Hellespont (the Black Sea).

In the Middle Ages, Romanians marketed their wines to countries ranging from Russia to the Republic of Venice and Poland.

Romania is currently the fifth-leading wine-producing country, between Portugal and Germany. Some 211 million gallons of wine are produced each year (11 percent of which is exported) and the vineyard—741,000 acres—is continuously expanding.

Various factors lie behind Romania's quality wines: it is on the same latitude as France; the continental climate with warm, dry summers is tempered by the Black Sea and the Carpathians; and the hillsides, which have soil rich in limestone, slope gently and have good exposure. The greatest vineyards are located south and east of the Carpathians, and are divided into six different regions.

In the northeast, covering the lower slopes of the Carpathians and extending the vineyard of Moldavia (territory that used to be Romanian and is a source of constant discord between the two countries), is an amphitheater-shaped vineyard, one of the most remarkable and oldest in Romania. The Cotnari vineyard produces a natural dessert wine, with a high alcohol content and more than 2 ounces of residual sugar per quart. It is truly an exceptional wine, with aromas of honey, orange rind and dried grapes, and was once as reputable as Tokay. The color is so deep that Grasà, which imparts the semi-sweet taste, could be compared to Furmint. Like Tokay, the wine keeps for many years.

On the southern slopes of the Carpathians, the vineyard of Dealul-Mare (meaning "Great Hill") northeast of Bucarest extends over 37 miles. It produces full-bodied, velvety red wines from Pinot Noir and Cabernet Sauvignon, including Valea

ROMANIAN GRAPE VARIETIES

Among white grapes, the famous Fetească-Albă (which is called Leanyka in Hungary and Fetească in Bulgaria) is predominant, particularly in the Banat and in Transylvania.

It is similar to Gewürztraminer, yielding a highly fruity wine with a hint of peach and apricot. One drawback is its lack of acidity to balance the bouquet.

Grasà imparts a semi-sweet taste to Cotnari and endows the wine with a fine capacity to age.

Ruländer, or Pinot Gris, produces heady, powerful wines.

Fetească Neagrà is the best known dark-skinned grape, yielding light, fruity wines to be drunk young.

Cabernet and Pinot Noir are becoming more and more popular, producing wines of excellent quality. Romania is one of the leading countries of Europe in cultivating Pinot Noir.

Calugareasca, one of the most popular wines in Romania.

The hills of Murfatlar near the Black Sea are bathed in sea breezes and yield a highly palatable dessert wine that has the slightest splash of orange blossom. The sun shines here an average 300 days a year, with long, warm autumns ideal for the development of noble rot. The region of Vrancea, in the center of the country, is Romania's largest viticultural zone and is known for its table wines.

In the heart of the Carpathians, the Banat estate is located in a region with plains and

RED WINE FROM THE DEALU MARE REGION

WILLOW RIDGE

PRODUCE OF
ROMANIA

MERLOT

1996

75cl   11.5%vol

ESTATE BOTTLED BY SERVE IN CEPTURA, ROMANIA.

hills and produces the famous Kadarka de Banat, a highly appreciated red wine harvested on the stony terraces of Minis.

In the central-western region, Transylvania is famous for its Tîrnave vineyard, and the dry wines produced from Fetească (Perla de Tîrnave) and Riesling. The semi-dry and sweet wines come from Sauvignon and Traminer.

MAJOR VITICULTURAL REGIONS OF ROMANIA

– **Banat** (southwest, on the border with the Yugoslav Federal Republic and Hungary)
• Teremia
• Recaş Tirol
• Mimiş Arad
– **Transylvania** (center of the country)
• Bistrita-Nāsăud
• Tîrnave
• Alba-Lulia-Aiud
• **Moldavia** (on the Moldavian border)
• Cotnari
• Dearlurile Moldovei
• Odobesti-Panciu-Nicoresti
• Tecuci Galati
– **Muntenia** (west of the Black Sea)
• Dealu Mare
– **Dobruja** (south of the Ukraine)
• Sarica-Niculitel
• Murfatlar
– **Oltenia** (north of Bulgaria)
• Drobeta-Turnu-Severin Corcova
• Segarcea
• Drăgăşani
• Arges-Stefăneşti

Produce of Romania

VALEVERDE

TAMAIOASA

Fine Sweet Wine

1997

PIETROASA

Controlled Appellation of Origin

SHIPPER · VINEXPORT, BUCHAREST · ROMANIA

Bulgaria

The borders of Bulgaria, whose Thracian populations first introduced the wine-making tradition, have fluctuated over the centuries. Today the Danube marks the northern boundary, the Black Sea marks the eastern frontier, and Macedonia and Greece the south. Two mountain chains traverse central Bulgaria from east to west; the Balkan Mountains, and farther south, the Rodopi Mountains, which run to the Aegean Sea. The vines are most dense in the valleys lying between the two mountain ranges.

Bulgaria, on the same latitude as Tuscany, cultivates sixty-two different grape varieties. It is the third-leading exporter of wines in Europe. Following the First World War, there was a revival in wine-

REGULATIONS

The earliest legislation regulating wines dates back to the tenth century; current legislation dates back to 1978. It demarcates four categories.
- **Vins de Pays,** or regional wines, which correspond to the French appellation. Some can be excellent;
- **Varietal wines,** made from a single grape variety;
- **Superior wines;**
- Topping the charts is the **appellation Controliran.** There are currently some thirty or so of these wines.

Two special mentions include Reserve and Special Reserve wines, which correspond to certain conditions for aging wines, notably in oak. To be consumed in moderation.

In contrast, the very promising indication of "young wine," which applies to Cabernet and Merlot wines.

making, after five centuries of occupation by the Turks. Today, as a result of an ongoing tradition and the introduction of modern production methods, the 400,000 winegrowers produce 106 million gallons of wine each year, most of which is exported to Russia and the former Soviet republics. Three-quarters of production is table wine. There are five viticultural zones in Bulgaria; but names and sites have little importance, for wines are classified by grape variety. Dimiat, a local grape, is the predominant variety; it is quite similar to Chasselas. It is as abundant and good in quality as Smederevka is in Serbia. Golden and harmonious, Dimiat thrives on the coast of the Black Sea. In general, white wines produced here are good and light; they are also rich in acidity, and therefore are easily exported.

Rosenthaler Riesling is produced in the rose valley of Kazanlŭk, and a kind of amber-colored Muscat from Misket called Hemus is made in Karlovo.

Melnik, a wine of superior quality that is dark and rather heavy and ages very well, comes from the southwestern area of the country, along the Greek border. The vineyards in the Thracian plain are

scattered along the Maritsa River, yielding primarily red wines from Pamid. But Gamza (in reality, a Kadarka) is the most highly appreciated grape. In the Danube Valley, it produces a dry wine with a remarkable bouquet.

BULGARIAN GRAPE VARIETIES

The most common grape variety is Cabernet Sauvignon, exceeding even Pamid, the Bulgarian red grape which yields popular wines of varying quality. Dimiat, a white grape, is to Bulgarian wines what Smederevka is to Serbian vintages. It yields a supple wine with an aroma of ripe fruit. It occupies 19,760 acres and is the second most predominant grape in Bulgaria, the first being Rka-Ziteli, originally from Georgia. Misket, with a perfume of Muscat (it is vinified in an identical fashion to Muscat), grows abundantly throughout Bulgaria. The planting of foreign grapes like Riesling and Welsch-Riesling proved disappointing at first for white wines, but the production of quality wines has shown some promise in recent years. It is linked to a grape that has adapted marvelously to the soil: Chardonnay, which gives only top-quality wines in the region of Varna and Khan (eastern region). Sauvignon, Muscat Ottonel and Aligoté are also found in Bulgaria.

Strong, dark wines are made from Mavrud, meaning "black," which keep several years in the cellar. Yet indigenous grapes are gradually being replaced by Cabernet Franc grapes, with a considerable degree of success. Cabernet Sauvignon, however, is most closely associated with Bulgaria. When well vinified and aged, it is a real treat, yielding an unctuous wine with a rich aroma of black currant. And it would be impossible to speak of Bulgarian wines without mentioning its sparkling wines (Champanski), produced in northern Bulgaria and marketed under the Iskra label.

Greece

Vines flourished in ancient Greece and were highly developed at the time. Hippocratus celebrated the virtues of wine, which still plays a major agricultural role in Greece today.

Running from the coast to the hilly slopes, the vines occupy some 235,000 acres of the Greek mainland. They grow in rocky, chalky soils and must be able to withstand the extremely dry climate and strong sunshine. The conditions produce grapes that are concentrated in sugar and high in alcohol content, hence the abundance of sweet wines as well as robust, hearty reds. Greece produces over 132 million gallons of wine annually from a great variety of indigenous high-yield grapes. It does not export much of the wine, however, only 10 percent of production. There are two types of Greek wines: commercial label wines and traditional appellation wines (AOC). Twenty-six AOCs exist in Greece, located in one of the eight wine-producing regions.

The Peloponnesus

The peninsula's 160,550 acres of vineyards produce over 25 percent of the total quantity of wine in Greece. Patras is the leading viticultural center, with four AOC wines produced here. Three of them are varietals: Mavrodaphne, an old grape variety that gives a heavy sweet red wine that is high in alcohol content, and the Muscats of Patras and Rion, yielding sweet white wines. The Patras appellation produces a light white wine as well. Two mountain varieties are also worth mentioning.

Nemea

The terraced vineyards of Neméa grow from 820 to 2,625 feet above sea level. The wine made from Agiorgitiko, which is spicy and so dark that it is nicknamed

"Hercules' blood," is one of Greece's finest wines. A few leading houses, including Papaioannou, Kourtakis, Kototos and Cambas, produce it. The best vineyards are located on slopes below the Asprokambos Plateau. It is a wine that keeps for many years.

Mantinea

This supple, light, aromatic white wine, which is either dry or semi-dry and made from Moscofilero, is produced in the center

of the Peloponnese. The wine has a very promising future.

Attica

This extremely arid region benefits from its proximity to Athens, from a commercial point of view. Savatiano is the predominant grape, and is used to make the world-famous Retsina wines. Its fame must not overshadow the red grape Mandilaria, or the Pallini, which yields the best white wine in the country.

Crete

Crete alone has 123,500 acres under vine, and the island is making a serious effort to protect the appellation of the wines. Top-quality red wines (those sold by Kourtaki are some of the finest) that are powerful and generous are produced from old Cretan grape varieties such as Archanes and Peza. Dry, assertive white wines come from Peza Blanc, as well as dessert wines from Sitía and Dafnes.

Macedonia, Thrace and Epirus

These regions receive more rainfall than the other regions, and the widely planted Xinomavro yields an excellent Naoussa, a

tannic red wine with a fruity nose, as well as two other wines, Goumenissa and Amynteon. Porto Carras, located in Sithoniá, is another leading wine center. Two French grapes, Cabernet Sauvignon and Cabernet Franc, have been planted in the north where it is somewhat cooler. The excellent AOC Côtes de Meliton is produced here, on the appellation's only estate. Two appellations in Epirus, a very mountainous region in northern Greece, deserve attention: Zitsa for a slightly sparkling white wine, and Metsovo, a prestigious red wine that is tannic and sturdy.

Ionian Islands

Robola, a white wine, is one of the best produced here, along with Muscat and Mavrodaphne from Kefallinía. AOC Verdea is one of the best white wines from Zákinthos, Leucadia and Corfu.

Leucadia also yields a good red wine that is powerful and dark, called Santa Mavra.

The Aegean Islands

The famous Muscat of Samos is produced on narrow, steeply terraced vineyards growing at altitudes of 2,625 feet above sea level. The wines are strictly regulated and are some of the finest in quality. Blending is illegal, as is the introduction of other Greek wines onto the island. The Muscat of Límnos is another good quality wine.

Dodecanese

Today only Rhodes continues the winemaking tradition that dates back to the Hospitalers. Generous red wines come from Amorgiano while dry whites are made from Athiri, like those of Lindos. Very little Muscat of Rhodes is produced however.

Cyclades Islands

Both dry and sweet wines are made from Assyrtico vines which flourish in the volcanic soil of Thíra. The dry white wine is assertive and high in minerals, while the sweet wine, or Vino Santo, is very high in alcohol. Wines produced in Páros come from a blend of two grape varieties, one white and one red, notably a "ruby" wine under the appellation of origin Páros.

MAJOR VITICULTURAL REGIONS OF GREECE

Attica and central Greece
- Kantza
- Céphalonia
- Ankalos
- Zitsa
- Rapsani

Macedonia and Epirus
- Goumenissa
- Amideo
- Naoussa
- Côtes de Meliton

Greek islands
- Rhodes
- Santorin
- Páros
- Samos
- Lemnos

Crete
- Sitia
- Peza
- Daphnès
- Archanès

Peloponnesus
- Nemea
- Mantinia
- Patras

Cyprus and Malta

Cyprus

This large eastern Mediterranean island, located off the coast of Syria and Lebanon, has been inhabited since the Mycenian era. Greeks and Phoenicians founded major settlements here. Cyprus has been a wine-making land since ancient times, when Aphrodite, the goddess of love, fertility and beauty, was worshiped in her temple at Paphos. (The name Cyprus, however, evokes copper, or *kyprosen* in Greek.) Today some 10 percent of the land is used for viticulture, with an annual production of 39.6 million gallons of wine.

The best vineyards grow in the volcanic soil of the southern foothills of the Troö-dos Mountains. Mount Olympus stands 6,400 feet high, between Limassol, which is nicknamed the "Bordeaux of Cyprus," and Paphos. Commandaria, a sweet wine made from sun-dried grapes, is harvested here; production is highly controlled. To protect against phylloxera, which has never hit the island, only traditional grape varieties are grown here. There are four main grapes: red Mavron (80 percent), white Xynisteri (a local grape), Marathef-ticon, a dark-skinned grape, and Ophtal-mo, a black grape that produces very deep-colored wines with a peppery taste. The other grape varieties, excluding Palo-mino, are originally from France (Cari-gnan, Grenache, Cuisalt, etc.).

Mavrons give dry, full-bodied wines with a high degree of tannin, such as Afames, Othello, Keo Ltd.'s Aphrodite and Etko's Semeli. Kokkineli, which is also found in Greece, is a very dry rosé with a deep color made from Mabron. A very popular wine, it should be drunk iced with a meal.

Cypriot vines, the pride of the island, were introduced into Madeira in the fif-teenth century to make the prestigious Madeira wine. Marsala from Sicily and Hungarian Tokay can trace a similar ori-gin. In ancient times, Hesiod wrote of how the legendary Nama was made from sun-dried grapes. During the Crusades, Richard the Lion-Hearted conquered the island and discovered this marvelous golden dessert wine. After Richard I gave the island to the Knights Templar, they renamed the wine Commandaria. It is said that the Turkish sultan Selim II captured Cyprus in 1571 to take control of the luscious dessert wine.

Today the legendary wine is just as fa-mous. Twenty or so villages, including Kalo-khorio, Zoopiyi and Yerassa, situated at altitudes of between 1,312 and 2,625 feet in the Troödos Mountains, are authorized to make the wine. The wine is a blend of Mavron and Xynisteri (red and white) grapes. Certain growers use the exact same

recipe that was used during Antiquity: the grape is always sun-dried. The wines are aged in huge earthenware jars that are coated with pitch, vine-ash and goat-hair, then buried in the earth. They are topped up with young wine each year. True Commandaria, velvety and supple, contains four times the amount of sugar that Port does. The amount of concentrated sugar must be a minimum 9 ounces per quart for Mavron and 7.5 ounces per quart for Xynisteri to obtain up to 16 ounces per quart once the grapes are sun-dried. Sometimes the wine is so concentrated that it must be diluted before being drunk. A more ordinary Commandaria is a palatable dessert wine similar to Sherry. Sherry is also produced on the island, ranging from very dry (finos) to very sweet (olorosos).

CYPRUS GRAPE VARIETIES

- Saved miraculously from the phylloxera plague, Cyprus's vineyard is based on two main grapes:
- Mavron (red): 80 percent of the vineyard. Produces robust, dry or semi-dry wines, powerful wines that lack a certain measure of finesse.
- Xynisteri: a local white grape used primarily for Commandaria. A rather flat, dark white wine is made from the grape as well.

MAJOR VITICULTURAL REGIONS OF CYPRUS

Troödhos Mountains (east to west)

– The highest vineyards
• Marathasa
• Pitsilia
• Commandaria (14 villages)
• Laona
• Kathikas
• Mount Afames
• Parraya (narrow terraced vineyards nearly 3,000 feet in altitude)

Malta

The 116-square-mile island of Malta is located south of Sicily in the middle of the Mediterranean. The heavy May rains that precede the torrid summers are not ideal for producing high-quality wines. Yet Malta (including the island of Gozo) has 3,700 acres under vine and produces 501,600 gallons of wine per year.

Most of the vineyards are located on the southern coast, in Burmarrad, Rabat and Siggiewi. Gamaru, Nigruwa and Dun Tumas grapes produce average-quality red and white wines that lack a certain meas-

ure of semi-sweetness. Two wines stand out from the others in terms of quality: Ghirgentina (white) and Gellewza (red). The Maltese government is making great efforts in promoting quality Muscat for exportation.

The Black Sea, Azov Sea and Caspian Sea region

After the collapse of the Soviet Union, a new winegrowing configuration was devised. It ran from the Romanian border and the Black Sea to the Azov Sea and the western shores of the Caspian. Vines have always flourished in this region. When Noah came ashore from the Ark on Mount Ararat, following the floods, he planted the first vines in what is now Armenia. Later, the ancient kingdom of Van, which extended from Armenia to southern Transcaucasia, made its fortune with wine. By Herodotus's time (460 B.C.), Armenian wines were very well known. Sulfur was used in treating vines even back then.

In the Odyssey, Homer lauded "the perfumed, spirited wines of Colchis, the land of golden grapes" (western Georgia, once the land of the Golden Fleece). Throughout history, winegrowing played a major role; in the past sixty years, however, the vineyards have more than quadrupled in size, particularly between the Black Sea and the Caspian Sea, in Armenia, Azerbaijan, Georgia and Crimea. Current production is 924 million gallons, with the vineyards occupying 3.5 million acres—ranking the region third among wine producers, behind Italy and France. East of the Azov Sea, in the Don Valley, red and white wines of the Donski appellation are produced from local grape varieties. Tsimlyansky Cherny (black) gives a sparkling red wine, Tsimlyanskoe. Let's begin with the Crimean vineyard, in the Ukraine, the leading viticultural sector of the three seas region.

Ukraine

It is impossible to mention the Ukraine without referring to the famous vineyards of Odessa, Ismalia and the Carpathians. The hybrids planted following the phylloxera plague have now been replaced by European plants throughout the region.

In Crimea, around Sevastopol and Simferopol, on the Black Sea, the coastal vineyards seem to stretch to infinity.

The entire wine-producing region developed thanks to the arrival of French growers in the early twentieth century, who acclimated the European grape varieties to the soil. Try the ruby-red wines

produced in the Crimea, which are very sturdy blends of Saperavi, Matrassa, Oleatica, Malbec and Cabernet. Today Massandra is the most famous Crimean wine. Found in Malta, it is a fortified Madeira-type wine with a stunning golden color. Other outstanding Crimean wines include Livadia, made from a warm Muscat, the dry white Sémillon Oreanda and the pink dessert wine Alupka. Yuzhnoverezhny, a concentrated wine that is high in alcohol content, is made from Saperavi. If sweet wines and dessert wines are most important in Crimea, the sparkling ones, such as the good Kaffia and Krimskoje, have contributed most to its reputation. These two wines are made according to the traditional methods using Chardonnay, Pinot, Riesling, Aligoté and Cabernet Sauvignon.

Moldavia

Moldavia, the former Romanian province of Bessarabia that was annexed by the

U.S.S.R., is a leading wine producer. The wine revolution is marching full steam ahead here, a movement launched in the early nineteenth century by Tsar Alexan-

GRAPE VARIETIES

In addition to the classic grape varieties of Western Europe, such as Cabernet, Sauvignon, Riesling and Merlot, there are 120 grape varieties, sixteen of which are of prime interest.

Among red grapes, Saperavi—meaning "dyer" (the grape enhances color in blends)—has a plum aroma and can be cellar-aged for many years. It is a late ripening grape and is high in sugar and very concentrated.

Khindogny occupies 70 percent of the Karabakh vineyard. It is a rather bitter, tannic grape that is used primarily in blending. Tsimlyansky Cherny is used in making sparkling wines, notably near the Don River.

Rka-Ziteli is the leading white grape (18 percent of all vineyards; it has only recently exceeded Ugni Blanc). It is indigenous to Georgia (its name means "red vine" in Georgian). It is the second-leading grape grown throughout the world and yields spirited wines with a spicy nose, somewhat similar to those of Alsace. Rka-Ziteli is used to produce dessert wines, fortified wines similar to Port, Madeira, Samos, Sherry and even Cognac, as it ages well in oak barrels.

Mzvane is the best grape of the region. Indigenous to Takhetia in Georgia, it yields wines vinified at low temperatures after a long maceration process. If drunk young, it is fruity and very aromatic.

der, who invited French wine specialists to come to the country and impart their wine skills and grapes. The Australian group Penfolds is continuing that tradition today. This vast vineyard is carrying out a campaign to improve quality by classifying fifteen Appellation Contrôlée zones. For white wines, Sauvignon and Chardonnay are abundant in the center of the country, near Kishinev; in the south, Aligoté is predominant, followed by Rka-Ziteli, Feteasca and Traminer. For reds, four grapes prevail: Merlot, Cabernet Sauvignon, Pinot Noir (called Pinot Franc here) and Saperavi. Two wines should top any list: Romanesti, a red wine produced north of the capital (the vineyards belonged to the Romanovs), for its quality and its history; and Negru de Purkar, a blend made from Cabernet and Saperavi with a splash of Feteasca Neagra.

Georgia

Georgia, between the Black and Caspian seas, has an infinitely rich vineyard. The best wines are produced in the Takhetia region, located in the northeastern part of the country on the mountainous slopes of the Caucasus. Some Georgian wines known abroad include Myshako Riesling, Ghurdjurni and Mzvane. Rka-Ziteli, a

white grape, is indigenous to Georgia (and is used in over one-half of all wine production). It yields refreshing wines with a spicy nose and a floral hint.

Armenia

Armenia is called "Fatherland of the Vine." Once the tiniest republic of the former U.S.S.R., it runs from Turkey to Iran. Major wine-producing centers include Oktemberyan, Vedi, Echmiadzin and Achtarak, which yield natural and fortified wines as well as brandy.

Russia

The region of Krasnodar near Anapa and Novorossiysk, east of the Black Sea and the Sea of Azov, produces good quality dry wines from Riesling, Aligoté, Sémillon, Cabernet Sauvignon, Sauvignon and Pinot. Fortified and dessert wines come primarily from the Kuban Valley. The zone of Stavropol in the northern Caucasus produces one of the best Rieslings in the country. Father north, on the Ukrainian border, the region of Rostov-on-Don is famous for its various sparkling wines made from the red Tsimlyansky grape. The vineyards of the Caspian Sea, south of Makhachkala, produce red wines and dessert wines.

In addition, Azerbaijan (near Iran), whose wine production dates back to the 1960s, is known for its table wines called Matrassa, Isabella and Bayan Shirey; Turkmenistan, with the introduction of irrigation, produces a fortified wine that is similar to Tokay; in Tadjikistan, north of Pakistan and Kashmir, dessert wine is produced; and in the vast area of Kazakhstan, running from the Caspian Sea to Mongolia, vine planting is currently expanding.

MAJOR VITICULTURAL REGIONS (Black Sea, Sea of Azov, Caspian Sea)

- **Moldavia** (between Romania and the Ukraine)
- Around Kishinev
- **Ukraine** (from Romania to Russia)
- Odessa
- Mouth of the Dnieper
- Southern Crimea

- **Russia** (between the Sea of Azov and the Caspian Sea)
- Rostov-on-the-Don (north of the Sea of Azov)
- Novorossiysk (on the Black Sea)
- Piatigorsk (north of the Caucasus)
- Makhachkala (on the Caspian Sea)

- **Georgia**

- **Armenia**
- West of Yerevan

- **Azerbaijan**
- Baku (on the Caspian Sea)

The Levant and the Far East

The earliest vines are believed to have grown wild in central Anatolia sometime around 4000 B.C. But Mesopotamia, Transcaucasia, Egypt and Greece also played major roles in the development of wine production.

The wines of Byblos (north of Beirut) were widely renowned. Phoenicians and Syrians shipped them throughout the Middle East and as far as India and China.

One wine has remained virtually the same since Antiquity: the Cypriot wine Commanderia, also known as the legendary Nama, which was Aphrodite's favorite wine.

Turkey has an immense vineyard, yet vinifies a mere 5 percent of its grape harvest. The Bekaa Plain in Lebanon has a *terroir* capable of producing the finest wines in the world. Farther south, Israel is making a spectacular effort to promote its top-quality wines. Mediocre grape varieties are being uprooted and replanted with Cabernet Sauvignon, Colombard and Sauvignon Blanc. Current production exceeds 9.5 million gallons for the country's 7,410 acres of vineyards, which are continuously expanding. Egypt has a few great vineyards. The one at Mariout, west of the Nile Delta, yields a very honest white wine from French grapes. Omar Khayyam is a somewhat average wine produced in the region of Alexandria.

Cappadoccia in Turkey is one of the oldest winegrowing areas in the world.

Turkey

In addition to the names and historic landmarks associated with Turkey—the Byzantine Empire, the Ottoman Empire, the fall of Constantinople—Turkey is also famous for being the site of what are believed to have been the earliest vines in the world, growing wild in the mountains of Anatolia. The first evidence of vinification was the discovery of barrels dating back at least four thousand years in a village in Middle Anatolia.

The Turkish vineyard prospered until the war between Greece and Turkey, after the First World War. Turkish wines were drunk and admired throughout Europe. Unfortunately, the departure of major Greek communities from Thrace and the Aegean coast caused a drop in wine production, and grapes were consumed as table fruit and dried to produce raisins. Wine production dropped from 79.2 million gallons to 528,000 gallons.

In response, the Turkish government nationalized the wine industry in 1927. In 1935, under Kemal Ataturk, a campaign to revive the vineyards and promote domestic wine consumption was launched. Today, although Turkey has the fifth-largest vineyard in the world, only 5 percent of its grape harvest is vinified. The domestic market is quite small: consumption per capita never exceeds 2 gallons a year. Yet Turkish wines are good. They are dry and are easy to drink.

The country is divided into four major viticultural regions: Thrace and Marmara, Aegean, Southeastern Anatolia and Middle Anatolia. The latter, located in Asia Minor near Ankara, produces Turkey's best wines, notably excellent white wines made in Nevşehir-Ürgüp, Niğde and Tokat from Emir and Narince. Red wines are produced from Kalecik and Cubuk. In southeastern Anatolia, Tekel, the state-owned company that operates over twenty centers, dominates the Turkish wine industry. It produces Buzbag, a deep-colored red wine that is sturdy and high in alcohol, made from Bogazkarasi. It is produced in

TURKISH GRAPE VARIETIES

Beside the well-known red grapes (Pinot, Cinsault, Gamay, Sauvignon, etc.), there are a great many regional grape varieties. The most famous are Papaz-karasi from Edirne-Kiklareli in Thrace, Kalecik and Karasi in Ankara, and Dimrit in Anatolia. The best white wines are produced from Emir near Hasandede and Nerince in Anatolia. Clairette, Chardonnay, Riesling and Sémillon are also found, particularly in Tekirdag in Thrace.

Elâziğ opposite the coast of Cyprus. If you are staying in Adana or Antakya (ancient Antioch) farther to the east, try one of the local red wines made from Sergi Karasi and Öküz-Gözü grapes.

Three-fifths of all Turkish wines come from Thrace and the Aegean coast. *Trakya kirmisi* means "red wine," produced by two predominant grapes, Papaz-Karasi and Adakarasi. White wine is *trakya beyaz*.

Sémillon is the primary grape found in Thrace and along the Marmara seaboard extending to the Bosphorus. The Aegean Sea region is well known for its Muscat wines, its highly fruity white wines that are drunk chilled, and its heady reds from Izmir (formerly Smyrna).

MAJOR VITICULTURAL REGIONS

- Thrace
- Sea of Marmara
- Aegean Sea
- Mediterranean Sea
- Black Sea
- Middle Anatolia (near Ankara)
- Eastern Anatolia
- Southeastern Anatolia (near Syria)

Lebanon and Syria

In ancient times, the area of Lebanon—originally meaning "White Mountain"—and Syria was occupied by the Canaanites, who founded the great Phoenician cities. It was one of the earliest winemaking regions of the world, producing such vintages as the wines of Helbon and the famous Chalybon (most likely a cooked white wine). The latter was the favorite wine of the Persians. It was exported by the Phoenicians and the Syrians as far as China. Its name was passed down over the centuries as one of the finest made in Antiquity. In Ezekiel: Chapter XXVII, Damascus is mentioned as a wine-producing center, and it still is today.

These two predominantly Muslim countries have always left winemaking to the Christians. The French troops stationed in Syria before and after the Second World War played a major role in the development of winemaking. Some 247,000 acres are under vine in the rocky regions of Aleppo and Homs, near Damascus, and in the northern part of the country on the coast, in Latakia.

Lebanese wine production is quasi-synonymous with the Bekaa Valley, notably the three vineyards of Kefraya, Ksara and Musar, which can produce some truly outstanding wines. The Lebanese vineyard is a tiny 1,750 acres—scarcely larger than the equivalent of thirty Bordeaux châteaux. The Bekaa Valley is a basin 3,000 feet in altitude between Mount Lebanon and the Anti-Lebanon mountain range, which tourists cross to visit the Roman temple at Baalbek, its music and theater festival and the legendary Hôtel Palmyra.

The red soil with white stones is fertile yet rugged. The winters are freezing, the summers torrid. But this soil is one of the best in the world for winegrowing (you'll find some plants with hallucinogenic effects growing here as well). The vineyards of Château Musar and Château Kefraya, east of Mount Baruk, tower some 3,280 feet above the Bekaa Valley. They benefit from

LEBANESE AND SYRIAN GRAPE VARIETIES

Before the arrival of imported French grape varieties like Cinsault, Cabernet, Sauvignon and Syrah, native white grapes were primarily used, including Méroué and Obaideh. Both have a low productive yield and may be associated with Chardonnay.

a relatively cool climate. Each year, grape pickers from Bedouin tribes pass through the valley, where the Roman temple to Bacchus is located, built in tribute to the wines of the land of Canaan that were exported from Byblos, Tyre and Sidon to Egypt, the land of the Pharoahs.

Charles Ghostine (Ksara), Michel de Bustros (Kefraya) and Serge and Ronald Hochar (Musar) are part of the new Lebanese wine union, located in the Christian quarter of Achrafieh in Beirut.

Château Musar

The name Musar is derived from the Arabic *m'zar*, meaning "a remarkably beautiful place." Was the wine intended to become Lebanon's Château Pétrus? Everything here is exceptional. First, the unusually long period of time that Château Musar wines spend in the cellars prior to being marketed: seven years. Next, the blending, which, according to Serge Hochar, is carried out to make wines that last.

The blending incorporates grapes from Bordeaux and the Rhône Valley, including Cabernet Sauvignon and Cinsault. The result: "A little Burgundy with a splash of Bordeaux." The wines are priced at nearly 70 dollars a bottle. The vineyard is located in the Bekaa Valley, and the eighteenth century castle, where the cellars and storehouses are located, is 30 miles away in Ghazir in the Christian zone. Between the two lies Dar el Beidar, a mountain pass 6,235 feet in altitude. In 1983, during the Lebanese war, the harvest took so long to reach the storehouses that it fermented in the containers.

Ksara

This wine estate, named after the *ksar* or fortress on the site at the time of the Crusades, lies in the heart of the Bekaa Valley near Baalbeck. Jesuit priests acquired Ksara in 1857 and carried on the winemaking tradition, notably planting new high-quality vines.

Ksara's wine cellar, extending nearly 2,000 yards, was a grotto discovered by the Romans, who consolidated part of the vault and dug narrow tunnels from the cave into the surrounding chalk. The tunnels served as a hideout for draft dodgers when the Ottomans called up men into service during the First World War.

The Jesuit Fathers sold off the estate in conformity with the directives of the Vatican II synod. Today, the "wine of the fathers" is run by Charles Ghostine. He is assisted by a team of investors including the owner of a Lebanon book store. This team hired James Palgé, cellar master at Château Prieuré-Lichine in Margaux. He has boldly mixed Cabernet Sauvignon, Merlot and thirteen southern grape varieties, including Syrah. The result is surprising and shows great promise indeed.

Kefraya

Lebanon's third-largest vineyard is run by Michel de Bustros, who has only a minority stake. The estate is owned by the family of Walid Jumblatt, the leader of the Druze community (70 percent). It is about 13 miles away from Ksara on the route to Damascus, near the large town of Chtaura. The 740 acres of vines were planted in 1951.

The first label, which was very much like a Bordeaux, appeared in 1979. The first *cuvée de prestige* is still aging in the barrel. It is the product of Jean-Michel Ferrandez, a French enologist and grower who boosted Château Citran's reputation and was headhunted in exchange for a significant sum of money while working at Château Gisors; both these châteaux are in the Bordeaux region of France.

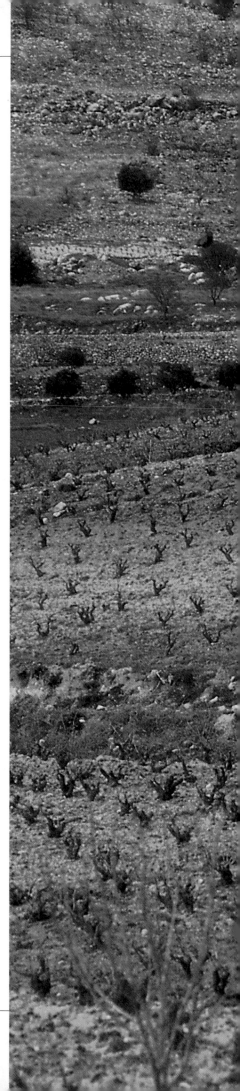

Israel

One name is intimately linked to the history of winegrowing in Israel: Baron Edmond de Rothschild. In 1882, well before the creation of the state of Israel, the earliest Zionists arrived in Palestine. Under the patronage of the baron, they planted the first *Vitis vinifera* vines (Alicante, Carignan, Petit Bouchet) in Shomron and in parts of Galilee. By 1890, there was beginning to be a surplus of wine, but phylloxera destroyed much of the vineyard. The baron not only taught the growers how to graft the vines onto American rootstocks, but offered them his cellars at Rishon-le-Zion, near Tel Aviv, and Zikhron-Yaacov, south of Haifa. These are still the primary wine-producing centers of Israel.

The history of the vines goes back to the book of Genesis. After the great flood, which occurred approximately in 2800 B.C., the first thing Noah did upon descending from the Ark was to plant a vine. A clay sign dating back to 1800 B.C. indicates that there was more wine than water in Palestine. The land was carpeted with vineyards, and the winegrowers' imagination was boundless. Wine was blended with honey and peppers, or boiled with asparagus to be used as a disinfectant or to dye fabrics.

By our era, the wines of Palestine were highly appreciated and were exported as far away as England. Crusaders found vineyards at Mount Carmel and in Bethlehem and Nazareth, run by Christians.

Since 1948 and the massive influx of new immigrants, viticulture has flourished, with an annual production of 5.3 million gallons* produced on 7,410 acres of vineyard. The Société Coopérative Vigneronne

THE WINE INSTITUTE

Created in 1957, the Israeli Wine Institute selects and tests the best grape varieties and wines suitable for the climate and soil. The newly created Israeli vineyard shows great promise as a result of its exceptional technical help and good equipment.

des Grandes Caves, known as Carmel, ensures 60 percent of production: Zikhron-Yaacov on the slopes of Mount Carmel, southeast of Haifa, and Rishon-le-Zion, near Tel Aviv. They are famous for their

rosé wines and the white wines vinified according to French methods. A new vineyard in northern Israel, in a steep region of Galilee, produces two excellent dry wines: Gamla and Yarden. In the foot-

ISRAELI GRAPE VARIETIES

All the major grapes that flourish in warm, dry climates grow in Israel. For red wines, there is Alicante, Grenache, Carignan (although it is becoming less popular, with more Colombard and Cabernet Sauvignon being planted, as they produce the best wines) and a local grape, Dabuki. For whites, Clairette, Muscat, Sémillon, Sauvignon and Ugni Blanc. Efforts to emphasize quality over quantity are being made, with Sauvignon and Chardonnay showing excellent results.

hills of Mount Hermon, the vines thrive in the volcanic soil. The high altitudes keep temperatures below 77° F, an ideal climate for Chardonnay, Sauvignon, Merlot and Cabernet. The region of Siddon-Gezer in central Israel is the country's second-largest vineyard and produces good red wines. And the area surrounding Jerusalem has been recently planted and shows great promise. There are many types of wines made in Israel: sweet dessert wines, slightly sparkling wines, sparkling wines; 70 percent of all wines are table wines. In the past, appellations often were borrowed from European countries, but today the wines have more Hebrew-sounding names: Adom Atic, Primor (formerly Pommard), Mont Rouge, Carmelith, Atzmon, etc.

Twenty percent is exported (Kosher wines) to the United States and Great Britain by the Carmel Wine Company.

Japan

Grape juice has always been used for medicinal purposes in Japan. Vines have been cultivated since the twelfth century; they gradually were extended during the nineteenth century with the arrival of Americans and Europeans. Today some 4 million gallons of wine are produced on 74,100 acres of vineyards (consumed as fruit and wine). The Japanese have devised an ingenious

technique called Tama-Zukuri, whereby the branches of the grape vines are trained along wires to allow them to fan out more easily. The leading vineyard is located on the island of Honshu, in the prefecture of Yamanashi near Kofu, some 60 miles west of Tokyo. There also are a few vineyards near Osaka, Yamagata and Nagano, northwest of Tokyo. The best wines are light and dry. They are somewhat similar to wines produced in Hunter Valley in Australia.

JAPANESE GRAPE VARIETIES

Ninety percent of Japan's vineyard is occupied by a dark-skinned grape, Campbell's Early, and four white grapes:
- Delaware, a hybrid from the U.S. state of Ohio, whose pale taste resembles that of sake;
- Koshu, considered the national grape of Japan. It belongs to the *vinifera* species and has been used in winemaking since the nineteenth century;
- Muscat Bailey, a hybrid grown on the southern coast;
- Neo-Muscat, which yields grapes consumed as table fruit in the coastal region of San Yo.

The remaining 10 percent are European grapes: Chardonnay, Cinsault, Cabernet Sauvignon, Merlot and Riesling.

The Japanese vineyard, although highly partitioned, is owned by three major companies: Suntory, Mercian and Manswine, which control 60 percent of the market.

Today, two American grapes, Delaware and Campbell's Early, occupy more than half of the vineyard, but are gradually being replaced by European varieties such as Sémillon, Chasselas, Chardonnay, Riesling and, for reds, Cabernet Sauvignon and Merlot. A local grape, Koshu, yields some good wines.

MAJOR VITICULTURAL REGIONS OF JAPAN
(south to north)

• Nagasaki	• Osaka	• Niigata
• Oita	• Shiga	• Yamagata
• Fukuoka	• Saitama	• Iwate
• Shimane	• Yamanashi	• Akita
• Tottori	• Nagano	• Aomori
• Hyogo	• Tochigi	• Hokkaido

China

The vine was introduced to China via the slow caravans that traveled from Persia around 130 B.C. They are believed to have been used for ornamental purposes. The Chin Dynasty in the twelfth century A.D. propagated the vine throughout the country and developed the art of vinification. During a trip to China, Marco Polo found vines growing abundantly in Chang-Si. Later, during the seventeenth century, Emperor K'ang-hsi imported grape varieties from Turkestan and planted the first great vineyards.

Although vines grow wild in southern China, the Chinese have never been great consumers of wine. Except for a few cour-tesans of the Imperial court and poets such as Li-Po, who recited poems lauding the merits of wine, the Chinese have always preferred rice alcohol and rice wine. Meals today are normally accompanied by beer or lemonade.

China has 160,550 acres under vine, one-fifth of which is vinified from either indige-nous grape varieties or European and American grapes. They are cultivated in the northwest of Sin-hiang, north of the Yang-tze River in central China, in the region of Yantai and along the Great Wall, near the Liao River and in the coastal provinces of Hebei, T'ien-tsin and Shandong. Red, white and rosé wines are produced; they can be dry, sweet or sparkling.

CHINESE GRAPE VARIETIES

China grows a dozen or so white grape varieties with such fanciful names as Cow's Teat, Dragon's Eye and Cock's Heart. Increasingly, traditional grapes are being replaced by Cabernet Sauvignon, Merlot, Pinot Noir, Carignan, Sauvignon, Gamay and notably Muscat Hamburg, which is marvelously successful.

The red grape Beichun, a hybrid be-tween the wild grapes of southern China (*Vitis amureusis*) and *vinifera*, is note-worthy. It appears to thrive in hot, humid climates. It is used to make dessert wines or in blends and has a very productive yield.

The predominant and oldest variety is Longyar (Dragon's Eye), grown in north-ern China and in southern Manchuria. It is a high altitude grape with a productive yield. It produces one of the best Chinese wines, nicknamed the Great Wall.

Tsingtao and Chefoo, cultivated along the same latitude as Gibraltar, yield wines that are similar to Sherry and light Port. The region of Beijing is known for its his-toric vineyard of Lung Yen, which pro-duced wines that were great favorites of the Ming emperors. More and more experi-mental wine centers are springing up in China. The French company Rémy Martin has been involved in a joint venture with T'ien-tsin since 1970 to produce a semi-sweet white wine called Dynastie, a blend of Muscat Hamburg and a local grape called Dragon's Eye.

There is a tendency to play down the Chinese aspects of wines these days, in favor of more European grapes, notably Chardonnay.

Africa

Between the Atlantic Ocean and the Libyan Desert lie three countries of the Maghreb: Morocco, Algeria and Tunisia. For centuries, the wines they produced were used in blending. The viticultural tradition is ancient, dating back to the establishment of the first Phoenician trading centers during the twelfth century B.C.

The Arab conquest in the eighth century marked the religious and cultural unification of North Africa, yet it eliminated all traces of the vine until the arrival of the French in the nineteenth century.

By colonizing the Maghreb, the French planted the great plains with grape varieties that have highly productive yields (Alicante-Bouschet, Carignan, Cinsault, etc.), resulting in a good number of European wines with higher alcohol content. When Algeria became independent in 1962, the country was producing the astronomical amount of over 422 million gallons of wine per year. Today the Maghreb vineyard covers just under 495,000 acres and produces 119 million gallons of wine annually. Governments throughout the region are emphasizing quality over quantity, placing stricter regulations on wine standards and establishing policies governing appellations.

Morocco produces heady red wines with incredibly complex bouquets.

Algeria

This Muslim country and former French colony inherited one of the world's leading vineyards when it gained independence in 1962. Despite major uprooting campaigns and a surge in Islamic fervor, Algeria still produces over 22 million gallons of wine on its 247,000 acres of vineyards, 40 percent of which is used in wine production. Nearly all wine is exported as most Algerians are Muslim and drinking alcohol is officially banned.

The history of Algerian wine dates back to the time when Algeria was a province of the Roman Empire. Following the Arab

ALGERIAN REGULATIONS

Like France with its VDQS classification, Algeria classifies its wines according to Vins d'Appellation d'Origine Garantie (VAOG), an appellation granted by the Institut Algérien de la Vigne and du Vin (IVV). They come from specific sites and are estate-bottled.

In 1970, Algerian authorities recognized seven major viticultural regions, three in the department of Alger and four in the department of Oran:
– Coteaux de Tlemcen
– Monts du Tessalah
– Coteaux de Mascara
– Dhara
– Coteaux du Zaccar
– Médéa
– Aïn-Bessem-Bouïra

ALGERIAN GRAPE VARIETIES

The main grape varieties date back to the colonial period and have been grafted onto American rootstocks.

They yield deeply colored wines that have a high alcohol content. Carignan, Cinsault, Grenache and Morrastel are among red grape varieties flourishing on the plain. Most of the hillside vintages come from Cabernet, Mourvèdre, Pinot and Syrah. White wines are made from Faranah (Coteaux de Tlemcen), Clairette, Ugni Blanc and Aligoté. The wines often give the appearance of having oxidized, given their color.

invasion, only table grapes were produced. Wine production did not resume in Algeria until the French arrived in the nineteenth century. After phylloxera devastated French vineyards, French growers settled in the colony beginning in 1842. They brought Pinot, Chasselas, Cabernet and Grenache grapes along with them, soon to be replaced by Alicante-Bouschet and Carignan, which were grafted onto American rootstocks when Algeria in turn was hit by the blight.

By the time Algeria gained its independence, 422 million gallons of wine were being produced annually, and 40 percent of the working population was employed in the wine industry. Today the vineyard has been drastically reduced. Sixty percent of production consists of deep-colored red wines that are high in alcohol (up to 15%); 30 percent are white wines that cannot be exported due to their color, which gives the impression that the wines have oxidized. The remaining 10 percent are rosé wines. Authorities are placing more emphasis on quality wines entitled to VAOG (Vins d'Appellation d'Origine Garantie) status. They are produced from grape varieties

that are a legacy of colonial times in the two former French departments of Alger and Oran. Seven delimited zones produce Vins d'Appellation d'Origine Garantie.

Department of Alger

Château Romain is a major estate in the Coteaux du Zaccar that produces a sturdy red wine with a very deep color from Pinot Noir, Syrah and Grenache grapes. Aïn-Bessem is a wild, mountainous region south of Alger. The vineyards running along the high plateau to Bouïra yield excellent rosé wines and well-balanced reds. Farther west, the vineyards of Médéa climb up to 4,265 feet—a record high for vineyards in Algeria.

Department of Oran

This district produces two-thirds of all Algerian wines. The conditions on the Coteaux de Mascara produce the country's best wine from the slopes around Mascara. It is an ideal habitat for wine production with a continental climate, sandy soil rich in sandstone and altitudes between 1,970 and 2,625 feet above sea level. The wines have a powerful bouquet and are surprisingly good. The Coteaux de Tlemcen, in southwestern Oran near the Moroccan border, also produce good wines on the sandstone and clayey soil, including two excellent crus: Lismara and Mansourah. In Dahra, on the slopes of what once were volcanoes, fruity, full-bodied reds and rosés are harvested. This was the region of the great wine estates prior to independence: Taoughrite (formerly Paul Robert), Aïn Merane (formerly Rabelais), Mazouna (formerly Renault) and Khadra Achaacha (formerly Picard).

There is also Mostaganem, which produces the famous fine, fruity wine. Finally, in Sidi bel Abbes, the Monts du Tessalah produce hillside wines that are dark and extremely robust.

Morocco

The Atlantic Ocean borders Morocco, the most western country in the Maghreb, to the west, while the Strait of Gibraltar and the Mediterranean lie to the north. Its wine tradition dates back to the Phoenicians, who established their first trading center in Lixus (what today is Larache) in the

REGULATIONS

Since 1956, when Morocco gained its independence, the Moroccan Ministry of Agriculture has regulated the quality and marketing of wines. Legislation in effect while the French occupied the country stipulates that all wine, even those for export, must be "healthy" and must contain at least 11% of alcohol (a minimum, as most reds are at least 14 or 15%). The legislation is less precise with respect to Appellations Contrôlées. The appellation of origin that appears on some labels merely indicates that it is a wine of superior quality.

seventh century B.C. It became a Roman province after Carthage, and was roughly coextensive with the province of Mauretania Tingitania, sending its finest vintages to Rome. This tradition was interrupted by the Arab conquests, and there was a hiatus in wine production for a thousand years.

In 1912, when France formed a protectorate, vine cultivation resumed and up to 148,200 acres were planted. Since independence, the winegrowing area has stabilized at 34,580 acres. Eighty percent of wines are reserved for domestic use; the remainder is exported to Europe to be used in blending.

Morocco produces heady reds with a very complex bouquet, although they lack a certain measure of finesse. They come from grape varieties that have high production yields. Varietal blending is based on Cinsault, Carignan, Grenache, Alicante-Bouschet and Cabernet. Rosés, which are popular, very palatable wines, are to be drunk young. White wines made from Clairette, Maccabeo, Grenache and Ximénez do not withstand the hot climate well and tend to maderize or oxidize too quickly. Vins Gris (a type of rosé made from Gamay) are a great Moroccan specialty, produced in districts south of Casablanca and east of Marrakech. The best are the driest and fruitiest ones produced by the El Jadida, Demnate and Guerrouane vineyards.

Morocco has two great viticultural zones located in flat regions: Berkane and Oujda, near Meknès and Fez, and farther west, the region of Rabat and Casablanca.

MOROCCAN GRAPE VARIETIES

Red grape varieties planted by the French between 1929 and 1935 have a high productive yield: Cinsault, Carignan, Cabernet, Mourvèdre, Grenache and Alicante-Bouschet. White grapes include Clairette, Maccabeo, Ximinéz and Grenache. The Rafsai white grape of the Riff mountain region is still grown, at least what survives following the phylloxera plague.

There are other smaller vineyards in the region of Mogador and on the slopes of the Atlas Mountains. No Grand Cru wines are produced in Morocco; the best rosé wines come from Berkane, in the northeast. Centrally located Taza is known for its powerful wines used in blending.

Meknès and Rabat produce Morocco's best red wines; they are exquisitely colored, and extremely full-bodied with a characteristic taste.

The Daïet slope vineyards (Roumi) and farther north, Dar Bel Hamri, near Sidi Slimane, are worthy of mention. One caveat: these wines need to be aged to reach their full maturity, and unfortunately, are often consumed too quickly. Rafsai is a rare native grape, as is the somewhat mysterious Plant X; both are white grapes. They share characteristics with Farranah grown on the slopes of Tlemcen in Algeria.

MAJOR VITICULTURAL REGIONS

- **Northeast region of the country, on the Algerian border**
  - Berkane
  - Angad

- **Between Rabat, Meknès and Fez**
  - Chellah
  - Zemmour
  - Guerrouane
  - Beni M'tir
  - Sais
  - Beni Sadden
  - Zerthoune
  - Gharb

- **Southeast of Casablanca**
  - Doukkala
  - Sahel
  - Zaer
  - Zenata

Tunisia

Tunisia is the easternmost North African state of the Maghreb. The nation, with its 8 million inhabitants, has had an exceptional past. When the Phoenician trading centers became emancipated in the sixth century B.C., Carthage became the capital of a vast maritime empire. The vine was present at the time and began to develop after the Punic Wars and the Roman victory over Carthage. An ingenious irrigation system was perfected that transformed the country into a superb vineyard admired throughout the Roman Empire.

A Carthaginian named Magnus wrote the first wine handbook in the fourth century B.C. But the Arab conquest cut short this expansion, and it wasn't until the French protectorate was established (1881-

REGULATIONS

In 1957, the Tunisian government established a system controlling appellation of origin and delimited zones. There are three official categories of wines, which are analyzed and subjected to a blind tasting by a panel of experts from the classifications commission.

The first category applies to superior wines, which must be from 11% to 13% in alcohol and aged at least one year. The vintage year and category must appear on the label.

The second category comprises the Muscats. Since 1947, the Appellation Contrôlée "Vin Muscat de Tunisie" was established. Wines are not restricted in terms of origin (except to Tunisia), but they must be made from Muscat d'Alexandrie, Muscat de Frontignan or Muscat de Terracina grape varieties. The third category includes Appellations d'Origine, such as Radès, Kelibia and Tébourba wines.

1954) that a revival in the Tunisian vineyard took place.

Today the vineyard covers some 74,100 acres, half of which produces grapes for wine. There are two major regions: the Cape Bon region, on the peninsula enclosing the Gulf of Tunis on the east; and the Medjerdah and Oued Miliane valleys, near Tunis. The grapes are European in origin, notably Carignan, Alicante-Bouschet and Cinsault for red wines.

One of the biggest threats to Tunisian vintners are the winds. The dry sirocco blows in from the desert, withering everything in its path. The vines must be sheltered and protected as much as possible. The climate and rapid maturation of the grapes alter the color of the wines, which tend to maderize. As a result, greater quantities of Pedro Ximénez, Ugni Blanc, Sémillon and Clairette are being grown for white wines; Pinot Noir, Cabernet, Mourvèdre and Nocera Noir for reds. With Alicante-Grenache, Tunisia produces one of the best rosé wines of Northern Africa (best drunk young before it oxidizes). Coteaux d'Utique, Carthage, Château Mornag (red and rosé), Tébourba in the Madjerdah Valley, Magon and Château

Thirbar are among Tunisia's best wines. Tunisia is particularly famous for its dry and richly sweet Muscat wines, Kelibia (Cape Bon), Radès and Thirbar. Powerful and fragrant, the wines produced can be as high as 18% in alcohol and contain at least 2.5 ounces of sugar per quart.

South Africa

In 1498, Vasco da Gama rounded the Cape of Good Hope and landed at Natal. But it wasn't until 1657 that Johan van Riebeeck established the first South African colony for the Dutch East India Trading Company. With him, he was carrying cuttings of vines from the Rhineland, most likely Muscatel (Hanepoot) and Steen (Steendruif in Afrikaans) grapes, the latter being similar to Sauvignon Blanc. The entry dated February 2, 1659, in van Riebeeck's diary read: "Today, praised be the Lord, wine was made for the first time from Cape grapes."

This first vine planted at the foot of the Tafelberg marked the beginning of what South Africa would become over three centuries later: a major wine-producing country.

There are five milestones in the history of South African winemaking. In 1684, Simon van der Stel, governor of the Cape of Good Hope, planted the most famous vineyard in the land: Groot Constantia, which produces the great sweet white wine. Napoleon and Bismarck were great fans of the wine. In 1688, Huguenots fleeing France following the revocation of the Edict of Nantes settled in the regions of Franschoek, Paarl, Drakenstein and Stellenbosch. They contributed greatly to the expansion of the South African vineyards. In 1885, phylloxera ravaged the Cape vineyards. In 1917, the vineyard was revived, but there was over-production and prices collapsed. In 1918, the Cooperative Wine Growers' Association of South Africa Ltd (K.W.V.) was founded.

Today, South Africa has some 260,000 acres under vine, for an annual production of 211 million gallons. It is the world's eighth-largest wine producer, yet is only thirtieth in terms of land area under vine. Yields can reach up to 3,740 gallons per acre, notably in irrigated areas like Orange River and Olifants River.

Great Britain is South Africa's chief export market for wines, but the K.W.V. boasts of exporting wines to over thirty

TYPICAL SOUTH AFRICAN GRAPE VARIETIES

Wines that South Africans call Riesling—South African Riesling, Cape Riesling, Paarl Riesling, Clare Riesling—are actually made from the same grape variety, Cruchen Blanc. The grape, meaning "firm and crisp," is originally from Gascony, a specialty of the Landes region. It is also known in France as Navarre Blanc and produces what is called Vin de Sables, a dry, fairly aromatic wine harvested in the region of Paarl and Stellenbosch. Pedro Luis, another white grape, is used in making Sherry. It thrives in the sandy soil near Paarl and Malmesbury. Chenel, a cross between Chenin and Ugni Blanc, is a vigorous grape with a productive yield that produces light, lively wines.

As for red wines, Pinotage illustrates the great originality of South African wines. It is a cross between Hermitage (actually Cinsault) and Pinot Noir (hence the name).

The grape was created in 1925 by Professor Perold and received recognition when a wine produced on the Bellevue Estate in Stellenbosch won first prize at the Cape Wine Exhibition in 1959. Although the wine is somewhat lacking in body, it has a lovely color and highly characteristic aroma.

Pontac, from Médoc, was believed to have been introduced by Huguenots. Today its popularity is waning due to its relatively limited yield. It produces a distinguished, invigorating, dark wine with a powerful bouquet. The wine ages very well.

countries. Wine consumption per capita is very low (just under three gallons) yet this is offset by a very high consumption of spirits (whisky, brandy, gin). This is changing, however, as natural and better-quality wines become more popular.

The Cape province can be divided into two viticultural zones: the Coastal Belt, extending from the coast to the first mountain range, and beyond, and the Klein Karoo, which extends beyond the Drakensburg Range to the Swartberg Mountains.

MAJOR VITICULTURAL REGIONS

West of the Cape
- Coastal region
  - Swartland
  - Tulbagh
  - Paarl
  - Stellenbosch
  - Constantia
  - Durbanville

- Breede Valley region
  - Worcester
  - Robertson
  - Swellendam

- Klein Karoo region

– Olifants River region (as well as Overberg and Piketberg regions)

North of the Cape
- Lower Orange River
- Douglas

The Coastal Belt

Stellenbosch, Paarl and Durbanville

The coast encompasses a vast zone that stretches around the Cape, separated from the Klein Karoo by the Drakensberg Mountains.

To the west lie the viticultural zones of Swartland, Malmesbury and Tulbagh;

238

farther east, Durbanville, Paarl, Franschoek, Stellenbosch and Walker Bay.

The Cape peninsula is the region of the famous Constantia Valley where South African wine production was born (the vineyards today are state-run in a pilot-phase operation). The Mediterranean-style climate of the southwest districts of the Cape, between latitudes 33° and 34°, provides an ideal habitat for South Africa's leading wine-producing region.

Yet the summers, which last from November to May, can be too hot. A cool wind originating in the Benguela Antarctic current provides relief. There are few poor vintage years; harvests begin in February or March, and the soil, climate and relief combine to produce excellent wines. Vineyards generally are found on

REGULATIONS

The Cooperative Wine Growers' Association of South Africa Ltd., better known as the K.W.V., was founded in 1918. Based in Paarl, it controls prices and absorbs surpluses. The K.W.V. currently groups over six thousand members and has five vinification centers. In response to K.W.V.'s demand, the state adopted a wine of origin system in 1972 (totally revamped in 1993). Fourteen production zones were delimited and fourteen wine estates were granted Wine of Origin status. The WO seal on the bottle guarantees the origin of the wine, the grape variety (or cultivar) and the vintage year on the label. The WOS seal indicates that the wine of origin is superior, and applies only to superior reserves.

The regulations sparked a small-scale revolution in the South African wine industry. To obtain the required quality, greater amounts of Sauvignon Blanc, Riesling, Chardonnay, Pinot Noir and Cabernet Sauvignon grapes are being planted.

Promoting grape varieties
Current wine policies emphasize grape variety over *terroir* or type of wine. The wines must comes from a minimum 75 percent of the indicated grape variety. When the estate appears on the label, all of the grapes used in making the wine must have been produced on the estate itself.

hillside slopes and produce a wide variety of wines: dry wines, fortified wines similar to Port or Sherry, light wines, full-bodied vintages, etc. Three major production zones are exceptional: the Paarl Valley, the regions of Stellenbosch (seat of the state research body, Nietvoorbij Institute for Viticulture and Technology) and Durbanville. There is one caveat however: the wines are too hearty and full-bodied for European tastes.

White wines predominate (80 percent): Cape Rieslings, Gewürztraminer, Colombards, Clairettes and excellent Chardonnays. Red wines, particularly Burgundy-style reds, come from Hermitage, Shiraz, Pontac and Gamay. Cabernet Sauvignon, Cabernet Franc and Merlot are becoming more fashionable grapes. Most Cape wines are good quality and well vinified. More rosés are being made as well, with some promising results. The soil of the coastal region is rich in sandstone mixed with organic silt or clay; the Klein Karoo, in contrast, is covered with a thick layer of fertile alluvial deposits.

Klein Constantia

Opposite False Bay and benefiting from the sea breeze that blows in from the ocean lies the legendary vineyards of Klein Constantia, which cling to the slopes of Constantiaberg, an extension of Table Mountain. Today the original estate is divided into two separate entities: Klein Constantia and Groote Constantia. The original estate was founded in the late seventeenth century by Simon van der Stel, governor of the Dutch Cape province. He secured a land grant from the Dutch East India Trading Company and founded an estate approximately as big as the city of Amsterdam. Thus began the extraordinary history of Constantia, the famous "wine of Constance," a naturally sweet wine made from Muscat d'Alexandrie and Muscat de Frontignan, among others. Today you can still see the Hanepoot and Frontignan grapes well aligned row after row on the Constantiaberg slopes. The grapes are

harvested in April, just as they achieve noble rot (*Botrytis cinerea*).

In 1980, Duggie Jooste bought Klein Constantia, an abandoned estate taken over by his son Lowell. The first vintage wines are very promising. Will we have to wait a good fifty years to taste this rare wine when it will have reached its peak? The wine enchanted poets and writers, from Dickens to Baudelaire, and was coveted by the princes of Europe and truly blessed by the gods. "The wine of Constance is of a highly superior quality in comparison to everything sent here up to now, and it is a pity that only such small quantities are available," maintained the first tasting review sent from Batavia, Holland, in 1692.

Klein Karoo, Worcester and Robertson

This area extends from beyond the Drakensberg Mountains (reaching 11,975 feet) to the Swartberg Mountains, encompassing the regions of Worcester, Robertson, Montagu, Oudtshoorem and Ladismith. The climate is rather harsh here, with the lack of humidity offset by irrigation. The alluvial soil has calcium deposits and is very fertile, however, and Hermitage, Steendruif, Hanepoot, Muscatel and Sultana grapes thrive here. The latter grape yields sweet Muscats when growing in the best soil; in impoverished soil, the wines are similar to Sherry and brandy. Everything is changing today, however. With the installment of good irrigation, Worcester, Olifants River and Robertson are beginning to produce light, fruity white wines that are very reasonably priced.

The Americas

Throughout the world, American wines generally are associated with the state of California, whose beauty was extolled by John Steinbeck in *The Grapes of Wrath:* " 'Jesus Christ! Look!' he said. The vineyards, the orchards, the great flat valley... Pa sighed: 'I never knowed they was anything like her...' and Ruthie whispered: 'It's California.' " California, the thirty-ninth U.S. state, is the seventh-leading economic area of the world. It produces 80 percent of American wines, more than the regions of Bordeaux and Burgundy combined. California's predominance is so great that it overshadows the other forty-three wine-producing states—from East Coast states like New York, to Ohio, the Pacific Coast and Washington State near the Canadian border.

The United States is the fifth-leading wine producer in the world. Just as the country has been a melting pot embracing the influx of immigrants over the centuries, the vineyards too are like a melting pot of diverse European grape varieties. These include Californian "Tokay," as well as American-type "Port," "Chianti," "Burgundy," "Champagne," "Sauternes," "Chablis" and others. Today, the United States wine market is a dynamic one, and wineries from the Golden State are forging their own viticultural traditions by creating vintages that are comparable in quality to the best produced in Europe.

The news hit like a bombshell

To commemorate the bicentennial of the Declaration of Independence in 1976, Steven Spurrier of the Académie du Vin organized a blind tasting in Paris of Californian Chardonnay and Cabernet Sauvignon wines, Bordeaux reds and Burgundy whites. The Californian wines were the winners by a landslide. The news had a major impact in the United States, and in 1980, wine consumption in the United States exceeded that of whisky.

There are two types of vines in the United States, the indigenous American, found wild in the east (essentially *Vitis riparia*) and *Vitis vinifera*, or the European variety, the backbone of the United States wine industry.

Historical archives in Basel, Switzerland, contain a very old map dating from the mid-fifteenth century and depicting land beyond Iceland and Greenland. This is the first representation of North America, discovered by the Vikings toward 1000, some four centuries earlier. They christened the land "Vineland" because of the wild vines growing there.

California, Napa Valley, young vines.

1562: the first American wine is drunk

The first American wine was tasted in 1562, made by Huguenots in Florida from Scuppernong, a variety of *Vitis rotundifolia.* Scuppernong was an Indian word meaning "vine" and the region in which it grew. According to one legend, the grapes were so powerfully heady and aromatic that they made passengers on arriving ships tipsy before they reached the port. The pilgrims from the *Mayflower* drank their first glass of wine in 1623 for the first Thanksgiving. The quality was of little importance. The first remotely palatable wine produced on the coast was made from the accidental crossing of an American grape and a European vine. It was called Alexander, named after its discoverer, John Alexander, William Penn's gardener. It all began with the inherent difficulties in acclimating the European vine *Vitis vinifera* to American soil. "It is useless to waste time and energy persisting over foreign grapes. It will take centuries for us to adapt them. Develop the indigenous plants instead," wrote Thomas Jefferson.

Phylloxera vastatrix

Jefferson was right, yet he was also wrong: several decades later, Californian wine producers succeeded in implanting *vinifera* vines. He was right because a burrowing plant louse named *Phylloxera vastatrix,* which systematically attacks the fragile roots of *vinifera,* destroyed all hopes of planting the vine in a few months' time. When phylloxera crossed the Atlantic and hit Europe in 1863, so much damage was wreaked that all of the vineyards were wiped out in only a few years. In 1880, a department of enology and viticulture was established at the University of California at Davis. The aim was to contain the devastating epidemic. The solution in part was to graft *vinifera* onto the hardy *labrusca* which, like all American grape varieties, had developed a resistance to phylloxera. Despite its resistance, *labrusca* has been criticized as being "foxy," having a pronounced and pungent taste that some compare to black currant, raspberry and waterfowl; others say it has the aroma of damp fur.

Prohibition

Just as the vineyards were being revived after the phylloxera disaster, a new catastrophe dealt the American wine industry a severe blow: the 1920 Prohibition Law. Prohibition was finally acknowledged as a failure (and lies behind America's penchant for shots of whisky and other spirits that can be knocked back quickly), and the Volstead Act was repealed in 1933. For a period, wines of inferior quality were hastily made and marketed, prices skyrocketed and an entire generation grew disillusioned with wine, even the subtle qualities of fine wines. The return of U.S. soldiers from Europe after the Second World War and the discovery of the Old Continent by American tourists broke down some of the barriers to wine consumption. The soldiers had gotten into the habit of drinking wine with meals—something totally unheard of in the past. And for the first time since Prohibition, wine consumption exceeded the consumption of fortified wines (Sherry, Port, Muscat and others) by the late 1960s.

APPELLATIONS

Forget the pale imitations of Sherry, Port, Tokay, Burgundy, Chablis, Sauternes, Beaujolais and other Champagnes produced daily in Californian wineries.

Fortunately, with the arrival of excellent grape varieties, California wineries are producing varietals, wines named after the predominant grape variety. Since 1983, a wine is a varietal if it is made from a minimum of 75 percent of a particular grape variety (the remaining 25 percent can be anything from Thompson Seedless to Concord). (The exception to this is *labrusca,* which has such a pronounced "foxy" taste that only 51 percent is required.) Another improvement lies in the highly regulated estate-bottled mention, indicating that the wine was entirely vinified on the estate possessing or controlling the vineyard.

American viticultural areas (AVA) have also been classified. There are some 130 AVAs regulated by the federal Bureau of Alcohols, Tobaccos and Firearms (BATF). Sixty of them are located in California. The regulations do not apply to grape variety or yield or quality controls, however. The zones have been delimited according to climatic conditions, topographic and pedological criteria. The BATF supervises the delimitation. A wine produced on an AVA must contain at least 85 percent of wine produced on the delimited zone. The most famous AVAs include: Napa Valley and Sonoma in California, and Finger Lakes in the state of New York.

Americans gradually became aware of the quality of the wine produced in the United States. There were forty winery estates in 1968; today there are over one thousand, most of which give quality top priority. Companies such as Gallo and Paul Masson, better known for their ordinary wines bottled in carafes, have begun to invest in varietals. French groups such as Moët-Hennessy, Mumm and Piper-Heidsieck have been present in Napa Valley for the past fifteen years, running bigger and bigger estates.

How to read a label

Three indications appear on labels.

1. Grape variety. Most American wines indicate the predominant grape variety on the label. The wine must contain a minimum of 75 percent of the grape. If the AVA is mentioned, 85 percent of the grape must have been produced in the area.

2. Region of origin and winery. Labels for ordinary wines—generally blends from one or several states, indicate "America" or the name of the state or county. If the state appears on the label, 100 percent of the grapes must be from that state; for a county, the minimal proportion is 75 percent, regardless of grape variety.

3. Obligatory details (valid only for the United States). Warnings must appear on all labels indicating the dangers of alcohol; the addition of any sulfates used as preservatives must appear as well. Consumer protection laws are far-reaching here, and soon may even require that all fifty authorized additives in wines (sugar, sulfur dioxide, etc.) be indicated.

How to read a label?

Predominant grape variety

Vintage year (optional)

Winery's region of origin

Obligatory specifications

United States

According to recent estimates, one-sixth of agricultural land in California will soon be covered with vines. Here winemaking is a booming business that reaps billions of dollars each year. Sixty-five percent of California wines are controlled by a few giant conglomerates: Seagram, which owns Paul Masson, and Heublien, of United Distillers, Almaden, Inglenook and Beaulieu. Nestle owns Beringer. The proprietors may change overnight as a result of new investment policies. What lies behind this California liquid gold rush?

California

California: a miracle of nature

California is a miracle of nature. The climate and soil make it one of the leading wine-producing areas in the world. But it hasn't always been this way.

In 1524, Cortez had just conquered Mexico and decided to transform the New World into one vast vineyard. He succeeded in doing so, to such an extent that the surplus in production a few years later posed a major threat to Spanish wines. To protect them, the king of Spain ordered the systematic uprooting of all vines from the new colonies in America. Baja California, which was too far away, escaped this fate.

The earliest vine: Mission

In 1697, a Jesuit priest, Father Juan Ugarte, planted what were likely the first vines on the west coast at Mission San Francisco Xavier in Baja California. The vine, European in origin, was named Mission and is still called this today. In 1769, a Franciscan monk from Majorca, Miguel José Serra, planted the grapes at Mission San Diego de Alcala in what is now California.

The grape harvest was superb, and excellent wines were produced. Fifty years later, twenty-one missions had been established along the Pacific Coast, all the way to Yerba Buena (San Francisco) and even Sonoma, the northernmost point of the Camino Real, or "King's Highway," which is still a major thoroughfare today. The San Gabriel Arcangel Mission near Los Angeles is worth a detour. It is claimed to be the site of the "first vine." Don't miss a visit to the small adobe building at the mission where Native-Americans once trampled the grapes. In 1850, the missions were secularized by the Mexican government and most of the vineyards were abandoned.

The age of the pioneers

A new chapter in history had begun, with the age of the pioneers. Jean-Louis Vignes, a Frenchman from Bordeaux, began a commercial venture on the site where the Los Angeles Union Station stands. He was the first to advocate the planting of noble grape varieties, which he brought over from France to Boston and then around Cape Horn to California. Another pioneer was William Wolfskill, a trapper from Kentucky who was famous for his huge wine cellar. In addition, two partners of German descent, Charles Kohler and John Frohling, opened the first wine shop in San Francisco.

Before the arrival of the father of California viticulture, Agoston Haraszthy, the Mission grape dominated northern and southern California. The robust grape had a prolific yield but produced mediocre wines that lacked a certain character.

The legend of Agoston Haraszthy, a Hungarian nobleman and colonel, began in 1851 when he decided to import European vines on a grand scale, notably the famous Zinfandel grape, which was planted for the first time in San Diego.

It took some thirty years for the famous dry red wine, now one of the leading Californian grape varieties, to gain ground. When Haraszthy died, he donated his 6,000-acre ranch to the Buena Vista

CALIFORNIA GRAPE VARIETIES

Californian grape varieties can be quite confusing, particularly to Europeans. A Californian Pinot Blanc has nothing to do with an Alsatian Pinot Blanc or an Italian Pinot Bianco. It is a Muscadet. Ditto for the Napa Gamay, rechristened Gamay 15, which is a very productive Aramon of southern France, or a Gamay Beaujolais, a mediocre variety of Pinot Noir and a curious blend, without any link to a French Gamay. What is called Gros Manseng in California is actually a Petit Verdot from the Gironde. A vast amount of *Vitis vinifera* has been planted over the past thirty years, at the expense of the very average Thompson Seedless and the common Mission grapes.

The white wine boom of the 1980s had major repercussions on the California vineyards. While red grape varieties increased by 15 percent during the same period, the land area for white grapes nearly doubled. French Colombard prevailed, with over 74,100 acres, followed by Chenin Blanc and Chardonnay. Other white grapes include Sauvignon Blanc, Sémillon, White Pinot, White Riesling (Johannisberg Riesling), Sylvaner and Traminer.

The most successful red grape varieties were Cabernet Sauvignon, Gamay, Beaujolais, Pinot Noir, Grenache and Barbera. Today, three grapes are predominant: Chardonnay, Cabernet Sauvignon and Merlot. Hybrids perfected by the University of California at Davis include Ruby Cabernet, a cross between Cabernet Sauvignon and Carignan, which has a very productive yield and can withstand intense heat. It has a very pronounced Cabernet Sauvignon taste.

Vinicultural Society, with its assortment of three hundred grape varieties planted around San Francisco. Haraszthy was the one who demonstrated that superior wines could be produced in the region, even without irrigation.

The liquid gold rush

The great liquid gold rush was fueled by legislation that provided growers with incentives to expand their vineyards. The great expansion ground to a halt, however, when phylloxera wiped out the vineyards in 1870.

Various wine boards and experimental grape-growing stations were established to assist winegrowers. The earliest wine laws regulating quality control date back to this period.

The vineyards had scarcely begun to be revived following the phylloxera plague when the wine industry was dealt a second blow: the Volstead Act and Prohibition. The production of wine dropped by one-half.

It took thirty years for the market to stabilize, but the involuntary downsizing proved to be a boon in the long run.

First, it helped reduce the proportion of Mission from northern California, which was gradually replaced by Cabernet Sauvignon, Pinot and Chardonnay. In addition, it raised awareness of the fact that the high yields of Carignan and Alicante-Bouschet were insufficient: there had to be a greater emphasis on producing quality vintages.

California is divided into five regions

Two researchers from the department of enology and viticulture at the University of California were the impetus behind this emphasis on quality.

Professor A. J. Winkler and Dr. Maynard Amerine established the first correlation between climate and the quality of wines (depending on grape variety) from various Californian regions. They maintained that the only climatic factor that influenced

vine-growing was temperature.

They divided California into five climatic regions based on daily temperatures averaging above 50° F, between April 1 and October 31.

Region 1: under 2,500 hours

Region 2: from 2,500 to 3,000 hours (Sonoma)

Region 3: from 3,000 to 3,500 hours (Napa Valley)

Region 4: 3,500 to 4,000 hours

Region 5: over 4,000 hours

The best wine regions are 1, 2 and 3.

The late 1980s: phylloxera strikes again

Phylloxera's latest attack, destroying nearly all of the Californian vineyards, occurred just over twenty years ago. Vineyards needed to be uprooted and replanted. Three grape varieties benefited from the attack: Chardonnay, Cabernet Sauvignon and Merlot, while such grapes as Syrah, Mourvèdre, Sangiovese, Marsanne and Rousanne suffered most.

The post-phylloxera period

In the 1990s, Chardonnay white grapes and Cabernet Sauvignon reds were replanted, as well as Merlot. The omnipotence of these three grapes, regardless of *terroir,* were influenced by certain local conditions such as climate and soil. Cabernet and Merlot grow very well in Napa and Sonoma, for example. Pinot Noir and Chardonnay thrive best in Los Carneros and Santa Maria Valley; Sauvignon Blanc flourishes in Stag's Leap; while Pinot Noir does very well in Santa Valley, halfway down the coast. Edna Valley, slightly farther north, is ideal for Chardonnay. Zinfandel seems to thrive throughout the state, particularly in Dry Creek Valley (Napa).

The five major winegrowing regions of California (AVAs)

- North coast
- Los Carneros
- Sonoma Valley
- Napa Valley
- Russian River
- Knights Valley
- Guenoc Valley
- Alexander Valley
- Dry Creek Valley
- Clear Lake
- McDowell Valley
- Mendocino
- Cole Ranch
- Anderson Valley
- Potter Valley

- Central Valley (south of Sacramento and north of Napa)
Between Napa and Vallejo
- Solano County Green Valley
- Suisun Valley

- South of Sacramento
- Lodi
- Clarksburg

- Sierra foothills (east of Sacramento)
- California Shenandoah Valley
- Fiddletown
- El Dorado

- Central coast (between San Francisco and Santa Barbara)
- Livermore Valley
- Santa Clara Valley
- Santa Cruz Mountains
- Mount Harlan
- Chalone
- Santa Lucia Highlands
- Carmel Valley
- Arroyo Seco
- San Lucas
- York Mountains
- Paso Robles
- Edna Valley
- Arroyo Grande
- Santa Maria Valley
- Santa Ynez Valley

- **Southern coast** (between Los Angeles and San Diego)
- Temecula
- San Pasqual Valley

Napa Valley

When you enter Napa Valley, you are in the heart of the most prestigious vineyard in the United States.

Cross the Golden Gate Bridge and, as you leave San Francisco, Napa is one hour away. The Wappo tribe, who first inhabited Napa Valley, gave the valley its name, meaning "land of plenty." The valley is 30 miles long and has Mediterranean-style vegetation. The vineyards occupy 29,640 acres.

Vines cover the hillsides and the narrow strip of land 3 to 4 miles wide in the valley basin, where the alluvial soil is composed of a mixture of sand and clay. Each year, Napa Valley produces on average 90,000 tons of grapes. The yield is fairly low: 535 gallons/acre, given the poor soil in certain areas. In 1836, G.C. Yount, an explorer from North Carolina, established the first local homestead in what is today Yountville and planted the first grapevines on a grant of 11,800 acres. The vines were Mission grapes. European varieties began to arrive beginning in 1850.

Charles Krug is credited with founding the first commercial winery in Napa Valley in 1861. It would become California's greatest vineyard.

Napa Valley

The great wineries classified according to subdistrict (from Napa going northwest)

- Hess Collection: Mount Veeder
- **Stag's Leap district**
- Shafer
- Stag's Leap Wine Cellars
- Clos du Val
- **Near Yountville**
- Chandon Estate
- **Oakville**
- Robert Mondavi
- Opus One
- Silver Oak
- **Rutherford**
- Niebaum-Commola
- Grigich Hills
- Beaulieu

- Frog's Leap
- **Near Santa Helena**
- Heitz
- Franciscan
- Joseph Phelps
- Sottswoode
- Berringer
- GraceFamily
- Duckhorn
- **Spring Mountain district**
- Newton
- **Howell Mountain**
- Dunn
- **Near Calistoya**
- Schramsberg
- Sterling
- Cuvaison
- Château Montelena

Growers and vintners

One grape variety is the king of Napa Valley—Cabernet Sauvignon, which is barrel-aged for up to four years. It occupies one-quarter of the land surface, notably the cooler areas of the valley. Each rootstock growing here is worth a fortune. The vines are heated in winter and moistened drop by drop during hot spells. Mechanization may have been launched and developed in California for grape harvests, but Napa relies on it with a degree of reserve, depending on the nature of the terrain.

In contrast to Europe (with the exception of the very great estates), a distinction is made between the grower and the vintner. The winery is where the wines are produced and aged. Vineyards that do not have their own winery often produce their wine in cooperatives which have large-scale equipment.

A valley divided into two zones

Napa Valley is divided into two zones, the upper and lower valley. The upper valley, with Santa Helena as its capital, runs for nearly ten miles from Calitoga to Rutherford and Oakville to the south. In contrast to the lower valley, the soil in the upper valley is stonier, the climate drier and the

vineyards grow on the hillsides. The area around the lower valley, which is more fertile and cooler due to its proximity to the San Francisco Bay, surrounds the city of Napa. It encompasses the basin of the valley and runs up to Sonoma.

Beaulieu Vineyard is one of the most beautiful vineyards of Napa Valley, occupying 988 acres in the middle of the valley. It produces Chardonnay, Pinot Noir, Sauvignon Blanc and Muscat de Frontignan. But Cabernet Sauvignon thrives here better than it does anywhere else. The Georges de Latour private reserve is the greatest red wine produced in the United States. Beaulieu owes its history and reputation to two men: Georges de Latour, a Frenchman who founded the estate in 1900, near Rutherford, and André Tchelistcheff, of Russian origin, raised in Czechoslovakia. After fighting in the White Army, he sought refuge in France, where he became assistant to the professor and enologist Paul Marsais. Hired by Georges de Latour in 1938, he proved to be a miracle man by raising Cabernet Sauvignon, Pinot Noir and Chardonnay to previously unknown standards.

Beringer Brothers is where any self-respecting tourist goes when visiting Napa. This winery, inspired by the Rhineland, was created in Santa Helena by Frederik and Jacob Beringer in 1876.

Château Montelena has a superb vineyard and produces excellent wines from Zinfandel, Cabernet Sauvignon and Johannisberg Riesling. The jewel in the crown of this estate is the Chardonnay, which is comparable to the greatest white Burgundies.

The Christian Brothers: The Christian Brothers were not only devoted to teaching but were gifted with an innate talent for business. They settled in California in 1869, at Mont la Salle, in homage to their founder, Saint Jean-Baptiste de LaSalle, along Redwood Road, on the outskirts of Napa Valley. With 1,235 acres of vineyards, a prestigious "grey stone" cellar in Santa Helena, wineries and a distillation company, they are currently one of the largest wine businesses in California. The

Christian Brothers are known especially for their brandy, vintage wines, and dessert and sparkling wines.

Domaine Chandon: This stunning estate of 1,482 acres, established by the French group Moët-Hennessy, has been specializing in the production of sparkling wines (the Champagne appellation is not authorized) made from Pinot Noir and Pinot Chardonnay grown at their Los Carneros vineyards since 1977.

Domaine Mumm was created following a joint venture between Seagram and the French Champagne makers Mumm. The estate is located next to the Sterling Winery, which Seagram already owns. In 1986, the famous "Domaine Mumm Cuvée Napa" was launched.

Freemark Abbey Winery is located north of Santa Helena. Notable wines produced here include Pinot Noir, Cabernet, Cabernet Sauvignon, Johannisberg Riesling and notably Pinot Chardonnay. The wines are all aged in oak barrels specially imported from Europe.

Inglenook Napa Valley Vineyards: The winery is in Rutherford and the vineyards on Mount Saint-Jean. Captain Gustav F. Niebaum founded the estate in 1879. It was purchased by a certain Inglenook in 1908.

The 222 acres of the estate have been entirely replanted with Cabernet Sauvignon, Pinot Noir, Sémillon, Pinot Chardonnay, Pinot Blanc and Traminer. Gamay and Merlot from Bordeaux were recently added. The estate prides itself on quality, to such an extent that today the oldest bottles of Cabernet Sauvignon fetch astronomical prices.

Charles Krug Winery: The winery boasts of being the oldest in the Napa Valley. It was founded in 1861, and the old vinification buildings are still standing along Highway 29 (the Napa Valley wine route), north of Santa Helena. Charles Krug, the founder, is a legendary figure in the valley. He was the disciple of Colonel Haraszthy and made his first wine in 1858 using a cider press. His name and his vintages spread very quickly throughout the United States and Europe. In 1943, Charles Krug was purchased by Mondavi and was

expanded by 495 acres in Oakville in 1962 following the annexation of the very famous historical To Kolon vineyard (said to be the best throughout the valley).

The first wine from Chenin Blanc was made at Krug. Chardonnay, Gewürztraminer, Johannisberg Riesling, Sémillon and Sauvignon Blanc were also planted. Red varieties include Cabernet Sauvignon, Gamay and Pinot Noir.

Robert Mondavi Winery (one of the five leading businesses in Napa), in Yountville, is a tourist hub for California with its Spanish architecture and famous bell tower.

Robert Mondavi is another leading figure in the Napa Valley. He started out working at Charles Krug before launching his own business in 1966. He and his children are constantly campaigning for quality and ecology. Many experts consider his varietal wines to be among the best in the United States. One reflection of this is the 20,000 *barriques* (220-liter barrels) that Mondavi had made of French oak (although American barrels are three times less expensive) and of white oak from the Black Forest for his Johannisberg Riesling. His goal is to stockpile 10 percent of his annual wine production for at least five years, and the wine is well worth the trouble. His Chardonnays are comparable to the best Burgundy whites; his Pinot Noir is on the same scale as a good Burgundy red.

But Mondavi's greatest success is his incomparable Sauvignon Blanc, particularly Stag's Leap. Mondavi, who did a great deal in improving the reputation of this grape variety in the United States, found the ideal microclimate in Stag's Leap for this wine: a perfect balance of mild and cool weather. Another marvelous wine is the Reserve Cabernet Sauvignon, undeniably one of the best red wines of California.

Although part of the 1,480-acre estate was bought by the Rainer Brewing Company in Seattle, Robert Mondavi still maintains control and is constantly innovating. To wit, his association with Baron Philippe de Rothschild, owner of the famous Châ-

teau Mouton-Rothschild, under the name Opus One. Together they have created a wine, Mondavi-Rothschild, produced on 150 acres and showing great promise. Robert Mondavi is one of the last of the great wine aristocrats (with Angelo Gaya, who produces Barbaresco in Piedmont, Italy). He skillfully created an exceptional estate and promoted his wines throughout the world. He has always had an obsession with quality. He has acted as a liaison between the Old World and California for nearly forty years.

Virtually nothing happens in Bordeaux or Burgundy without Robert Mondavi being there to learn firsthand about it and ultimately improve his wines. He sees wine as culture, an art de vivre on a scale with painting, music (hence the music festival he organizes, one of the most popular in the region) and cuisine. He tries to share this philosophy with the people around him. Long live Robert Mondavi!

Opus One

Baron Philippe de Rothschild had a clear idea of what he wanted when he proposed to Robert Mondavi in 1970 that they work together to create a joint venture between Bordeaux and Napa: produce one of the best red wines in the world. Opus One is made with three grape varieties: a predominant Cabernet Sauvignon (80 to 97 percent of the blend), Cabernet Franc and Merlot. This Premier Grand Cru, a wine to be laid down in all its splendor, deserved a futurist winery. It was inaugurated in 1991. The first vintage dates from 1979.

Stag's Leap Wine Cellar

Stag's Leap is the name that Native-Americans gave to the cliff bordering the vineyard between Yountville, in the north, and Napa. One name and a key day mark this magnificent estate. The name: Warren Winiarski ("made from wine" in Polish), a former classics professor at the University of Chicago. The date: 1976, when during a blind tasting in Paris, his second vintage wine (1973) was chosen as the best red

wine made from Cabernet Sauvignon. To top it off, another Napa wine that same year won first place for whites from Chardonnay: Château Montelena.

Today, his wines are among the greatest and most expensive in the United States (notably Cask 23, a truly exceptional Cabernet Sauvignon).

Louis M. Martini Winery: The Martinis are one of the great families of the valley. The winery's founder, Louis M. Martini, was born in Italy and came to the United States in the early twentieth century. He created his company in Santa Helena just before Prohibition was repealed. Today the reputation of the wines produced on this immense 2,470-acre estate (region of Los Carneros, Sonoma, Santa Helena and Healdsburg) has spread throughout the entire United States (Chardonnay and Cabernet in Napa; Cabernet Sauvignon, Zinfandel, Chenin Blanc and Johannisberg in Santa Helena; Merlot, Gamay, Gewürztraminer and Zinfandel in Sonoma).

Mayacamas Vineyards. In an effort to give as broad an overview as possible, the following must be mentioned: The superb terraced vineyards (and their remarkable Zinfandel rosé wine) of Mayacamas Vineyards; the 125 acres west of Yountville purchased by Moueix and the descendants of John Daniel (Christian Moueix, son of one of the owners of Château Pétrus, produces a Cabernet called Dominus); Francis Ford Coppola's investment in the **Domaine Niebaum** in a great Cabernet Sauvignon; the association of the owners of **Schramsberg** Vineyards with Rémy Martin, the French Cognac producer, to produce an eau-de-vie that is 100 percent American; the famous viticultural (and tourist) center of **Sterling Vineyards** and its funicular at the top of the valley; the excellent Chardonnay and Pinot Noir of the **Domaine Trefethen;** and, lastly, a very surprising association between the greatest restaurants in the region and Robert Mondavi to buy the **Vichon Winery,** with the aim of promoting their Chardonnay, Cabernet Sauvignon and Chevrignon—a blend of Sauvignon Blanc and Sémillon.

Sonoma

The Sonoma and Napa valleys are separated by the famous Mayacamas Mountains. Jack London described it as the "valley of the moon." He was inspired by its Native-American name, "Valley of the Seven Moons," called this because of the moon dipping in and out from behind each of the valley's seven hills.

Los Carneros

The region of Los Carneros runs south of Sonoma and Napa and the foothills of the Mayacamas and Sonoma mountains, between the cities of Napa and Sonoma. The cool air blowing in from the ocean via the Bay of San Francisco is engulfed in the two valleys. It tempers the excessive heat of summer nights with fog, enveloping the vineyards with a protective shroud until the late hours of the morning.

Russian River Valley, Dry Creek Valley, Alexander Valley

The small Russian River acts as a breach, letting the cool air flow in from the ocean. It links these three sectors. Things change drastically once you reach Healdsbury. Up until recently, Chardonnay and Pinot Noir had been the dominant grapes. Today, Cabernet prevails on one side along a small valley facing north west, Dry Creek Valley, and on the other to the north, Alexander Valley.

Los Carneros and Sonoma Valley

The greatest wineries (from south to northwest).

– Los Carneros
- Bouchaine
- Kent Rasmussen
- Acacia
- Buena Vista
- Saintsbury
- Domaine Carneros
- Carneros Creek

– Sonoma Valley
- Gundlach-Bundschu
- Ravenswood
- Lauren Glen (District of Sonoma Mountain)
- Carmenet
- Kistler
- Château St Jean
- St Francis

– Russian River Valley
- Green Valley district

- Marimar Torres
- Iron Horse
- Dehlinger
- De Loach
- Davis Bynum
- William Selyem
- Hop Kiln
– **District of Choltk Hill**
- Rodney Strong
- Piper-Sonoma
– **Dry Creek Valley**
- Lytton Springs
- Nalle
- E & J Gallo
- Dry Creek
- Rafanelli
- Preston
- Duxoup
- Ferrari Carano
– **Alexander Valley**
- Seghesio
- Jordan
- Murphy-Goode
- Clos du Bois
- Geyser Peak

The pioneer of California winegrowing, Colonel Agoston Haraszthy, and his estate, the **Buena Vista Winery & Vineyards,** located southeast of Sonoma, deserve a great tribute. Despite the phylloxera plague, earthquakes and successive ownerships, the company is thriving and producing excellent wines from Pinot Noir, Cabernet Sauvignon, Traminer and Riesling.

The Korbel Brothers, originally from Czechoslovakia, made their first "champagne" in the late nineteenth century, in Guerneville in Sonoma county. F. Korbel & Bros, still located on the Russian River, produces sparkling wines (70 percent of production), including Korbel Brut, Korbel Extra, Extra Dry, Korbel Rosé, Korbel Sec and a Blanc de Blanc made from Pinot Noir and Chardonnay. This superb company has belonged to Jack Daniel's distillery since 1966.

The history of the **Sebastiani family** is a perfect example of an American success story. An Italian immigrant, Samuele Sebastiani—the father of the dynasty—managed to start his own company in Sonoma a few years after arriving in the United States. His wine trade (sold in bulk) was so prosperous that he set up shop on the historical square of Sonoma, in the same spot where Sonoma was made capital of California in 1840. The 740 acres of his estate produce good Zinfandel, Chardonnay, Cabernet Sauvignon and Barbera (a souvenir of his Italian origin) wines. One of the founder's grandsons launched his own company, San Sebastiani Vineyards, in 1986.

Other wineries

A look at the biographies of various wine producers reveals the diverse origins of Colonel Haraszthy's descendants:

Jean-Jacques Michel, a banker from Geneva, Switzerland, founded the **Domaine Michel** in 1985 in Dry Creek Valley. James D. Zellerbach, a former United States ambassador to Italy, created **Hanzell Vineyards,** modeled after Clos de Vougeot. The property was bought by the Countess Barbara de Brye. A professional dancer acquired the **Rodney Strong Vineyards,** today owned by a New York importer and Piper-Heidsieck (under the name Piper-Sonoma).

Bruce Cutter-Jones, a former fighter pilot, purchased 495 acres of vineyards in the Russian River Valley; and in Los Carneros, the **Sonoma-Cutter Vineyards,** whose specialty is Chardonnay. A newspaper publisher, Frank H. Bartholomew, after having been the owner of the prestigious Buena Vista, sold it to acquire the **Hacienda Wine Cellars,** a 110-acre viticultural center in the heart of the Valley of the Moon.

Mendocino

Mendocino, located northwest of Sonoma, was for years neglected by its wine producers due to irrigation problems. Today, due to the installation of water reserves, the vineyard has grown from 1,235 acres in 1970 to 12,350 today, planted primarily with Gamay Beaujolais (actually, a variety of Pinot Noir), Cabernet Sauvignon, Zinfandel and Pinot Chardonnay. The Cresta Blanca Winery was one of the first wineries based in California. Formerly located in the Livermore Valley, today it extends north of Ukiah. Founded in 1882 by

Charles Wetmore, the Cresta won several awards at the Universal Exhibition held in Paris in 1900. Currently the owner of the Guild Wine Company, it is known for its very honest varietal wines.

Central Valley

The central area of the coast and its different viticultural areas (AVAs):
• Livermore Valley (east of the San Francisco Bay, between Oakland and Alamera)
• Santa Cruz Mountains (between San Francisco and Santa Cruz)
• Santa Clara Valley (south of the San Francisco Bay, along Coyote Creek)
• Mount Harlan (east of Salinas)
• Carmel Valley (southeast of Monterey)
• Santa Lucia Highlands (west of Soledad)
• Arroyo Seco (between Soledad and Greenfield)
• Chalone (northeast of Soledad)
• San Lucas

Livermore

This valley in Alameda county, whose vineyard is under 1,975 acres southeast of San Francisco, owes its reputation to its full-bodied, sweet white wines that are slightly reminiscent of Sauternes. Cresta Blanca, originally located in the valley, planted cuttings from Bordeaux, notably from Château d'Yquem. The southern region of Livermore, which is nearly adjacent to the San Francisco Bay, produces as many red wines as white, as well as sparkling wines, dessert wines and aperitif wines.

The Weibel Vineyards specialize in bottle-fermented champagnes and has become the nation's leading producer of sparkling wines.

At Wente Bros, the type of wine produced is indicated on the label (not the original European appellation). Good varietals, similar to Graves and Sauternes, are produced.

Santa Clara and Santa Cruz

These regions cover thousands of acres south of San Francisco. The Los Gatos-Saratoga area, in the foothills of Santa Cruz Mountain, produces the best table wines in California, at the Evergreen vineyards, located east of San José on the slopes of Mount Hamilton.

In 1982, the BATF authorized a new winegrowing zone in San Benito, which has 4,445 acres of varietals (a large section belonging to Almaden Vineyards): Lime Kiln Valley (2,225 acres) and an appellation that is Chalonnais in origin (8,645 acres) in San Benito County.

Almaden Vineyards, located in outer San José, is a historical estate. In the beginning, the Almaden vineyard in the Santa Cruz foothills was planted in 1852 with European grape varieties by two men from Bordeaux, Charles Le Franc and Étienne Thée. The rocky slopes of Almaden are tempered by the nighttime mists from the Pacific, ideal for a few good Pinot Chardonnay and Cabernet Sauvignon wines.

Paul Masson, a Frenchman from Burgundy who arrived in California in 1878, founded his company in Santa Clara.

His wines and champagnes were so popular that he built an actual château and vinification center in the midst of the vineyards. He was the first to produce a Gamay Beaujolais from French plants (actually Pinot Noir), which has been an ongoing source of controversy for years.

Paul Masson Vineyards, now owned by Seagram, has transferred a great deal of its wine activities to Monterey. It is known for its "exclusive" blends made from hybrids like Rubion or Emerald Dry (created by the University of California at Davis). Paul Masson also make varietal wines, fortified wines, champagnes and brandies.

Ridge Vineyards

This amazing vineyard is an immense landscaped region located 2,625 feet above sea level in the heart of the Santa Cruz Mountains south of San Francisco. Ridge

Vineyards was founded by Osae Perrone, an Italian immigrant, in 1885. His vineyard, which runs along a crest called Monte Bello, basks in an ideal climate. The

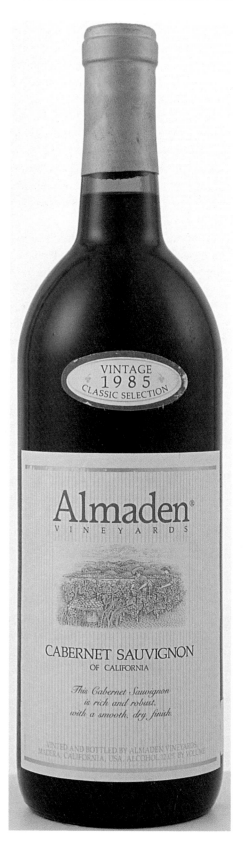

San Andreas fault lies just below the vineyard on the seaward side. Silicon Valley is located nearby in the valley below. Three Stanford University engineers bought the estate in 1959. Ten years later, Paul Draper, a philosopher and enologist, joined the venture. He created two extraordinary wines from Zinfandel, the Californian grape par excellence: Geyserville and Lytton Springs. The wines have a fabulous concentration of fruit and spices and an incredibly rich bouquet that only vines over 100 years old could produce.

Monterey, Sacramento Valley, San Joaquin Valley

The region of **Monterey,** south of San Francisco near Sacramento Valley, shows great promise for the future. It has just under 29,650 acres under vine in the Salinas Valley—dubbed the "salad bowl of America" due to the abundant fruit and vegetables produced here. The vines grow mainly on the hills of Soledad and around Pinnacles National Monument. Upper Monterey in the northwest has a cool climate (Regions 1 and 2) and produces Pinot Noir, Gewürztraminer and Riesling; the warmer regions in the southeast are more conducive to Cabernet Sauvignon, Merlot, Zinfandel and Sauvignon Blanc.

The Sacramento Valley, northeast of San Francisco Bay, has a relatively cool climate. The 2,470 acres under vine are clustered around San Joaquim and Sacramento, the state capital (heading farther south toward the city of Elk Grove), with production zones for table wines, fortified wines (similar to Port) and dessert wines.

San Joaquin Valley: This region is known for the area of Escalon-Modesto, south of Stockton, in the southern part of the county of San Joaquin. Modesto is the seat of the biggest wine-producing company in the world, **E. & J. Gallo Winery,** which presses 500,000 tons of grapes each year.

Gallo bottles nearly one-fourth of wines consumed in the United States. For Americans, Gallo is the generic name for popular, inexpensive wines. This family, originally from the Piedmont region of Italy, settled in the San Joaquin Valley in 1933. They placed great emphasis on dessert wines in the 1950s, then began producing the faddish, highly aromatic Pop'Wines (a marketing ploy), which mixed fruit-based wines with small quantities of alcohol. Today the company is shifting upscale, more toward varietals bearing the label "Wine Cellars of Ernest & Julio Gallo." It now has a superb wine cellar, and the wines are stored in barrels made of oak from France and the Balkans.

Gallo is a wine empire with some 3,000 employees and some of the top laboratories in California (chemistry, enology and microbiology).

Guimarra Vineyards are located in the region of Fresno in the San Joaquin Valley (the central area of the great inner valley, which has a tropical climate). The 7,410-acre estate was created in 1910 by "Papa Jo" Guimarra, a Sicilian immigrant. The wines produced under the Central Coast appellation are honest wines. They are primarily Johannisberg, Chenin Blanc, Cabernet, Riesling and Colombard.

East Coast

Maryland is the land of Catawba (a hybrid of the *labrusca* and *riparia* grapes whose golden age was during the nineteenth century). Yet only a few vineyards remain in the state, clustered around Baltimore.

Farther west, Ohio was the leading winemaking state of the Union, with over 5 million gallons produced annually, mostly from the famous area nicknamed "the American Rhine," near Cincinnati and Ripley. The first American champagne was produced here, called Sparkling Catawba. Michigan has a few vineyards in the south of the state, in Paw-Paw and Benton Harbor. They yield very ordinary wines from Concord, Catawba and Delaware. One exception currently being tested is a wine called Lake Michigan Shores.

New York State

The state of New York is the second-leading wine state in the United States, after California. Some 31.7 million gallons are produced on 19,760 acres of vines. There are 75 wineries in the state, and wine is made according to the following breakdown: 50 percent of *labrusca*; 40 percent of hybrids and 10 percent of *vinifera*.

During Peter Stuyvesant's time, around 1650, vines flourished in Manhattan, Brooklyn and Long Island. They thrived until the mid-nineteenth century. Brotherhood Winery was the first viticultural company created in the Hudson River region in 1839. Today New York wines have a reputation for being sweet and foxy, as is characteristic of *Vitis labrusca,* such as

AMERICAN VITICULTURAL AREAS (AVA)

- The Hamptons (eastern end of Long Island)
- North Fork of Long Island (northern end of Long Island)
- Hudson River Region (between New York and Albany)
- Cayuga Lake (Finger Lakes, south of Rochester)
- Finger Lakes
- Lake Erie (between Buffalo and Port Clinton)

RED GRAPE VARIETIES

Concord is the principal grape found east of the Rocky Mountains, a variety of *labrusca* that gives off a pronounced foxy taste. Of the 29,640 acres of Concord under vine in New York State, only one-fifth is used in making wine. The wine is generally sweet, light red in color and sometimes slightly sparkling.

Catawba is a *labrusca* hybrid that is even older than Concord. Among other hybrids, Baco Noir (approximately 990 acres) is a cross between Folle Blanche and *riparia*. Chancellor, which was widely planted in France before the Second World War, is still grown in all of the states along the Eastern seaboard of the United States. Like Maréchal Foch, it is highly resistant to the cold; it ripens early and has a high degree of sugar. It is used to deepen the color and strength of certain varietal wines.

Cabernet Sauvignon is also found, as well as Merlot, Cabernet Franc and Pinot Noir.

those produced from Concord, a typically New York grape variety. The grape imparts a certain musky aroma to the wines, almost as if it came from damp fur (hence the allusion to the fox). So will the future be *Vitis labrusca* or *vinifera* and hybrids? Only time can tell.

The climate presents another problem. The autumns are rainy and the winters too harsh, with early thaws, which means that grape-growing is a risky business.

In addition, the only way of stabilizing the vintages from year to year is by chaptalization. Consensus has it that white wines are best adapted to this type of intervention (for example, the very honest sparkling wines), even if efforts are underway to develop red wines that are similar

to Italian Lambruscos—pleasant, fresh and semi-sparkling.

Finger Lakes. Located on 39,520 acres of vineyards on the east coast (including Lake Erie and Long Island), one area is particularly famous: the Finger Lakes, around Hammonds Port and Pleasant Valley, 185 miles north of New York.

Eleven long, narrow glacial lakes make up the Finger Lakes region of New York; seen from an aerial shot, the five biggest Finger Lakes fan out like the fingers of a hand.

The vines here thrive in the volcanic soil and the climate, which is tempered by the lakes. The lakes all have Native-American names, such as Keuka, Seneca, Cayuga (which has its own AVA), Skaneateles, etc. The Finger Lakes region has a reputation for producing honest sparkling wines from Catawba, Delaware and Elvira, blended with more neutral wines from California.

The Pleasant Valley Wine Company located here makes the Great Western New York State, the state's most famous sparkling wine.

WINE-PRODUCING STATES AND THEIR AVAs

– Massachusetts
- Martha's Vineyard (north of Cape Cod)

– New Jersey
- Central Delaware Valley
- Warren Hills

– Pennsylvania
- Lancaster Valley

– Maryland
- Linganore
- Catoctin
- Cumberland Valley

– Virginia
- Virginia's East Shore
- Monticello
- Rocky Knob
- Kanawha River Valley
- Northern Neck
- Shenandoah Valley

– Ohio
- Isle St George
- Grand River Valley
- Loramie Creek
- Ohio River Valley

Canada

Canada could still be called Vineland.*
According to the Norse Sagas, Leif the
Lucky landed on what was believed to be
the northern coast of Newfoundland in the
tenth century and saw such an abundance
of wild vines (in reality, blueberry bushes)
growing that he named the country Vineland.

It was officially recognized five centuries
later, in 1497, following its discovery by
John Cabot, a Venetian navigator working
for the services of the British crown. Canada, called New France at the time, was
officially colonized in 1608, when Samuel
de Champlain founded Quebec. It is said
that among his companions, a certain man
named Pontrincourt planted a few rootstocks. Canadian viticulture became com-
mercially important, however, only after
John Schiller, an ex-corporal of the German
army, settled in Cooksville, near Toronto,
in 1811, and set up a vineyard and a small
winery. Today the Canadian vineyard
occupies 44,460 acres and produces
approximately 21.1 million gallons each
year, primarily in four provinces: Ontario,
British Columbia, Quebec and Nova
Scotia.

Ontario

Three regions of Ontario form what is
called the Designated Viticultural Areas
(DVA), where the wines are produced
exclusively from *vinifera* on a 9,880-acre
area:
- Niagara peninsula
- Lake Erie North Shore
- Pelee Island.

Niagara peninsula

Four-fifths of the Canadian vineyard is
located in the Niagara peninsula. The rich
alluvial soil borders on Lake Ontario. It is
linked to Lake Erie by the Niagara River,
which is 35 miles long and famous for

WHITE GRAPE VARIETIES

The climate and schistous soil seem ideal
for New York Riesling, which is pleasantly aromatic, but also for Chardonnay,
Gewürztraminer, Seyval Blanc and a
number of hybrids, like Cayuga (the name
of a Finger Lake wine perfected at the
nearby experimental station in Geneva)
and Vidal Blanc, a cross based primarily
on Ugni Blanc that yields wines that are
high in acidity and very fruity and have a
good level of sugar.

Hudson Valley, another well-known
region located north of New York between
Highland and Newburgh, has 990 acres of
vineyards that produce mainly red wines.
Here the valley is deep and narrow, the climate is maritime and the soil composed of
a mixture of shale, clay and slate. The characteristics of the valley provide an ideal
habitat for producing wines, which have
been made here on a regular basis since
1677.

New York State's two most recent AVAs
are located at the tip of Long Island: some
1,482 acres of vineyards divided between
North Fork and the Hamptons. Curiously
enough, there is a similarity between the
soil here and the soil of Bordeaux, to such
an extent that recent tests on Cabernet and
Merlot appear to be very promising. But
the vineyard's most extraordinary results
have been achieved with Chardonnay. If
one place had to be designated as the
"American Médoc" region, it would be the
northern section of the island around Cut-
chogue.

Niagara Falls. All the great vineyards are located here, west of the falls. The proximity of the lakes creates an ideal climate for wine production. The winters are moderate, as is precipitation, summers are warm and autumns pleasant. As in other regions east of the Rockies, *Vitis labrusca* has been predominant on the Niagara peninsula for years, mainly with two grapes, Concord and Niagara, which have a musky aroma. But today's tastes demand better quality wines. Greater amounts of *vinifera* are being planted. Today 60 per-

REGULATIONS

Wine laws require that wines be marketed by the winery producing them. In all provinces, except Ontario, wineries can sell strictly to Liquor Control Boards or Commissions which sell retail to consumers and hotels and restaurants. The system is different in Ontario, where wineries sell to the Liquor Control Board, which operates a chain of 600 retail stores, and to consumers through a given number of cooperative-run retail stores.

Vintners Quality Alliance (VQA)

This quality control system for wines is unusual. It is closer to a moral control between the consumer and the wine producer. Geographic specifications are insufficient. Regulations set a minimum ripening degree for each grape variety.

- The VQA label is granted only to the best wines after a blind tasting conducted by a jury.

- The wines must be made from *vinifera* grape varieties, the exception being for Icewine, made from Vidal, a hybrid.

cent of the vines are planted with Riesling, Chardonnay, Franco-American hybrids, Seyval and Maréchal Foch. Merlot and Cabernet Franc appear to be off to a very good start as well.

Extraordinary Icewine

Icewine is undeniably Canada's most astonishing wine. Like Eiswein produced in Germany, Austria and Switzerland, from Riesling, the wines are shaped by the great winter cold. Here, on the banks of the Niagara River, the grape variety used is a hybrid of Ugni Blanc, the highly resistant Vidal grape. The grapes remain on the stocks until midwinter. Just imagine the overripe grapes subjected to frosts and thaws day after day. The sugar becomes incredibly concentrated. The grapes are harvested in late November or early December and pressed while still frozen. Eighty percent of the liquid is eliminated, leaving an extraordinarily sugary syrup

that is phenomenally powerful in aroma. The juice ferments for several months and yields a wine that is low in alcohol but highly concentrated in aromas. Very little of the wine is produced, and prices often can be unreasonably high. Among Canada's sixty or so leading wine producers, one name symbolizes the evolution of Canadian viticulture: TG Bright and Co, near Niagara Falls. This company, the largest in the country, is known for its sparkling wines made from Pinot Chardonnay and Pinot Noir. Château-Gai, founded in 1890, was the first to make "champagne" by using the Charmat process. Jordan and St. Michelle Cellars in Sainte-Catherine on Lake Ontario are worth mentioning as well.

British Columbia

Okanagan Valley

The other major winemaking area is the Okanagan Valley in British Columbia, located 155 miles east of Vancouver, between the Trepanier Plateau and the Monashee Mountains. The proximity of Lake Okanagan creates a milder climate and provides enough humidity for the vines during dry spells. California grapes are no longer imported to be blended with native grapes, as they once were. Wine laws stipulate that wines must have a minimum of 80 percent of Okanagan grapes, a de facto acknowledgement of the major efforts of the valley's growers, who have successfully planted *Vitis vinifera*: Riesling, Chardonnay, Pinot Blanc, Gewürztraminer and hardy hybrids like Seyval Blanc, which appear to be as popular as they are 1,550 miles away in the Niagara Peninsula. Just forty years ago, nearly all wine production was geared toward fortified wines similar to Port. Today table wines represent 90 percent of all wine production.

CANADIAN GRAPE VARIETIES

The Canadian vineyard is going through a great many changes ever since the Free Trade agreement was reached with the United States, and Californian wines have been imported en masse. The native *Vitis labrusca* grapes, Concord (the red grape with the particular foxy taste), Niagara and Elvira (the latter two white grapes) are becoming less and less popular. Consumer tastes are leaning more toward finer wines made from European *Vitis vinifera* grapes like Chardonnay, Riesling, Gewürztraminer and Pinot Noir, as well as hybrids (mainly Franco-American). The excellent Seyval Blanc, a descendant of Chardonnay, adapts well to the terrain and ripens early. Vidal Blanc, a hardy cross based on Ugni Blanc, produces good sugar levels in cold climates.

Quebec

Quebec's vineyard covers some 250 acres, with a dozen or so growers located primarily in the region of Dunham, on the 45th parallel along the United States border. This small vineyard has a microclimate with barely 1,200 hours of sunshine a year and only a four-month growth season, yet it produces some dry slightly fruity white wines that are worthy of note: Orpailleur vineyards, Dietrich-Joos and Cep d'Argent.

The Ontario Department of Agriculture Experimental Station at Vineland, Ontario, has tested over three hundred different grape varieties.

Chile

Vines were introduced in the sixteenth century by Spanish missionaries who followed the Conquistadores. They began by planting Muscat d'Alexandrie and a grape named Pais, the origin of which is not clear. For years the vines were cultivated around monasteries, to be used in making altar wines. The vineyard expanded to such an extent that in 1840 Chile became the main wine-producing country in Latin America. In 1851, Silvestre Ochagavia launched a small-scale revolution with respect to the Chilean vineyard. He brought viticultural experts over from France and had them plant the great French grape varieties in the central valley (still Chile's leading vineyard): Cabernet Sauvignon, Pinot Noir, Sauvignon Blanc, Semillon, Merlot, Riesling, Chardonnay and Gewürztraminer. Here, in the region surrounding the Maipo River near Santiago, the Bordelais vines thrived in an ideal habitat of soil, climate and sunshine.

Chile is such an ideal site for wine production that the vines were planted directly into the soil, without first being grafted onto rootstocks; they remained resistant to mildew and phylloxera. Chile is one of the few countries in the world not to have been hit by these two epidemics.

To revive the Bordeaux vineyards ravaged by phylloxera in the late nineteenth century, these same grape varieties were reintroduced into their original *terroir*.

Chile currently has 172,900 acres under vine that produce 132 million gallons of wine each year. The average annual consumption per capita is 9.25 gallons. Some 5.8 million gallons of wine are exported each year, double the amount exported in the early 1980s. Chile's efforts to produce better quality wines have paid off: Chilean wines are now recognized throughout the world, and the country is the third-largest supplier of wine to the United States and the leading wine exporting country in Latin America.

Wines are produced from a wide variety of grapes. In general, they are full-bodied

CHILEAN GRAPE VARIETIES

Païs, a native red grape, represents some 30 percent of all production. It originated in Spain, perhaps the Canary Islands. According to legend, the dried raisins eaten by sailors during their voyage were planted when the Conquistadores landed here; they grew phenomenally well. Païs yields a rustic wine that matures very quickly. It makes up a good proportion of Vino Piperro, a popular wine in Chile. If the vineyard is irrigated, its yield can reach astronomical quantities. Better quality wines are produced on the less fertile soils of the Cordillera de la Costa, in areas without irrigation.

wines with complex aromas and a good bouquet. Some fault them for a slight woody taste due to processing methods.

The introduction of French barrels, however, is improving the taste of the wines. There are basically no differences in the wines from year to year, as the climate remains more or less the same, with an equal amount of sunshine and rains that are never excessive.

The quality-price ratio of Chilean wines is unbeatable. Leading American companies such as Mondavi and Gallo, as well as the Australian giant Penfolds, are beginning to invest in the Chilean vineyard.

In the eight principal winemaking valleys of the country, which are divided into three major regions located between the 32nd and 38th south parallels, the grapes are harvested from February to March for white wines, and in March and April for reds. In addition to its excellent climate and soil, Chile has another advantage:

natural barriers protecting the vines from all angles. The Atacama Desert in the north, the Pacific Ocean in the west, the cold regions of Patagonia in the south and the Andes to the east shelter the wine-growing areas. The country was spared the phylloxera blight that hit in 1877.

THE THREE MAJOR VITICULTURAL REGIONS

(concentrated along a 315-mile-area in the center of the country, between Valparaiso and Concepción)

– Aconcagua and Casablanca
• Aconcagua Valley (northeast of Valparaiso)
• Casablanca Valley (east of Lake Peñuelas)

– Central Valley (between the Maipo River and the Maulé Basin)
• Maipo Valley (southwest of Santiago)
• Rapel Valley
• Curicó Valley
• Maulé Valley

– Southern region
• Itata Valley
• Bío Bío Valley

REGULATIONS

To control alcoholism, Chile has established one of the strictest regulated systems in the world. Each grower has a production figure they cannot exceed. If they do exceed the limit, they must try to export it or sell it off for industrial purposes. Yet the dumping of wine is highly restricted by the National Council of External Commerce. White wines must have a minimum 12% in alcohol content; red wines must have a minimum 11.5%. Each wine must be clear, healthy and at least one year old.

Wines for the export market are classified by age: Courant refers to wines one year old; Special to two-year-old wines; Reserve for four-year-old wines (often the best produced in Chile); and Gran Vino for wines six years old or more.

Aconcagua and Casablanca valleys

The northern region of the country runs from the Atacama Desert to the Chapa River. Rainfall is minimal, and the survival of the vines depends on irrigation and the climate tempered by cold currents along the Chilean coast.

This area is 50 miles north of Santiago; on the horizon, the huge, grandiose Aconcagua culminates nearly 23,000 feet above sea level. The vineyards flourishing beneath it are planted mainly with Cabernet Sauvignon, which are fed by an irrigation system due to the intense dry spells.

Farther west toward Valparaiso lies Casablanca Valley, which is more affected by the ocean climate. This valley has sandy soil and is one of the best white wine terrains of Chile. It is occupied nearly 80 percent by Chardonnay.

Central Valley

The central region is located between two rivers, the Aconcagua and the Maulé, and includes the areas around Santiago, O'Higgins, Colchagua, Curicó and Talca. The influence of Bordeaux is predominant in the grape varieties and vinification methods. The soil composition and climate are similar to those of Bordeaux, but the vineyards here are irrigated.

The upper Maipo Valley, often compared to the Médoc region of France, lies southeast of Santiago. It produces the best wines of Chile, notably Cabernet Sauvignon and Sauvignon Blanc.

There are no cold or hot zones here or red and white growing areas, but a great variety of microclimates. The Maipo Valley, where the most prestigious vineyard is located a few miles from Santiago, owes its reputation to the fertile alluvial soil and the waters of the Maipo. They flow down from the Andes, around Santiago, irrigating the vineyards, then flow into the Pacific.

The greatest estates are found here: Santa Rita, Don Melchor, Antiguas Reservas, Cousiño Macul, Santa Ines, Concha y Toro and Viña Carmen.

Southern area

The southern region is located between the Maulé and Bío-Bío rivers. The vineyards yield red wines that are less interesting than those produced in the central regions, and light whites that are low in alcohol. This is the land of Païs, a grape variety that has a productive yield and, when blended with other wines, produces the vintage that Chileans consume on a daily basis.

Argentina

In 1516, Diaz de Solis sailed in on the Rio de la Plata and a few years later the viticultural history of Argentina began. In 1556, in the region of Cuyo, Jesuits planted the first vines in the country, the forefather of the Criollas Grande and Cereza. These two local grape varieties currently represent 30 percent and 10 percent, respectively, of the highly productive Argentinian vineyard.

Among European grape varieties, Malbec and Syrah are the most widely planted. For whites, Sémillon, Chenin Blanc and Ugni Blanc exceed Chardonnay by far. In general, these wines are marked by a taste of overripe fruit and lack a certain measure of acidity. The vineyards occupy 741,000 acres and produce an annual 370 million gallons of wine, ranking Argentina as the fourth-leading wine-producing country after Italy, France and Spain. This enormous quantity of wine is earmarked exclusively for the domestic market. There are 30 million Argentinians, who consume 18.5 gallons per capita each year, thus explaining the small amount of wine exported. What little is exported goes to North America. This is a far cry from the period just after the Second World War when Argentina exported one fourth of its wine production to Great Britain. Here wine is produced on an industrial scale. The leading winery of Mendoza alone handles 26.4 million gallons of wine each year, and ferments and ages 264,000 gallons. It is easy to see why ordinary wines represent some 70 percent of national production.

The two major winegrowing regions are Mendoza and San Juan provinces in northwestern Argentina. The vast vineyards are set in the foothills of the Andes at 500 feet in altitude. The population, many of whom are of Italian and Spanish descent, brought with them production methods that emphasized quantity over quality. Winemaking policies are changing, however, thanks in part to the efforts of French wine experts to improve the quality of wines, the investment of Moët & Chandon being one example.

Mendoza

Located 620 miles west of Buenos Aires, the region of Mendoza devotes 40 percent of its arable land to vineyards. It produces 70 percent of Argentinian wine and 90 percent of its fine wines. Grape varieties such as Criollas, Malbec and Pedro Ximénez are widely planted thanks to irrigation from the two rivers of the region: the Tunuyán and the Mendoza.

Today three sectors of the Mendoza region are entitled to an appellation (they are the leading regions of the country):

Argentina's wine laws are somewhat vague. Grape varieties are rarely indicated on labels; the name of the estate appears instead. Malbec, which produces two-thirds of red wine in Argentina, is most often blended with Barbera or Syrah. If you drink an Argentinean Riesling, most likely you will be drinking Sylvaner. Pinot Blanc can be Chenin Blanc, and Cabernet Sauvignon is either a crude wine or an excellent vintage that is nearly comparable with Médoc. Be aware of some rather odd blends, notably the unnatural marriage between Riesling and Chardonnay. Ask for advice from wine producers and exporters of quality wines.

San Rafael: The soil here is better suited to reds, notably Malbec and Cabernet.

Luján de Cuyo: At 3,280 feet above sea level, the relatively cool climate is conducive to the production of Chardonnay, Sauvignon and Riesling.

Maipú: The vineyards, 2,297 feet high, are relatively well suited for Malbec and Cabernet.

Dominated by the Andes mountain chain, the snowy, majestic Tupungato Valley southwest of Mendoza produces excellent white wines, notably the remarkable Sauvignon de Trapiche from the Bodegas Peñaflor. They are comparable to the extraordinary Salta vineyards in the northern tip of the country, near the Bolivian border. They are said to be the most beautiful vineyards in the world and the highest (just over 6,000 feet), and produce the best white wines of Argentina.

The province of Mendoza has forty thousand vintners for every one thousand bodegas, or small wineries; a dozen or so major wine companies supply one fourth of all wine production and market the wines (Seagram in San Rafael, Peãflor, Orfila, etc.).

MAJOR ARGENTINIAN WINE-PRODUCING REGIONS

– Near the Chilean border
- Mendoza
- San Juan

– Heading up toward Bolivia
- La Rioja
- Catamarca
- Tucumán
- Salta

– Farther south, around the city of Neuquén (between Colorado and Rio Negro)
- La Pampa
- Rio Negro

ARGENTINEAN GRAPE VARIETIES

Red wines are produced from six grape varieties: Malbec, Bonarda, Tempranillo, Cabernet Sauvignon, Merlot and Barbera, but two indigenous grapes, Criollas Grande and Cereza, dating back to 1556, occupy 30 percent and 10 percent respectively of the Argentinian vineyard. These two varieties of *vinifera* are perfectly adapted to the climate and region of Mendoza, where the irrigated yields reach 2,080 gallons per acre. They yield rustic wines for everyday consumption. They are gradually being replaced by imported grape varieties that are higher in quality.

White grape varieties include Pedro Ximénez, Chenin, Sémillon, Tokay and Pinot Blanc.

San Juan

San Juan, north of Mendoza, is the other major viticultural region of Argentina. It is closer to the equator and its hotter climate produces wines that are stronger. Twenty percent of Argentinian wines are produced here in the Zonda, Ullun and Tulun valleys. The vines are irrigated. They yield a majority of white wines from Moscatel, Pedro Ximénez and Ugni Blanc. Red grape varieties include Barberas, Nebbiolo, Lambrusco and Malbec; rosé wines are made from Criollas. In addition, the provinces of Rio Negro and Neuquén, in the southern regions of the country are worthy of mention, as is La Rioja, farther north. The ensemble represents 44,460 acres of vines.

Australia and New Zealand

The Australian vine dates back to the early years of the young British colony itself, when Captain Arthur Philip set sail from the Thames with a fleet of eleven ships in 1788. Upon landing, he planted a few rootstocks where the Botanical Gardens of Sydney now stand. Australia is filled with superlatives, but that is only natural, as it is the world's biggest island at 2.93 million square miles and a continent in its own right.

Who is the actual father of Australian viticulture? John McArthur who planted the first vineyard at Camden Park 30 miles from Sydney? His two sons, James and William? Or Gregory Blaxland, who was the first grower to export his wine to London, a quarter-pipe of red wine, from his Panamatta vineyard? He became even more famous after embarking on an adventure with Lawson and Wentworth to cross the immense Blue Mountains west of Sydney and explore the fertile plains that lay beyond.

Consensus has it that James Busby was the true viticultural father of Australia: He arrived in Sydney one fine day in 1824. He was Scottish, only 24 years old and had an incredible amount of chutzpah. Having spent only a few months in French wine districts, he arrived with the wild notion of converting Australia into a paradise of wine. As a first step, he wrote a book entitled *A Treatise on the Cultivation of the Vine and the Art of Making Wine.* He soon received a grant of 2,000 acres of land in Hunter Valley, which he christened Kirkton. He imported the best grape varieties from France and Spain to acclimate them and joined up with Blaxland and McArthur to distribute the grapes to whomever would plant them.

The Barossa Valley, near Adelaide, is Australia's richest wine-producing region.

Australia

For years, nearly all wines exported by Australia were Burgundy-type vintages sold exclusively in Great Britain, by companies like P.B. Burgoyne with Harvest and Tintara, and Gilbey's with Rubicon. After the First World War, Bruce Page's government encouraged returning soldiers to work in the vineyards planting vines. The campaign soon led to a surplus of wine. Two measures were enacted in response: export bounties were granted to create new markets and the excise tax on fortifying spirit used for this new market was lowered, thus cutting the cost of making and exporting fortified wine.

As a result, beginning in 1936, Australia became a leading exporter of Sherry-type fortified wines, which were very popular among the British and Canadians, with 4.49 million gallons produced yearly.

CLASSIFICATION AND APPELLATION

A new delineation of zones and subregions came into effect following a European Union agreement in 1994. Interregional blends now appear on all labels. Grapes blended by the major wineries usually come from different regions or states. The name and origin of the grapes now must be indicated. Brand names are not obligatory, however. Small wineries are not bound to indicate these details, either. But if the information does appear, the wine must be made from a minimum of 85 percent of the grape variety grown in the stated region.

Until the 1960s, little wine was consumed. In the early 1970s, there was a turnabout and dry wines began to grow more popular, to such an extent that producers had difficulty meeting demand. They discovered cooler sites and began to produce lighter, more assertive wines.

Today, Australian viticulture is booming and always looking to expand to new territory.

Wine is produced in all states, including those located in the north, but most particularly in the southern regions of the country, where the climate is cooler.

Although the climate is generally too hot, too humid and too dry, the vine flourishes on 172,900 acres, benefiting from the variety of microclimates and ideal soil types, ranging from alluvial, argilous or sandy to volcanic. Some 79.2 million gallons of wine are produced each year. "Each year is a good year for wine," as the saying goes in Australia, which has thirty-three distinct wine-producing regions (the figure is always changing). There are seven thousand vineyards for six hundred wineries. But four of them alone represent 80 percent of Australian wine production: Penfolds, BFL Hardy, Orlando and Mildara Blass.

There are brand labels for wine, such as Koonunga Hill and Jacob's Creek. The labels on Australian wines indicate the name of the grape variety, yet blends are authorized. The results can be exceptional at times, yielding wines that are comparable to the best produced in the world at very reasonable prices.

Annual per capita wine consumption today is 5.6 gallons. The demand is so high

that good quality Australian wines are rarely exported.

What does the label indicate?

Labels are systematically verified according to the Label Integrity Program (LIP), guaranteeing the grape variety, vintage year and origin.

Produce of Australia without any indication of origin or grape variety. This is the leading category for Australian wines.
South-Eastern Australia: a category superior to the previous one. It applies to most of Australia's wine-producing regions.
State of origin: indicates in which state the wine was produced.
Zones: these are the traditional major wine-producing regions, which are then broken down into wine-producing areas.
Regions: a more specific appellation with respect to the preceding one. For example, Clare Valley in South Australia.
Subregions: a subdivision that is more specific. For example, the Southern Wales region in southern Australia (south of Adelaide) and the subregion of Langhorne Creek, on the Fleurien peninsula.

The major viticultural regions

Western Australia (from Perth in the north and Albany in the south)
- Swan Valley
- Perth Hills
- South-West Coastal Plain
- Margaret River
- Lower Great Southern Region

South Australia
- Clare Valley
  • Barossa Valley
  • Eden Valley
- Metropolitan Adelaide
- Adelaide Hills
- Southern Wales
- Riverland

- Langhorne Creek
- Padthaway
- Coonawarra

Victoria (around Melbourne)
- Drumborg
- Great Western
- Pyrenees
- Bendigo
- Goulburn Valley
- Macedon
- Central Victoria
- Greelong
- Mornington Peninsula
- Yarra Valley - Gippsland
- North-Eastern Victoria
- Murray River

PETER LEHMANN

1985
BAROSSA VALLEY
SHIRAZ DRY RED

PETER LEHMANN WINES PTY. LTD., TANUNDA • S.A • ALCOHOL 13.0% BY VOLUME
750 ml • WINE MADE IN AUSTRALIA

AUSTRALIAN GRAPE VARIETIES

Australia specialized in dessert wines for many years (Port- and Sherry-type wines), a tradition dating back to the nineteenth century inherited from Spain, Portugal and France.

In the hottest regions, Muscat d'Alexandrie (Gordo Blanco) is as widely planted as Riesling. But there is also Palomino, Pedro Ximénez and Doradillo.

One-third of varietal blending for red wines is Shiraz (actually Syrah), which is considered to be an ordinary table wine in Autralia (the yields are forced and vinification occurs at too high temperatures). For white grapes, Riesling is predominant to such an extent that Australians have become great specialists (note the Rieslings from the Barossa Valley).

Lighter, fresher, dryer wines are becoming increasingly popular. The country produces a great variety of wines due to the many microclimates, particularly in the southwest. Chardonnay, Sauvignon Blanc and Sémillon are planted here, notably in Adelaide Hills, Upper Hunter and Margaret River.

New South Wales (between Canberra and Brisbane)
- Riverina
- Canberra district
- Mudgee
- Upper Hunter Valley
- Lower Hunter Valley

Queensland
- Granite Belt

Tasmania (island of Tasmania, off the coast from Melbourne)
- Launceston
- Hobart

Western Australia

Western Australia is a gigantic state located in the western part of the country, with the Indian Ocean bordering along much of it and the Timor Sea to the north. The western half is desert land. The vineyards, which produce an annual 1.32 million gallons of wine, occupy only a very small section between Perth, the capital, and Albany.

Swan Valley

Swan Valley is a legendary valley with scorched earth. In January and February, temperatures can rise as high as 113° F and the area has extremely low rainfall despite the cool breeze near the Swan estuary. A few large vineyards are located in the valley, slightly east of Perth, and are run by such groups as Hardy and Sandalford.

The wines produced here are Burgundy-type vintages that are vigorous, full-bodied and a touch velvety. Their highly characteristic aroma is similar to that of Hunter Valley wines in New Wales. They are made from Pinot Noir, Malbec, Cabernet Sauvignon, Shiraz and Merlot. The white wines are much finer and elegant. For years, Honghton White Burgundy, made from Chenin Blanc, Muscadelle and a small amount of Chardonnay, was Australia's most famous white wine. The Chenin grape is an extraordinary one, and although it is thousands of miles away from its native Loire, it produces in this sun-scorched soil a hint of acidity in an intense, generous golden wine.

Another sector worthy of note is Margaret River southwest of Perth, which benefits from the maritime climate.

There is a great future in store for this region, which produces an excellent Pinot Noir, as well as Cabernet, Hermitage and Zinfandel, and Sémillon and Sauvignon. Keep an eye on this region!

South Australia

Bordering on the Great Australian Bight and the Indian Ocean, this state alone produces 40 percent of Australian wines. It has a Mediterranean-type climate and is relatively flat, except for Flinders Range, a chain of mountains 2,950 feet in altitude running north-south from the bay to the outskirts of Adelaide. Adelaide (population: 1 million) is the gastronomical center of Australia. It offers visitors a Mediterranean-style atmosphere, with Chinese, Japanese and Vietnamese influences. This culinary melting pot offers up a variety of national specialties like seafood, kangaroo, emu and crocodile dishes in the city's best restaurants. Huge cooperatives such as Seppelt's, Grant Burge and Penfold's run the vineyards.

A fair share of Australian table wine comes from the irrigated vineyards in Murray Valley, near the border of Victoria State.

Penfolds Grange

Adelaide, the capital of South Australia, boasts of its Grange Hermitage, Australia's most illustrious red wine. It is owned by Penfolds.

It was named after Grange Cottage, a farm owned here by wine creator Max Shubert, combined with the term Hermitage, which Australia then gave to all wines coming from the Syrah grape. Today, the grape's origin is irrelevant, whether they come from the hills that serve as a backdrop to the city or the Kalimna vineyard in Barossa Valley, or even Clare Valley. Max Shubert's sole criteria was the meticulous selection of the best grapes, coupled with a "perfect" vinification. The result is an exceptional Shiraz that offers Australia its best red wine.

Adelaide Hills

Adelaide Hills, located just twenty minutes southeast of Adelaide, is a chic spot with a temperate zone ideal for wine production. Here, the Shiraz is slightly sparkling, the Cabernet Sauvignon has a characteristic light chocolate flavor and the Riesling is astonishingly fresh with a light splash of lemon blossom. The quality of the wines is reflected in the many prizes and awards won: an Abott's Prayer that won the Henschke Prize for best vintner of the year in 1994, and a Lenswood Sauvignon Blanc 1993 that won the International Wine Challenge's Sauvignon Trophy in 1994.

The entire coastal area is cool and damp; it yields wines that resemble vintages produced in Bordeaux and Port-type wines (in Vintage or Tawny). The winegrowing district of McLaren Vale, tempered by the sea breezes of the Saint-Vincent Gulf, is the best example, with the famous Old Reynella.

The vineyards in the north run all the way to Clare (60 miles from Adelaide) and Coonawarra, located in the extreme southeast region of the state, 245 miles from the capital.

Barossa Valley

Between Clare and Adelaide, Barossa Valley is the most touristy county in Australia, and is famous for its grape harvests. The area has four hundred vintners, making Barossa one of the leading winemaking valleys in the world. German immigrants settled here during the nineteenth century, speaking what is called the Barossa Valley Deutsch dialect. The region has a vast number of vineyards and some thirty wineries. Barossa is the land of Penfolds, Australia's biggest winery. Riesling, grown on the slopes of Burings, Orlando and Yalumba, is comparable to the best German Ries-

lings. It is delicate and fruity, a truly exceptional wine. But keep an eye on the Shiraz produced in Barossa, as it is showing great promise.

Coonawarra

Farther south, Coonawarra has been having an ongoing love affair with Cabernet Sauvignon for decades.

This wine-producing zone is well delimited, flowing along the 9-mile-long and 2,625-foot-wide Terra Rossa belt composed of limestone and fertile alluvial soil irrigated by an underground water table. The new Chardonnay plants are so promising that leading wineries like Lindemans, Wynns, Midara and Penfolds have expanded into the area. The region, located 235 miles south of Adelaide, has soil that is similar to that found in Bordeaux, and the red wines which are produced here are frequently exceptional, with a rich leafy, almost minty flavor. Most wine producers have adopted the Bordelais methods of blending Merlot, Cabernet Franc and Cabernet Sauvignon.

Australia's best Chardonnays are produced here, notably at Padthaway.

Clare Valley

Just one hour and a half from Adelaide, the landscape of Clare Valley, 15 miles long, will take your breath away. Its 4,940 acres of vineyard are divided among some

thirty wine cellars producing sprightly white wines that are elegant and rich in bouquet. Reds, which are produced from Cabernet Sauvignon, Shiraz and Grenache, are powerful, full-bodied wines. A Hardy Laesmigham 1995, pure Shiraz, has such complexity and intensity, with subtle notes of pine, that it rivals the great Syrah wines produced in the Rhône Valley. The northern area, as you approach Clare Valley-Watervale, is associated with Sevenhill Estate, operated by the Aloysius Jesuit College since 1840. They produce altar wines. This fairly warm, windy region yields dry highly aromatic white wines from Riesling.

New South Wales

Hunter Valley

New South Wales is the birthplace of Australian viticulture, best symbolized by Hunter Valley. This valley, located 112 miles north of Sydney, is a nearly legendary site. The first vines were planted here in 1828. The white wine they produced was so rich and golden that they called it "Hunter's Honey." Syrah (actually a Hermitage called Shiraz here) and Sémillon are very popular. But when Tyrrell's, one of the leading vintners in the region, planted Chardonnay, it was a magical stroke. The local woods were not suitable for making good barrels, so they were brought here from France and the United States. Today, many enologists rank the Chardonnays and Sémillons of Hunter Valley alongside the best produced in the world. Large producers like Lindemans (Lindeman's Ben Ean), McWilliams (McWilliams Mount Pleasant), Tulloch, Draytons Family, Wyndham Estate and Sutherland control major areas of the valley. There are also newer, smaller wineries as well, such as Brokenwood, Peterson's Allandale, Lake's Folly and Hunter Estate, which add just the right amount of innovation in creating new wines.

Hunter Valley is divided into two zones. Upper Hunter Valley, in the north around Denman, has a basaltic soil rich in limestone that produces excellent Chardonnays and Sémillons by Roxburgh de Rosemount. Lower Hunter Valley, before the Hunter River flows into the Pacific Ocean at Newcastle, has many terraced vineyards on the slopes of the Brokenback Mountains. The soil here is rich in red volcanic silt. The small Mountview chain of mountains, west of Cassock, and the hillsides of Mount Pleasant are the best situated.

Mudgee

The new elevated wine zone of Mudgee, on the western slopes of the Australian cordilleras, has a certified appellation wine system, one of the first in Australia. The

Cabernet and Shiraz wines here are hardy and robust with powerful aromas.

Victoria State

Famous for its gold mines, Victoria State, where the oldest vineyard at Yering near Lilydale dates from 1838, was the leading wine-producing region of Australia in the early twentieth century. There were some 1,200 vineyards scattered throughout the state at the time. They produced 70 percent of Australian wines before phylloxera wiped out nearly all of the vines.

Fifty years later, all that remained were the irrigated zones of Mildura and Swan Hill. A few great names survived: Château Tahbilk, in Victoria Central, and Great Western, near Ararat. The latter, a dry region, produces Great Western Champagne on its limestone soil (the best sparkling wine in the country). In the northeast, Wangaratta, Milawa and Glenrowan

are known for their dessert wines and full-bodied red vintages. In Rutherglen and Glenrowan, Muscat de Frontignan yields the famous Muscat dessert wine, which can be barrel-aged for up to fifty years. These sweetly rich wines are called "stickies" here.

In the western part of the state, the Swiss planted the famous Mont Grampian vineyards in the mid-nineteenth century, which produce light white wines from Riesling and robust reds with a complex bouquet. Today some one hundred wineries are grouped by region, the biggest being Mildura-Robinvale (10 percent of national production). Others include Murray Valley, Goulburn Valley, Bendigo Central Highlands and the Victorian Pyrenees.

With the revival of wine production dating from the 1960s, there are only highly selected wines: Cabernet Sauvignon, Pinot Noir, Chardonnay, Sauvignon Blanc and Riesling, produced in Geelong or in the Mornington peninsula, east of Port Philip Bay.

Yarra Valley

Melbourne is in the southwest, while the mountains of the Australian cordillera lies in the northeast. In between is the Yarra Valley, a virtual garden of Eden. The vineyard around Dixon Creek, Warramote Hills and Coldstream benefits from elevated land that has very good drainage. The cool climate produces everything from richly sweet wines and excellent red wines to very reputable sparkling wines. Pinot Noir, which thrives in this type of climate, occupies one-fourth of the vineyard. One third is planted with Chardonnay.

New Zealand

New Zealand boasts of having the youngest vineyard in the world—the only one in any case, besides Australia and Chile, that is located between the 35th and 40th parallels in the southern hemisphere. It is a surprising country in many respects.

The island was discovered by the Dutch navigator Abel Tasman in 1642. The Treaty of Waitangi (1840) guaranteed the Maori tribes full possession of their land in exchange for recognition of British sovereignty (the treaty was never respected, however). New Zealand became a British colony in 1851.

Vines began to be cultivated due to the influence of two Australian pioneers and a

REGULATIONS

Wine production traditionally has focused on dessert wines and Sherry-type wines. In 1946, wine authorities claimed that the country was too cold and damp to obtain quality dessert wines, as the sugar concentration in the grapes couldn't reach optimal levels. Since then, wine production has shifted toward table wines, notably white wines, and an appellation of origin system is being established (indicated on labels).

- **Certified origin:** guarantees that the wine is made from a minimum 85 percent of a single grape variety grown in the same geographical area in the same year.
- **Geographical denomination:** a broad denomination, New Zealand, as well as a more specific origin, North Island or South Island, with sixteen specific regions following by specific place names and vineyards.

French bishop. Samuel Marsden, a chaplain from the New South Wales government, and James Busby, the first British resident of New Zealand, settled in the Bay of Islands in the early nineteenth century and introduced the first vine cuttings. In 1835, Monseigneur Pompallier, a French bishop and missionary who led a congregation of Marist brothers, introduced vines into Hawke Bay. Enologist Romeo Bragata provided the real foundation for New Zealand's wine industry. Vineyards quickly sprang up in the North and South islands. French and German colonists settled in Akaroa and Nelson. The expansion came to a halt when phylloxera and Prohibition hit. In 1923, there were only 445 acres under vine, largely in the hands of Yugoslav immigrants and Marist fathers living in Greenmeadows, in Hawke Bay. The revival of New Zealand's vineyards dates from the Second World War, when the country had to survive on its own resources.

Annual wine production today is an estimated 15.8 million gallons for 9,880 acres of vineyards planted 95 percent with *Vitis vinifera* (notably Chardonnay, Riesling, Sauvignon and Sémillon). The maritime

climate is temperate. The two main islands running north to south along 930 miles are swept by the damp Westerlies winds that make New Zealand so green. Although Jade Island in the south is too cold for winegrowing (except for the areas near Marlborough and Nelson) some excellent Cabernet wines, a very honest Riesling and a very promising Sauvignon Blanc are produced in the region.

Cloudy Bay

The Cloudy Bay winery produces one of the very best Sauvignon Blanc wines in the world, and one of the most sought-after in North and South America. You have to cross Cook Strait between North Island and South Island to reach Cloudy Bay. The region of Marlborough is the most recent major winemaking district of New Zealand. All of the vineyards were planted after 1973. Cloudy Bay is located in the Wairau Valley, a mountainous landscape that protects the vineyards from heavy rains and winds that blow in from the ocean. When David Hohnen and Kevin Judd produced the first vintage in 1985, it was a smash hit and served as a model for other New Zealand wines. Sauvignon Blanc is better here than it is anywhere else. The color is pale with a greenish tinge. The nose is filled with fresh fruity notes of gooseberries, kiwi, apple and passion fruit, and the wine has a touch of roundness.

North Island

New Zealand's most picturesque vineyards are found in the area between Auckland and Hamilton in the Waikato Valley; in the districts of Henderson, Hawke Bay and Poverty Bay; and around the cities of Napier and Gisborne on the east coast. New Zealand receives more annual sunshine than Switzerland or Germany, notably the region of Blenheim (Marlborough County). Hawke Bay is often compared with Burgundy, and the Cabernet Sauvignon produced here often comes out as a frontrunner in world competitions.

NEW ZEALAND GRAPE VARIETIES

Nearly all hybrids (there are some 6 percent remaining) were uprooted and replaced by *vinifera,* notably Müller-Thurgau, which supplies half of the yearly grape harvest. But the grape is becoming less popular.

New Zealanders are developing a taste for dryer white wines made from Sauvignon Blanc (the most brilliantly successful), Gewürztraminer, Chenin Blanc and Chardonnay. Oddly enough, Riesling is less successful here than it has been in Australia, although the climate here is more similar to that of Germany. There is a surprising blend of Merlot and Cabernet in the area around Auckland, made by Te Mata, the oldest winery in the country dating back to 1896.

Good red wines are made from Pinot Noir, Pinot Meunier, Hermitage and Pinotage (a South African grape variety). The drawbacks of certain young wines—too high a degree of acidity, a lack of body, too astringent—are becoming less and less a problem. The white wines produced here tend to be better in quality: Pinot, Chardonnay, Traminer and notably Riesling-Sylvaner, the famous Müller-Thurgau-one of the most popular white wines of New Zealand.

The annual wine consumption per inhabitant (4.5 gallons) pales in comparison to beer consumption (34 gallons). New Zealanders tend to prefer fortified wines like Madeira, Port and Sherry, obtained by adding cane sugar.

The climate, however, is more suitable for light white wines (representing 75 percent of production).

Much of the vineyard belongs to major Australian producers such as Montana Wine Ltd. in Auckland, part of the Joseph Seagram group, as well as other companies like MacWilliams and Corbans.

Bibliography

ADAMS Leon D, *The Wines of America*, New York, 1985.

AMBROSI Hans, *Welt-Atlas des Weines*, Bielefeld, 1983.

ANDERSON Burton, *The Pocket Guide to Italian Wines*, New York, 1982.

ANDERSON Burton, *Vino: the Wine and Winemakers of Italy*, Boston, 1980.

ASPLER Tony, *Vintage Canada*, Scarborough, 1983.

Atlas Hachette des vins de France, 1989.

BENSON Robert, *Great Winemakers of California*, Santa Barbara, 1977.

BRADLEY Robin, *The Small Wineries of Australia*, Melbourne, 1982.

BROADBENT Michael, *Pocket Guide to Wine Tasting*, London, 1982.

CHAPTAL, *L'Art de faire du vin*, Paris, 1981.

CITÉ DE LA VILLETTE, *La Vigne et le Vin*, Paris, 1988.

CLUB DES GOURMETS, *Guia Practica de los Vinos de España*, Madrid, 1983.

COBBOLD David, *The Great Wines and Vintages*, Paris, 1997.

CRESTIN-BILLET Frédérique and PAIREAULT Jean-Paul, *Les Grands Crus classés du Médoc*, Paris, 1988.

CRESTIN-BILLET Frédérique and PAIREAULT Jean-Paul, *Les Grands Crus classés des Graves et Sauternes*, Paris, 1990.

CRESTIN-BILLET Frédérique and PAIREAULT Jean-Paul, *Les Grands Crus classés du Saint-Émilion*, Paris, 1989.

DOVAZ Michel, *Encyclopédie des crus bourgeois du Bordelais*, Ed. de Fallois, 1988.

DOVAZ Michel, *Encyclopédie des vins de Champagne*, Julliard, 1983.

DOVAZ Michel, *Les Grands vins de France*, Julliard, 1987.

ENJALBERT Henri, *Histoire de la vigne et du vin, l'avènement de la qualité*, Paris, 1975.

EVANS Len, *The Complete Book of Australian Wine*, Melbourne, 1985.

FLETCHER Wyndham, *Port: an Introduction to its History and Delights*, London, 1978.

GEORGE Rosemary, *Guia de los Vinos y Bodegas de España*, Barcelona, 1984.

GOL and NIAUD, *Petit Guide des vins d'Espagne*, Ed. Milan, 1983.

GOLD Alec, *Wines and Spirits of the World*, Coulsdon, 1972.

GUNYON REH, *The Wines of Central and South-Eastern Europe*, New York, 1971.

HALASZ Zoltan, *Hungarian Wines Through the Ages*, Budapest, 1962.

HALLGARTEN FL and SF, *The Wines and Wine Gardens of Austria*, London, 1979.

HALLYDAY James, *Wines and Wineries of New South Wales*, St Lucia, 1980.

HAZAN Victor, *Italian Wine*, New York, 1982.

HEINEN Winifried, *Rheinpfalz : Gesamtwerk Deutscher Wein*, Essen, 1980.

HUTCHINSON Ralph, *A Dictionary of American Wines*, New York, 1985.

HYAMS Edward, *Dionysos, a Social History of the Wine Vine*, London, 1965.

IBAR Leandro, *El Libro del Vino*, Barcelona, 1982.

JAMES Walter, *Wine in Australia*, Melbourne, 1963.

JAMIESON Ian, *Pocket Guide to German Wines*, London, 1984.

JOHNSON Hugh, *L'Atlas mondial du vin*, Ed. Laffont, 1986.

JOHNSON Hugh, *The Atlas of German Wine*, London, 1986.

JOHNSON Hugh, *Le Guide mondial du connaisseur du vin*, Ed. Laffont, 1986.

JOHNSON Hugh, *The Wine Companion*, London, 1983.

LÉGLISE Marc, *Une initiation à la dégustation des grands vins*, Jeanne Laffitte, Marseille, 1984.

LICHINE Alexis, *Encyclopedia of wines & spirits*, New York, 1967.

LICHINE Alexis, *Guide to the Wines and Vineyards of France*, New York, 1979.

MAYNE Robert, *The Great Australian Wine Book*, New South Wales, 1985.

MOORE RODRIGO Alvarado, *Chile, Tierra del Vino*, Santiago, 1985.

NAVARRE J-P, *Manuel d'œnologie*, Paris, 1979.

PENNING-ROWSELL Edmund, *The Wines of Bordeaux*, London, 1985.

PEPPERCORN David, *Pocket Guide to the Wines of Bordeaux*, New York, 1986.

PEYNAUD Émile, *Connaissance et travail du vin*, Paris, 1981.

PEYNAUD Émile, *Le Goût du vin*, Paris, 1983.

PIALLAT R, and DEVILLE P, *Œnologie et Crus des vins*, Paris, 1983.

PLATTER JOHN, *John Platter's South African Wine Guide*, Cape, 1989.

RAY Cyril, *Robert Mondavi of the Napa Valley*, Novato, 1984.

READ Ian, *Pocket Guide to Spanish Wines*, London, 1983.

READ Ian, *The Wines of Portugal*, London and Winchester, 1982.

READ Ian, *The Wines of Spain*, London and Winchester, 1982.

RENOUIL Yves, *Dictionnaire du vin*, Bordeaux, 1962.

RIBEREAU-GAYON J, PEYNAUD E, SUDRAUD P, *Sciences et Techniques du vin*, Paris, 1975.

ROBINSON Jancis, *Le Livre des cépages*, Hachette, 1988.

RONCARATI Bruno, *Viva Vino, DOC, Wines of Italy*, London, 1976.

SAUNDERS Peter, *A Guide to New Zealand Wine*, Auckland, 1982.

STABILISIERUNGSFONDS für Wein, *German Wine Atlas*, London, 1977.

SUTCLIFFE Serena, *André Simon's Wines of the World*, New York, 1981.

SUTCLIFFE Serena, *The Wine Handbook*, New York, 1987.

THOMPSON Bob, *The Pocket Encyclopedia of California Wines*, New York, 1980.

TORRES Miguel, *Los Vinos de España*, Barcelona, 1983.

Vins et vignobles de France, Larousse, 1987.

WOUTTAZ Fernand, *Dictionnaire des appellations*, Ed. Marabout, 1987.

Index

Photograph credits

Jean-Paul Paireault, Hubert Josse, Pix, Gamma and Matthieu Prier

Acknowledgements

Copyright would like to thank the following for their collaboration:

L'Office national de commercialisation des produits viti-vinicoles, 112, quai Sud-Alger, 16000 Algiers, Algeria;
Ri-Wine, St. Mary's Road – South Ascot – Bershire SL 5 9 AX, South Africa;
Springfield Estate, P.O . Box 770, Robertson, 6705 South Africa;
Badischer Wein, Kesslerstrasse 5, 76185 Karlsruhe, Germany;
Einig-Zenzen, P.O. Box 1254, 56756 Kaisersesch, Germany;
Koll, P.O. Box 1305, Ravenestrasse 35, 56812 Cochem, Germany;
Rheinhessen Winzer, Wöllsteiner Strasse 16, 55599 Gau-Bickelheim, Germany;
Wolfenweiler, 79225 Schallstadt-Wolfenweiler, Germany;
Bodegas de Crianza de Castilla la Vieja, Ctra, La Coruna, Km. 170,6, 47790 Rueda, Spain;
Parxet, Mas Parxet, 08391 Tiana (Barcelona), Spain;
Torres, Apartado 13, 08720 Vilafranca del Penedés, Spain;
Beaulieu Vineyards, 1960 St. Helena Hwy, P.O. Box 219, Rutherford, CA 94573, United States;
Cakebread Cellars, 8300 St. Helena Highway, Rutherford, CA 94573, United States;
Château Woltner, 3500 Silverado Trail, St. Helena, CA 94574, United States;
Tokaj Ormeus, Tolscva, Bajcsy-Zs, Ut 45. 3934 Hungary;
Compagnie médocaine des grands crus, 7, rue Descartes, BP 119, Zi, 33294 Banquefort cedex (Hungarian Tokaj);
Gam Audy, Château Jonqueyres, 33750 Saint-Germain-du-Puch
(Hungarian, Argentinian and South African wines);
Chirag, 1, rue Gabriel-Lame, quai 20, 75012 Paris (Greek wines);
Epsilon, 18-20, rue des Marguettes, 75012 Paris (Greek wines);
Carmel, 25, HaCarmel, P.O.B. 2, Rishon-le-Zion, 75100 Israel;
Golan Heights Winery, P.O.B. 183, Katzrin, 12900 Israel;
Boscaini, 37020 Valgatara di Marano, Verona, Italy;
Enotria, 12, rue Baudoin, 75013 Paris (Italian wines);
Vinitalia, 160, chaussée Jules-César, 95130 Le Plessis-Bouchard (Italian wines);
Sartori, 37024 S. Maria di Negrar, Italy;
Umani Ronchi, S.S. 16 km 310+400, 60027 Osimo, Italy;
Bernard Massard, 8, rue du Pont, 6773 Grevenmacher, Luxembourg;
Montana Wines, 171 Pilkington Road, Glenn Innes Auckland 6, New Zealand;
Saint-Clair, 739 New Renwick Rd, RD 2 Blenheim, New Zealand;
SERVE, Romania;
Henri Badoux, avenue du Chamossaire 18, case postale 448, Switzerland;
Les Frères Dubois, Le Petit-Versailles, 1096 Cully, Switzerland.

And lastly, Benoît Calvet (Bordeaux, France); Giovanni Cancelarra (Italia import, France);
M. Jarousse (Paris, France); Caves Nicolas (Paris, France);
the shop Geneviève Lethu (95, rue de Rennes, 75006 Paris);
the shop Lescene-Dura (63, rue de la Verrerie, 75004 Paris); Professor Thomasson (Treize-Vents, France);
Miodrag Draganic and Zivadin Mitrovic (Yugoslavia).